# Bilingual
## VISUAL
# dictionary

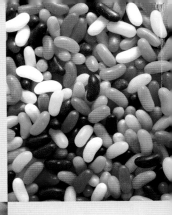

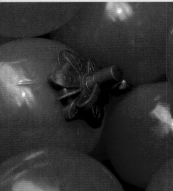

# Bilingual

## VISUAL

# dictionary

A DORLING KINDERSLEY BOOK

**London, New York, Melbourne, Munich, Delhi**

**Senior Editor** Angeles Gavira
**Senior Art Editor** Ina Stradins
**DTP Designers** Sunil Sharma, Balwant Singh,
Harish Aggarwal, John Goldsmid, Ashwani Tyagi
**DTP Coordinator** Pankaj Sharma
**Production Controller** Liz Cherry
**Picture Researcher** Anna Grapes
**Managing Editor** Liz Wheeler
**Managing Art Editor** Phil Ormerod
**Category Publisher** Jonathan Metcalf

**Designed for Dorling Kindersley by WaltonCreative.com**
**Art Editor** Colin Walton, assisted by Tracy Musson
**Designers** Peter Radcliffe, Earl Neish, Ann Cannings
**Picture Research** Marissa Keating

**Language content for Dorling Kindersley by**
**g-and-w PUBLISHING**
**Managed by** Jane Wightwick, assisted by Ana Bremón
**Translation and editing by** Christine Arthur
**Additional input by** Dr. Arturo Pretel, Martin Prill,
Frédéric Monteil, Meinrad Prill, Mari Bremón,
Oscar Bremón, Anunchi Bremón, Leila Gaafar

First published in Great Britain in 2005
by Dorling Kindersley Limited,
80 Strand, London WC2R 0RL
Copyright © 2005 Dorling Kindersley Limited
A Penguin Company
20  19  18  17  16  15  14  13  12  11
040-BD221-Aug/05
Content first published as
*5 Language Visual Dictionary* in 2003
Copyright © 2005 Dorling Kindersley Limited, London

ISBN-13:  978-1-4053-1104-5

Colour reproduction by Colourscan, Singapore
Printed and bound by L Rex

See our complete catalogue at
# www.dk.com

# Inhalt
## contents

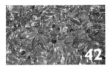

**die Gesundheit**
health

**auswärts essen**
eating out

**die Freizeit**
leisure

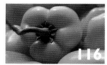

# die Menshen •
## people

# die äußere Erscheinung • appearance

# die Gesundheit •
## health

# das Haus • home

# die Dienstleistungen • services

# der Einkauf •
## shopping

# die Nahrungsmittel • food

deutsch • english

# auswärts essen •
## eating out

# das Lernen • study

# die Arbeit • work

# der Verkehr •
## transport

# der Sport • sport

# die Freizeit • leisure

# die Umwelt •
## environment

# die Information •
## reference

# über das Wörterbuch

Bilder helfen erwiesenermaßen, Informationen zu verstehen und zu behalten. Dieses zweisprachige Wörterbuch enthält eine Fülle von Illustrationen und präsentiert gleichzeitig ein umfangreiches aktuelles Vokabular in zwei europäischen Sprachen.

Das Wörterbuch ist thematisch gegliedert und behandelt eingehend die meisten Bereiche des heutigen Alltags, vom Restaurant und Fitnesscenter, Heim und Arbeitsplatz bis zum Tierreich und Weltraum. Es enthält außerdem Wörter und Redewendungen, die für die Unterhaltung nützlich sind und das Vokabular erweitern.

Dies ist ein wichtiges Nachschlagewerk für jeden, der sich für Sprachen interessiert – es ist praktisch, anregend und leicht zu benutzen.

## Einige Anmerkungen

Die zwei Sprachen werden immer in der gleichen Reihenfolge aufgeführt – Deutsch und Englisch.

Substantive werden mit den bestimmten Artikeln, die das Geschlecht (Maskulinum, Femininum oder Neutrum) und den Numerus (Singular oder Plural) ausdrücken, angegeben, zum Beispiel:

**der Samen**   **die Mandeln**
seed        almonds

Die Verben sind durch ein (v) nach dem englischen Wort gekennzeichnet:

**ernten** • harvest (v)

Am Ende des Buchs befinden sich Register für jede Sprache. Sie können dort ein Wort in einer der zwei Sprachen und die jeweilige Seitenzahl nachsehen.
Die Geschlechtsangabe erfolgt mit folgenden Abkürzungen:

m = Maskulinum
f = Femininum
n = Neutrum

# about the dictionary

The use of pictures is proven to aid understanding and the retention of information. Working on this principle, this highly-illustrated bilingual dictionary presents a large range of useful current vocabulary in two European languages.

The dictionary is divided thematically and covers most aspects of the everyday world in detail, from the restaurant to the gym, the home to the workplace, outer space to the animal kingdom. You will also find additional words and phrases for conversational use and for extending your vocabulary.

This is an essential reference tool for anyone interested in languages – practical, stimulating, and easy-to-use.

## A few things to note

The two languages are always presented in the same order – German and English.

In German, nouns are given with their definite articles reflecting the gender (masculine, feminine or neuter) and number (singular or plural), for example:

**der Samen**   **die Mandeln**
seed        almonds

Verbs are indicated by a (v) after the English, for example:

**ernten** • harvest (v)

Each language also has its own index at the back of the book. Here you can look up a word in either of the two languages and be referred to the page number(s) where it appears. The gender is shown using the following abbreviations:

m = masculine
f = feminine
n = neuter

**deutsch** • english

# die Benutzung des Buchs

Ganz gleich, ob Sie eine Sprache aus Geschäftsgründen, zum Vergnügen oder als Vorbereitung für einen Auslandsurlaub lernen, oder Ihr Vokabular in einer Ihnen bereits vertrauten Sprache erweitern möchten, dieses Wörterbuch ist ein wertvolles Lernmittel, das Sie auf vielfältige Art und Weise benutzen können.

Wenn Sie eine neue Sprache lernen, achten Sie auf Wörter, die in verschiedenen Sprachen ähnlich sind sowie auf falsche Freunde (Wörter, die ähnlich aussehen aber wesentlich andere Bedeutungen haben). Sie können ebenfalls feststellen, wie die Sprachen einander beeinflusst haben. Englisch hat zum Beispiel viele Ausdrücke für Nahrungsmittel aus anderen europäischen Sprachen übernommen und andererseits viele Begriffe aus der Technik und Popkultur ausgeführt.

## Praktische Übungen
• Versuchen Sie sich zu Hause, am Arbeits- oder Studienplatz den Inhalt der Seiten einzuprägen, die Ihre Umgebung behandeln. Schließen Sie dann das Buch und prüfen Sie, wie viele Gegenstände Sie in den anderen Sprachen sagen können.
• Schreiben Sie eine Geschichte, einen Brief oder Dialog und benutzen Sie dabei möglichst viele Ausdrücke von einer bestimmten Seite des Wörterbuchs. Dies ist eine gute Methode, sich das Vokabular und die Schreibweise einzuprägen. Sie können mit kurzen Sätzen von zwei bis drei Worten anfangen und dann nach und nach längere Texte schreiben.
• Wenn Sie ein visuelles Gedächtnis haben, können Sie Gegenstände aus dem Buch abzeichnen oder abpausen. Schließen Sie dann das Buch und schreiben Sie die passenden Wörter unter die Bilder.
• Wenn Sie mehr Sicherheit haben, können Sie Wörter aus einem der Fremdsprachenregister aussuchen und deren Bedeutung aufschreiben, bevor Sie auf der entsprechenden Seite nachsehen.

# how to use this book

Whether you are learning a new language for business, pleasure, or in preparation for a holiday abroad, or are hoping to extend your vocabulary in an already familiar language, this dictionary is a valuable learning tool which you can use in a number of different ways.

When learning a new language, look out for cognates (words that are alike in different languages) and false friends (words that look alike but carry significantly different meanings). You can also see where the languages have influenced each other. For example, English has imported many terms for food from other European languages but, in turn, exported terms used in technology and popular culture.

## Practical learning activities
• As you move about your home, workplace, or college, try looking at the pages which cover that scene. You could then close the book, look around you and see how many of the objects and features you can name.
• Challenge yourself to write a story, letter, or dialogue using as many of the terms on a particular page as possible. This will help you retain the vocabulary and remember the spelling. If you want to build up to writing a longer text, start with sentences incorporating 2–3 words.
• If you have a very visual memory, try drawing or tracing items from the book onto a piece of paper, then close the book and fill in the words below the picture.
• Once you are more confident, pick out words in a foreign-language index and see if you know what they mean before turning to the relevant page to check if you were right.

**die Menschen**
people

# der Körper • body

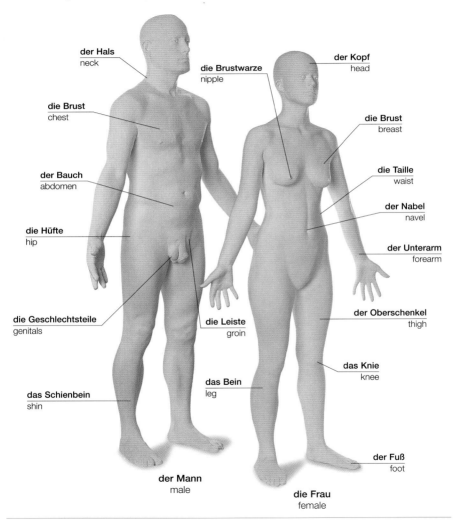

**der Hals**
neck

**die Brustwarze**
nipple

**der Kopf**
head

**die Brust**
chest

**die Brust**
breast

**die Taille**
waist

**der Bauch**
abdomen

**der Nabel**
navel

**die Hüfte**
hip

**der Unterarm**
forearm

**die Geschlechtsteile**
genitals

**die Leiste**
groin

**der Oberschenkel**
thigh

**das Knie**
knee

**das Bein**
leg

**das Schienbein**
shin

**der Fuß**
foot

**der Mann**
male

**die Frau**
female

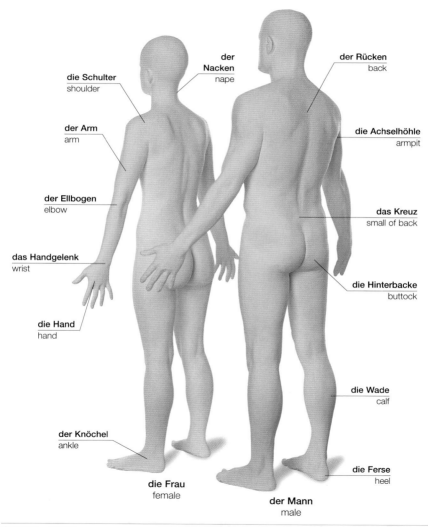

**die Schulter**
shoulder

**der Nacken**
nape

**der Rücken**
back

**der Arm**
arm

**die Achselhöhle**
armpit

**der Ellbogen**
elbow

**das Kreuz**
small of back

**das Handgelenk**
wrist

**die Hinterbacke**
buttock

**die Hand**
hand

**die Wade**
calf

**der Knöchel**
ankle

**die Ferse**
heel

**die Frau**
female

**der Mann**
male

# das Gesicht • face

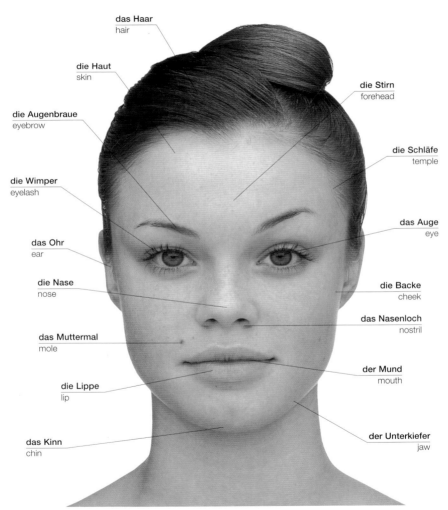

**das Haar**
hair

**die Haut**
skin

**die Augenbraue**
eyebrow

**die Wimper**
eyelash

**das Ohr**
ear

**die Nase**
nose

**das Muttermal**
mole

**die Lippe**
lip

**das Kinn**
chin

**die Stirn**
forehead

**die Schläfe**
temple

**das Auge**
eye

**die Backe**
cheek

**das Nasenloch**
nostril

**der Mund**
mouth

**der Unterkiefer**
jaw

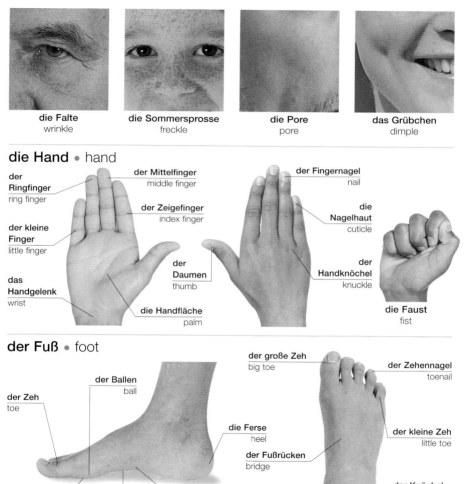

**die Falte**
wrinkle

**die Sommersprosse**
freckle

**die Pore**
pore

**das Grübchen**
dimple

## die Hand • hand

der
**Ringfinger**
ring finger

der **Mittelfinger**
middle finger

der **Zeigefinger**
index finger

der **Fingernagel**
nail

der kleine
**Finger**
little finger

die
**Nagelhaut**
cuticle

das
**Handgelenk**
wrist

der
**Daumen**
thumb

der
**Handknöchel**
knuckle

die **Handfläche**
palm

**die Faust**
fist

## der Fuß • foot

der **große Zeh**
big toe

der **Zehennagel**
toenail

der **Ballen**
ball

der **Zeh**
toe

die **Ferse**
heel

der **Fußrücken**
bridge

der **kleine Zeh**
little toe

die **Fußsohle**
sole

der **Spann**
instep

das **Gewölbe**
arch

der **Knöchel**
ankle

# die Muskeln • muscles

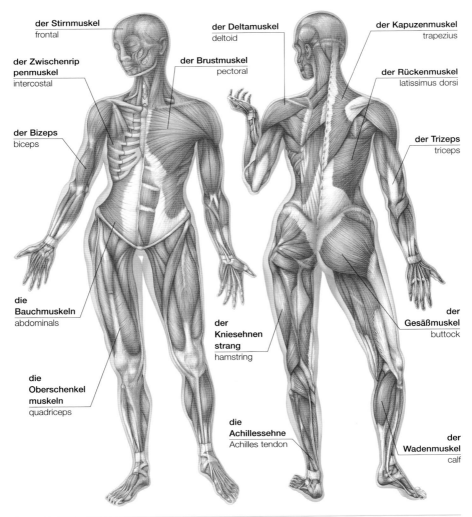

der Stirnmuskel
frontal

der Deltamuskel
deltoid

der Kapuzenmuskel
trapezius

der Zwischenrip
penmuskel
intercostal

der Brustmuskel
pectoral

der Rückenmuskel
latissimus dorsi

der Bizeps
biceps

der Trizeps
triceps

die
Bauchmuskeln
abdominals

der Kniesehnen
strang
hamstring

der
Gesäßmuskel
buttock

die
Oberschenkel
muskeln
quadriceps

die
Achillessehne
Achilles tendon

der
Wadenmuskel
calf

# das Skelett • skeleton

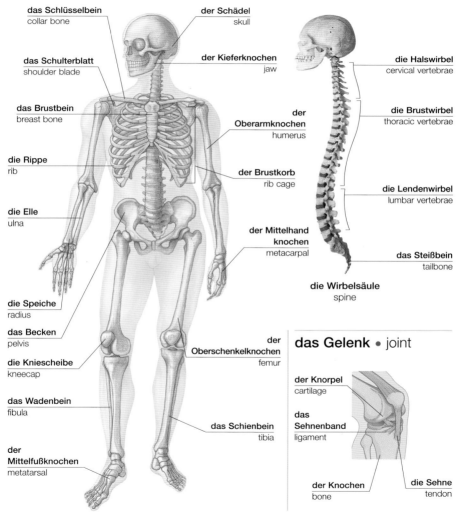

das Schlüsselbein
collar bone

der Schädel
skull

das Schulterblatt
shoulder blade

der Kieferknochen
jaw

die Halswirbel
cervical vertebrae

das Brustbein
breast bone

der Oberarmknochen
humerus

die Brustwirbel
thoracic vertebrae

die Rippe
rib

der Brustkorb
rib cage

die Elle
ulna

die Lendenwirbel
lumbar vertebrae

der Mittelhand knochen
metacarpal

das Steißbein
tailbone

die Wirbelsäule
spine

die Speiche
radius

das Becken
pelvis

der Oberschenkelknochen
femur

# das Gelenk • joint

die Kniescheibe
kneecap

das Wadenbein
fibula

der Knorpel
cartilage

das Schienbein
tibia

das Sehnenband
ligament

der Mittelfußknochen
metatarsal

der Knochen
bone

die Sehne
tendon

# die inneren Organe • internal organs

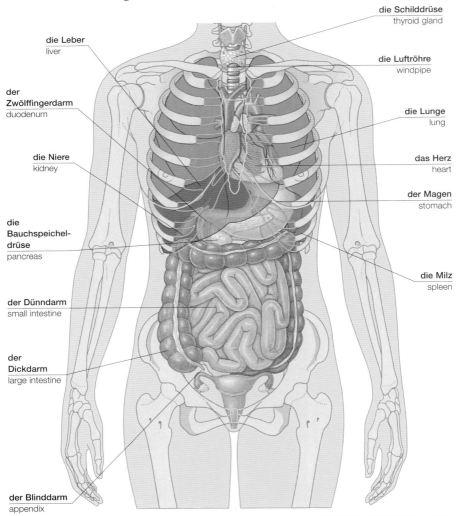

die Schilddrüse
thyroid gland

die Leber
liver

der
Zwölffingerdarm
duodenum

die Luftröhre
windpipe

die Lunge
lung

die Niere
kidney

das Herz
heart

der Magen
stomach

die
Bauchspeichel-
drüse
pancreas

die Milz
spleen

der Dünndarm
small intestine

der
Dickdarm
large intestine

der Blinddarm
appendix

# der Kopf • head

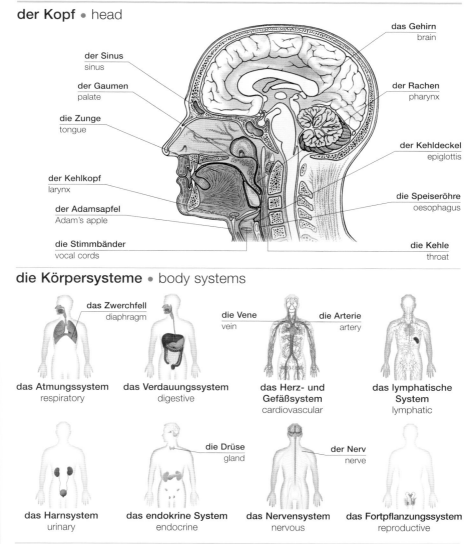

**das Gehirn**
brain

**der Sinus**
sinus

**der Gaumen**
palate

**die Zunge**
tongue

**der Rachen**
pharynx

**der Kehlkopf**
larynx

**der Adamsapfel**
Adam's apple

**der Kehldeckel**
epiglottis

**die Speiseröhre**
oesophagus

**die Stimmbänder**
vocal cords

**die Kehle**
throat

# die Körpersysteme • body systems

**das Zwerchfell**
diaphragm

**die Vene**
vein

**die Arterie**
artery

**das Atmungssystem**
respiratory

**das Verdauungssystem**
digestive

**das Herz- und Gefäßsystem**
cardiovascular

**das lymphatische System**
lymphatic

**die Drüse**
gland

**der Nerv**
nerve

**das Harnsystem**
urinary

**das endokrine System**
endocrine

**das Nervensystem**
nervous

**das Fortpflanzungssystem**
reproductive

# die Fortpflanzungsorgane • reproductive organs

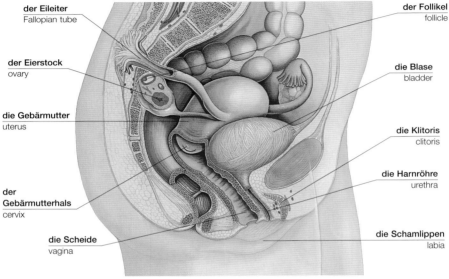

der Eileiter
Fallopian tube

der Eierstock
ovary

die Gebärmutter
uterus

der
Gebärmutterhals
cervix

die Scheide
vagina

der Follikel
follicle

die Blase
bladder

die Klitoris
clitoris

die Harnröhre
urethra

die Schamlippen
labia

**weiblich** | female

## die Fortpflanzung • reproduction

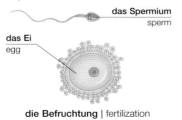

das Spermium
sperm

das Ei
egg

**die Befruchtung** | fertilization

**Vokabular** • vocabulary

| | | |
|---|---|---|
| **steril**<br>infertile | **impotent**<br>impotent | **die Menstruation**<br>menstruation |
| **fruchtbar**<br>fertile | **empfangen**<br>conceive | **der Geschlechtsverkehr**<br>intercourse |
| **das Hormon**<br>hormone | **der Eisprung**<br>ovulation | **die Geschlechtskrankheit**<br>sexually transmitted disease |

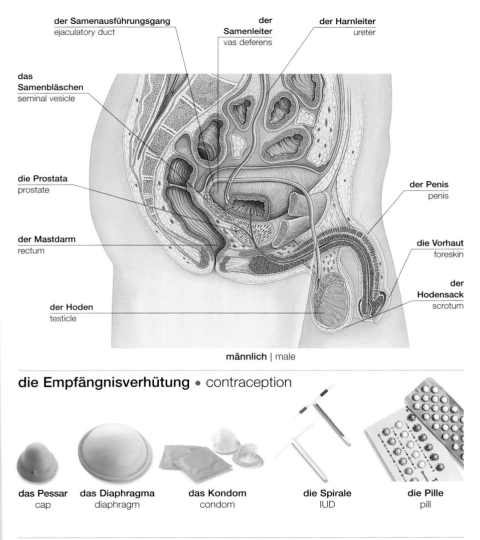

**der Samenausführungsgang**
ejaculatory duct

**der Samenleiter**
vas deferens

**der Harnleiter**
ureter

**das Samenbläschen**
seminal vesicle

**die Prostata**
prostate

**der Mastdarm**
rectum

**der Hoden**
testicle

**der Penis**
penis

**die Vorhaut**
foreskin

**der Hodensack**
scrotum

**männlich** | male

# die Empfängnisverhütung • contraception

**das Pessar**
cap

**das Diaphragma**
diaphragm

**das Kondom**
condom

**die Spirale**
IUD

**die Pille**
pill

# die Familie • family

**die Großmutter**
grandmother

**der Großvater**
grandfather

**der Onkel**
uncle

**die Tante**
aunt

**der Vater**
father

**die Mutter**
mother

**der Cousin**
cousin

**der Bruder**
brother

**die Schwester**
sister

**die Ehefrau**
wife

**die Schwiegertochter**
daughter-in-law

**der Sohn**
son

**die Tochter**
daughter

**der Schwiegersohn**
son-in-law

**der Enkel**
grandson

**die Enkelin**
granddaughter

**der Ehemann**
husband

## Vokabular • vocabulary

| die Großeltern grandparents | die Verwandten relatives | die Enkelkinder grandchildren | die Stiefmutter stepmother | die Stieftochter stepdaughter | die Generation generation |
|---|---|---|---|---|---|
| die Eltern parents | die Kinder children | der Stiefvater stepfather | der Stiefsohn stepson | der Partner/die Partnerin partner | die Zwillinge twins |

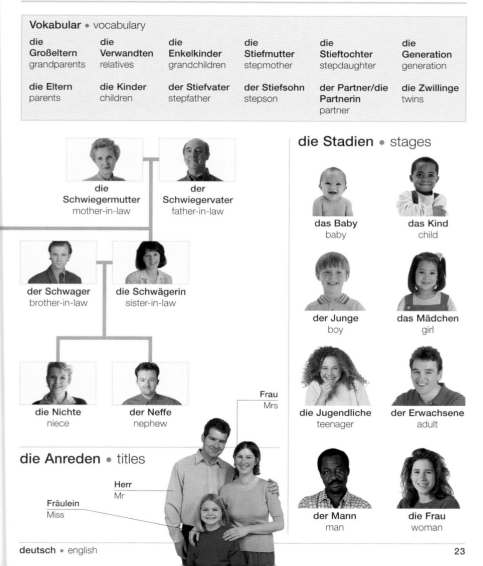

die
Schwiegermutter
mother-in-law

der
Schwiegervater
father-in-law

der Schwager
brother-in-law

die Schwägerin
sister-in-law

die Nichte
niece

der Neffe
nephew

## die Anreden • titles

Herr
Mr

Fräulein
Miss

Frau
Mrs

## die Stadien • stages

das Baby
baby

das Kind
child

der Junge
boy

das Mädchen
girl

die Jugendliche
teenager

der Erwachsene
adult

der Mann
man

die Frau
woman

# die Beziehungen • relationships

der Chef
manager

die Assistentin
assistant

die Geschäftspartnerin
business partner

die Arbeitgeberin
employer

der Arbeitnehmer
employee

der Kollege
colleague

**das Büro** | office

**der Nachbar**
neighbour

**der Freund**
friend

**der Bekannte**
acquaintance

**der Brieffreund**
penfriend

der Freund
boyfriend

die Freundin
girlfriend

der Verlobte
fiancé

die Verlobte
fiancée

**das Paar** | couple

**die Verlobten** | engaged couple

# die Gefühle • emotions

das Lächeln
smile

**glücklich**
happy

**traurig**
sad

**aufgeregt**
excited

**gelangweilt**
bored

**überrascht**
surprised

das Stirnrunzeln
frown

**erschrocken**
scared

**verärgert**
angry

**verwirrt**
confused

**besorgt**
worried

**nervös**
nervous

**stolz**
proud

**selbstsicher**
confident

**verlegen**
embarrassed

**schüchtern**
shy

## Vokabular • vocabulary

| | | | |
|---|---|---|---|
| **bestürzt** upset | **schreien** shout (v) | **lachen** laugh (v) | **seufzen** sigh (v) |
| **schockiert** shocked | **gähnen** yawn (v) | **weinen** cry (v) | **in Ohnmacht fallen** faint (v) |

# die Ereignisse des Lebens • life events

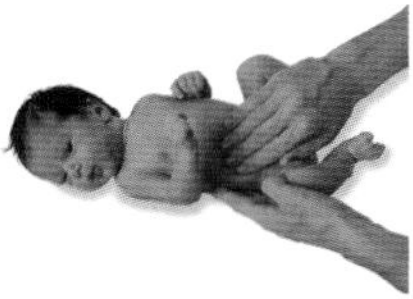

**geboren werden**
be born (v)

**zur Schule kommen**
start school (v)

**sich befreunden**
make friends (v)

**graduieren**
graduate (v)

**eine Stelle bekommen**
get a job (v)

**sich verlieben**
fall in love (v)

**heiraten**
get married (v)

**ein Baby bekommen**
have a baby (v)

**die Hochzeit** | wedding

**die Scheidung**
divorce

**das Begräbnis**
funeral

## vokabular • vocabulary

| | |
|---|---|
| **die Taufe**<br>christening | **emigrieren**<br>emigrate (v) |
| **die Bar Mizwa**<br>bar mitzvah | **sterben**<br>die (v) |
| **der Hochzeitstag**<br>anniversary | **die Hochzeitsfeier**<br>wedding reception |
| **in den Ruhestand treten**<br>retire (v) | **die Hochzeitsreise**<br>honeymoon |
| **sein Testament machen**<br>make a will (v) | **die Geburtsurkunde**<br>birth certificate |

# die Feste • celebrations

**die Geburtstagsfeier**
birthday party

**die Karte**
card

**der Geburtstag**
birthday

**das Geschenk**
present

**das Weihnachten**
Christmas

**das Neujahr**
New Year

**der Karneval**
carnival

**der Umzug**
procession

**das Band**
ribbon

**der Thanksgiving Day**
Thanksgiving

**das Ostern**
Easter

**das Halloween**
Halloween

# die Feste • festivals

**das Passah**
Passover

**der Ramadan**
Ramadan

**das Diwali**
Diwali

**die äußere Erscheinung**
appearance

# die Kinderkleidung • children's clothing

## das Baby • baby

**der Schneeanzug**
snowsuit

das
**Hemdchen**
vest

der
**Druckknopf**
popper

der
**Strampelanzug**
babygro

**der Schlafanzug**
sleepsuit

**der Spielanzug**
romper suit

**das Lätzchen**
bib

die
**Babyhandschuhe**
mittens

die
**Babyschuhe**
booties

die
**Stoffwindel**
terry nappy

die
**Wegwerfwindel**
disposable nappy

das
**Gummihöschen**
plastic pants

## das Kleinkind • toddler

**die Latzhose**
dungarees

**das T-Shirt**
t-shirt

**der Sonnenhut**
sunhat

**die Shorts**
shorts

**der Rock**
skirt

**die Schürze**
apron

# das Kind • child

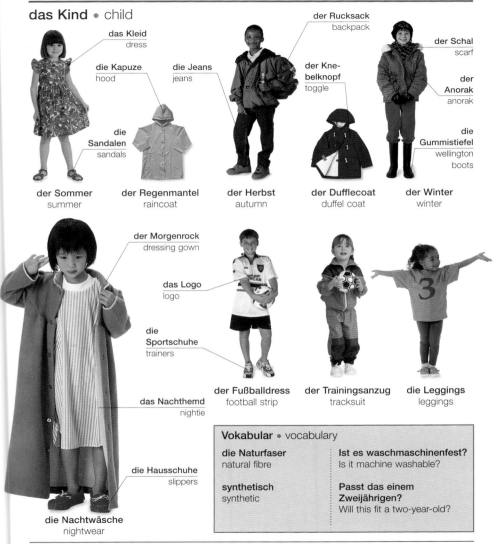

**das Kleid**
dress

**die Kapuze**
hood

**die Jeans**
jeans

**der Rucksack**
backpack

**der Knebelknopf**
toggle

**der Schal**
scarf

**der Anorak**
anorak

**die Sandalen**
sandals

**die Gummistiefel**
wellington boots

**der Sommer**
summer

**der Regenmantel**
raincoat

**der Herbst**
autumn

**der Dufflecoat**
duffel coat

**der Winter**
winter

**der Morgenrock**
dressing gown

**das Logo**
logo

**die Sportschuhe**
trainers

**das Nachthemd**
nightie

**die Hausschuhe**
slippers

**die Nachtwäsche**
nightwear

**der Fußballdress**
football strip

**der Trainingsanzug**
tracksuit

**die Leggings**
leggings

| **Vokabular** • vocabulary | |
|---|---|
| **die Naturfaser**<br>natural fibre | **Ist es waschmaschinenfest?**<br>Is it machine washable? |
| **synthetisch**<br>synthetic | **Passt das einem Zweijährigen?**<br>Will this fit a two-year-old? |

# die Herrenkleidung • men's clothing

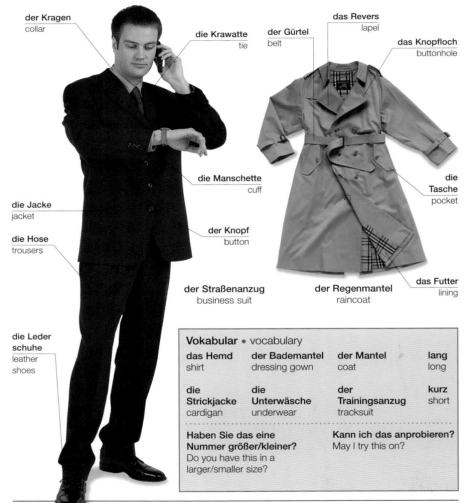

**der Kragen**
collar

**die Krawatte**
tie

**der Gürtel**
belt

**das Revers**
lapel

**das Knopfloch**
buttonhole

**die Manschette**
cuff

**die Jacke**
jacket

**die Hose**
trousers

**der Knopf**
button

**die Tasche**
pocket

**die Leder schuhe**
leather shoes

**der Straßenanzug**
business suit

**der Regenmantel**
raincoat

**das Futter**
lining

---

**Vokabular** • vocabulary

| | | | |
|---|---|---|---|
| **das Hemd** shirt | **der Bademantel** dressing gown | **der Mantel** coat | **lang** long |
| **die Strickjacke** cardigan | **die Unterwäsche** underwear | **der Trainingsanzug** tracksuit | **kurz** short |

**Haben Sie das eine Nummer größer/kleiner?**
Do you have this in a larger/smaller size?

**Kann ich das anprobieren?**
May I try this on?

der V-Ausschnitt
v-neck

der runde
Ausschnitt
round neck

**der Blazer**
blazer

**das Sportjackett**
sports jacket

**die Weste**
waistcoat

das T-Shirt
t-shirt

**der Anorak**
anorak

**das Sweatshirt**
sweatshirt

**die Windjacke**
windcheater

die Trainings
hose
sweatpants

**der Pullover**
sweater

**der Schlafanzug**
pyjamas

**das Unterhemd**
vest

**die Freizeitkleidung**
casual wear

**die Shorts**
shorts

**der Slip**
briefs

**die Boxershorts**
boxer shorts

**die Socken**
socks

# die Damenkleidung • women's clothing

der Ausschnitt
neckline

die Jacke
jacket

die Naht
seam

trägerlos
strapless

ärmellos
sleeveless

der Ärmel
sleeve

knöchellang
ankle length

das Abendkleid
evening dress

das Kleid
dress

der Rock
skirt

die Bluse
blouse

knielang
knee-length

die Hose
trousers

der Saum
hem

die Strumpfhose
tights

die Schuhe
shoes

leger
casual

# die Unterwäsche • lingerie

# die Hochzeit • wedding

**der Träger**
strap

**das Negligé**
negligée

**der Unterrock**
slip

**das Mieder**
camisole

**der Strumpfhalter**
suspenders

**das Bustier**
basque

**die Strümpfe**
stockings

**die Strumpfhose**
tights

**das Unterhemd**
vest

**der Büstenhalter**
bra

**der Slip**
knickers

**das Nachthemd**
nightdress

**der Schleier**
veil

**die Spitze**
lace

**das Bukett**
bouquet

**die Schleppe**
train

**das Hochzeitskleid**
wedding dress

## Vokabular • vocabulary

| | |
|---|---|
| **das Korsett**<br>corset | **gut geschnitten**<br>tailored |
| **rückenfrei**<br>halter neck | **das Strumpfband**<br>garter |
| **der Rockbund**<br>waistband | **der Sport-BH**<br>sports bra |
| **das Schulter polster**<br>shoulder pad | **mit Formbügeln**<br>underwired |

# die Accessoires • accessories

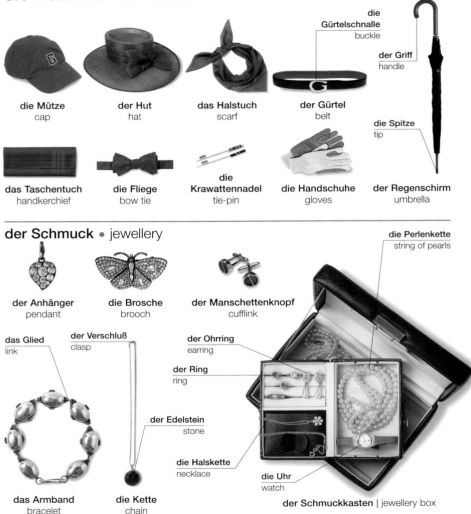

**die Mütze**
cap

**der Hut**
hat

**das Halstuch**
scarf

**der Gürtel**
belt

**die Gürtelschnalle**
buckle

**der Griff**
handle

**die Spitze**
tip

**das Taschentuch**
handkerchief

**die Fliege**
bow tie

**die Krawattennadel**
tie-pin

**die Handschuhe**
gloves

**der Regenschirm**
umbrella

## der Schmuck • jewellery

**der Anhänger**
pendant

**die Brosche**
brooch

**der Manschettenknopf**
cufflink

**die Perlenkette**
string of pearls

**das Glied**
link

**der Verschluß**
clasp

**der Ohrring**
earring

**der Ring**
ring

**der Edelstein**
stone

**die Halskette**
necklace

**die Uhr**
watch

**das Armband**
bracelet

**die Kette**
chain

**der Schmuckkasten** | jewellery box

# die Taschen • bags

der Verschluss
fastening

der Schulterriemen
shoulder strap

die Griffe
handles

**die Brieftasche**
wallet

**das Portemonnaie**
purse

**die Umhängetasche**
shoulder bag

**die Reisetasche**
holdall

**die Aktentasche**
briefcase

**die Handtasche**
handbag

**der Rucksack**
backpack

# die Schuhe • shoes

der Schnürsenkel
lace

die Zunge
tongue

die Öse
eyelet

die Sohle
sole

der Absatz
heel

**der Schnürschuh**
lace-up

**der Wanderschuh**
walking boot

**der Sportschuh**
trainer

**der Lederschuh**
leather shoe

**die Strandsandale**
flip-flop

**der Schuh mit hohem Absatz**
high heel shoe

**der Plateauschuh**
platform shoe

**die Sandale**
sandal

**der Slipper**
slip-on

**der Herrenhalbschuh**
brogue

# das Haar • hair

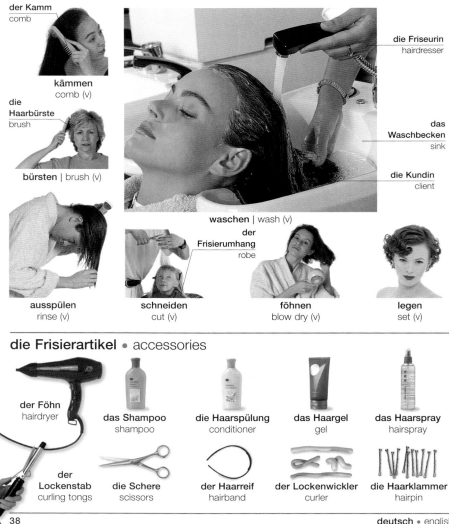

**der Kamm**
comb

**kämmen**
comb (v)

**die Haarbürste**
brush

**bürsten** | brush (v)

**ausspülen**
rinse (v)

**die Friseurin**
hairdresser

**das Waschbecken**
sink

**die Kundin**
client

**waschen** | wash (v)

**der Frisierumhang**
robe

**schneiden**
cut (v)

**föhnen**
blow dry (v)

**legen**
set (v)

# die Frisierartikel • accessories

**der Föhn**
hairdryer

**das Shampoo**
shampoo

**die Haarspülung**
conditioner

**das Haargel**
gel

**das Haarspray**
hairspray

**der Lockenstab**
curling tongs

**die Schere**
scissors

**der Haarreif**
hairband

**der Lockenwickler**
curler

**die Haarklammer**
hairpin

# die Frisuren • styles

das
**Band**
ribbon

**der Pferdeschwanz**
ponytail

**der Zopf**
plait

**die Hochfrisur**
french pleat

**der Haarknoten**
bun

**die Schwänzchen**
pigtails

**der Bubikopf**
bob

**der Kurzhaarschnitt**
crop

**kraus**
curly

**die Dauerwelle**
perm

**glatt**
straight

die **Wurzeln**
roots

**die Strähnen**
highlights

**kahl**
bald

**die Perücke**
wig

| Vokabular • vocabulary | |
|---|---|
| **das Haarband** hairtie | **fettig** greasy |
| **nachschneiden** trim (v) | **trocken** dry |
| **der Herrenfriseur** barber | **normal** normal |
| **die Schuppen** dandruff | **die Kopfhaut** scalp |
| **der Haarspliss** split ends | **glätten** straighten (v) |

# die Haarfarben • colours

**blond**
blonde

**brünett**
brunette

**rotbraun**
auburn

**rot**
ginger

**schwarz**
black

**grau**
grey

**weiß**
white

**gefärbt**
dyed

# die Schönheit • beauty

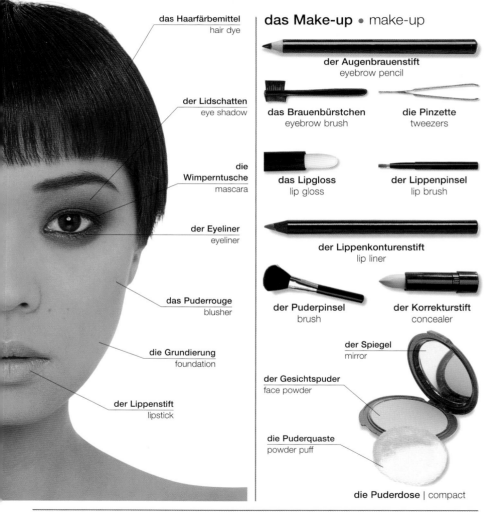

das Haarfärbemittel
hair dye

der Lidschatten
eye shadow

die Wimperntusche
mascara

der Eyeliner
eyeliner

das Puderrouge
blusher

die Grundierung
foundation

der Lippenstift
lipstick

## das Make-up • make-up

der Augenbrauenstift
eyebrow pencil

das Brauenbürstchen
eyebrow brush

die Pinzette
tweezers

das Lipgloss
lip gloss

der Lippenpinsel
lip brush

der Lippenkonturenstift
lip liner

der Puderpinsel
brush

der Korrekturstift
concealer

der Spiegel
mirror

der Gesichtspuder
face powder

die Puderquaste
powder puff

die Puderdose | compact

## die Schönheitsbehandlungen •
beauty treatments

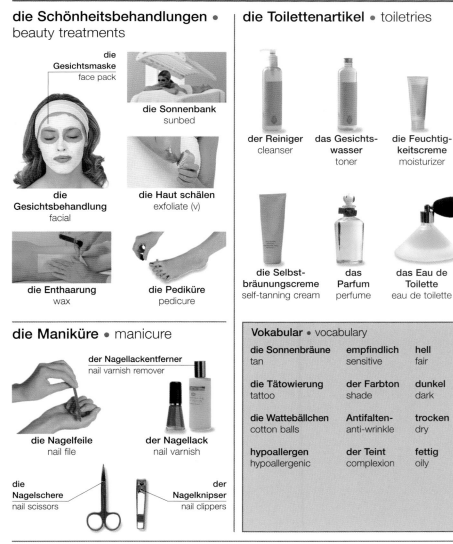

**die Gesichtsmaske**
face pack

**die Sonnenbank**
sunbed

**die Gesichtsbehandlung**
facial

**die Haut schälen**
exfoliate (v)

**die Enthaarung**
wax

**die Pediküre**
pedicure

## die Maniküre • manicure

**der Nagellackentferner**
nail varnish remover

**die Nagelfeile**
nail file

**der Nagellack**
nail varnish

**die Nagelschere**
nail scissors

**der Nagelknipser**
nail clippers

## die Toilettenartikel • toiletries

**der Reiniger**
cleanser

**das Gesichts-wasser**
toner

**die Feuchtig-keitscreme**
moisturizer

**die Selbst-bräunungscreme**
self-tanning cream

**das Parfum**
perfume

**das Eau de Toilette**
eau de toilette

**Vokabular • vocabulary**

| | | |
|---|---|---|
| **die Sonnenbräune** tan | **empfindlich** sensitive | **hell** fair |
| **die Tätowierung** tattoo | **der Farbton** shade | **dunkel** dark |
| **die Wattebällchen** cotton balls | **Antifalten-** anti-wrinkle | **trocken** dry |
| **hypoallergen** hypoallergenic | **der Teint** complexion | **fettig** oily |

**die Gesundheit**
health

# die Krankheit • illness

**das Fieber** | fever

**die Kopfschmerzen**
headache

**das Nasenbluten**
nosebleed

**der Husten**
cough

der Inhalations apparat
inhaler

**das Niesen**
sneeze

**die Erkältung**
cold

**die Grippe**
flu

**das Asthma**
asthma

**die Krämpfe**
cramps

**die Übelkeit**
nausea

**die Windpocken**
chickenpox

**der Hautausschlag**
rash

---

**Vokabular • vocabulary**

| | | | | | |
|---|---|---|---|---|---|
| **der Herzinfarkt**<br>heart attack | **die Allergie**<br>allergy | **das Ekzem**<br>eczema | **die Verkühlung**<br>chill | **die Epilepsie**<br>epilepsy | **der Durchfall**<br>diarrhoea |
| **der Blutdruck**<br>blood pressure | **der Mumps**<br>mumps | **der Virus**<br>virus | **die Migräne**<br>migraine | **sich übergeben**<br>vomit (v) | **die Masern**<br>measles |
| **der Schlaganfall**<br>stroke | **die Zucker krankheit**<br>diabetes | **die Infektion**<br>infection | **die Magenschmerzen**<br>stomach ache | **in Ohnmacht fallen**<br>faint (v) | **der Heuschnupfen**<br>hayfever |

---

# der Arzt • doctor
## die Konsultation • consultation

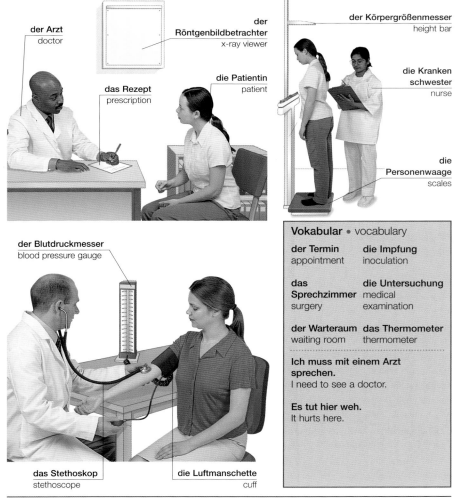

**der Arzt**
doctor

**der Röntgenbildbetrachter**
x-ray viewer

**das Rezept**
prescription

**die Patientin**
patient

**der Körpergrößenmesser**
height bar

**die Kranken schwester**
nurse

**die Personenwaage**
scales

**der Blutdruckmesser**
blood pressure gauge

**das Stethoskop**
stethoscope

**die Luftmanschette**
cuff

**Vokabular** • vocabulary

| | |
|---|---|
| **der Termin**<br>appointment | **die Impfung**<br>inoculation |
| **das Sprechzimmer** surgery | **die Untersuchung** medical examination |
| **der Warteraum** waiting room | **das Thermometer** thermometer |

**Ich muss mit einem Arzt sprechen.**
I need to see a doctor.

**Es tut hier weh.**
It hurts here.

# die Verletzung • injury

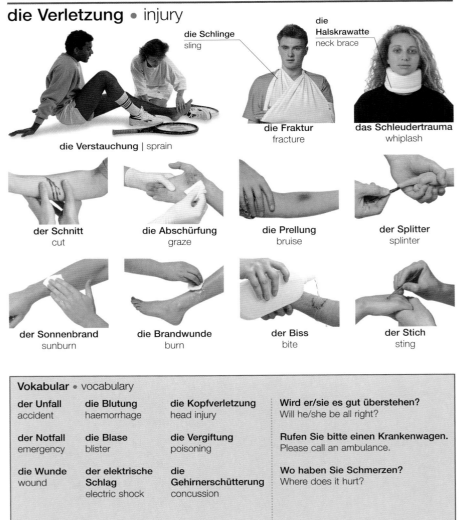

die Schlinge
sling

die Halskrawatte
neck brace

**die Fraktur**
fracture

**das Schleudertrauma**
whiplash

**die Verstauchung** | sprain

**der Schnitt**
cut

**die Abschürfung**
graze

**die Prellung**
bruise

**der Splitter**
splinter

**der Sonnenbrand**
sunburn

**die Brandwunde**
burn

**der Biss**
bite

**der Stich**
sting

---

**Vokabular** • vocabulary

| | | | |
|---|---|---|---|
| **der Unfall**<br>accident | **die Blutung**<br>haemorrhage | **die Kopfverletzung**<br>head injury | **Wird er/sie es gut überstehen?**<br>Will he/she be all right? |
| **der Notfall**<br>emergency | **die Blase**<br>blister | **die Vergiftung**<br>poisoning | **Rufen Sie bitte einen Krankenwagen.**<br>Please call an ambulance. |
| **die Wunde**<br>wound | **der elektrische Schlag**<br>electric shock | **die Gehirnerschütterung**<br>concussion | **Wo haben Sie Schmerzen?**<br>Where does it hurt? |

---

# die erste Hilfe • first aid

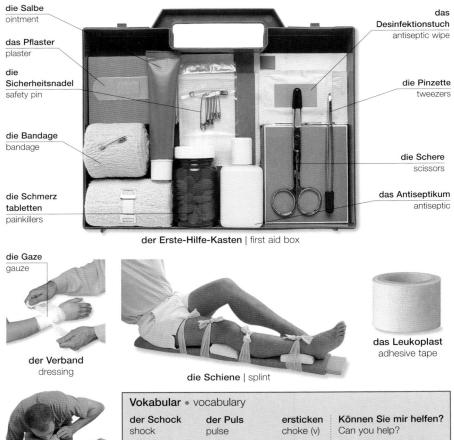

**die Salbe**
ointment

**das Pflaster**
plaster

**die Sicherheitsnadel**
safety pin

**die Bandage**
bandage

**die Schmerz tabletten**
painkillers

**das Desinfektionstuch**
antiseptic wipe

**die Pinzette**
tweezers

**die Schere**
scissors

**das Antiseptikum**
antiseptic

**der Erste-Hilfe-Kasten** | first aid box

**die Gaze**
gauze

**der Verband**
dressing

**die Schiene** | splint

**das Leukoplast**
adhesive tape

**die Wiederbelebung**
resuscitation

**Vokabular** • vocabulary

| | | | |
|---|---|---|---|
| **der Schock**<br>shock | **der Puls**<br>pulse | **ersticken**<br>choke (v) | **Können Sie mir helfen?**<br>Can you help? |
| **bewusstlos**<br>unconscious | **die Atmung**<br>breathing | **steril**<br>sterile | **Beherrschen Sie die Erste Hilfe?**<br>Do you know first aid? |

# das Krankenhaus • hospital

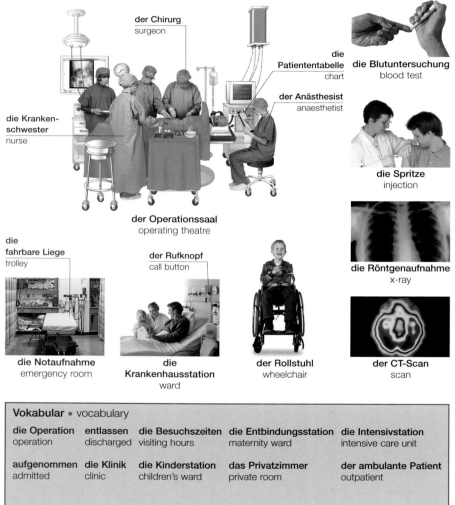

**der Chirurg**
surgeon

die
**Patiententabelle**
chart

**der Anästhesist**
anaesthetist

**die Kranken-
schwester**
nurse

**der Operationssaal**
operating theatre

**die Blutuntersuchung**
blood test

**die Spritze**
injection

**die Röntgenaufnahme**
x-ray

die
**fahrbare Liege**
trolley

**der Rufknopf**
call button

**die Notaufnahme**
emergency room

**die
Krankenhausstation**
ward

**der Rollstuhl**
wheelchair

**der CT-Scan**
scan

## Vokabular • vocabulary

| | | | | |
|---|---|---|---|---|
| **die Operation**<br>operation | **entlassen**<br>discharged | **die Besuchszeiten**<br>visiting hours | **die Entbindungsstation**<br>maternity ward | **die Intensivstation**<br>intensive care unit |
| **aufgenommen**<br>admitted | **die Klinik**<br>clinic | **die Kinderstation**<br>children's ward | **das Privatzimmer**<br>private room | **der ambulante Patient**<br>outpatient |

# die Abteilungen • departments

**die HNO-Abteilung**
ENT

**die Kardiologie**
cardiology

**die Orthopädie**
orthopaedy

**die Gynäkologie**
gynaecology

**die Physiotherapie**
physiotherapy

**die Dermatologie**
dermatology

**die Pädiatrie**
paediatrics

**die Radiologie**
radiology

**die Chirurgie**
surgery

**die Entbindungsstation**
maternity

**die Psychiatrie**
psychiatry

**die Ophthalmologie**
ophthalmology

---

**Vokabular • vocabulary**

| | | | | |
|---|---|---|---|---|
| **die Neurologie** neurology | **die Urologie** urology | **die plastische Chirurgie** plastic surgery | **die Pathologie** pathology | **das Ergebnis** result |
| **die Onkologie** oncology | **die Endokrinologie** endocrinology | **die Überweisung** referral | **die Untersuchung** test | **der Facharzt** consultant |

---

# der Zahnarzt • dentist

## der Zahn • tooth

der Zahnschmelz
enamel

das Zahnfleisch
gum

der Nerv
nerve

die Zahnwurzel
root

der vordere Backenzahn
premolar

der Schneidezahn
incisor

der Backenzahn
molar

der Eckzahn
canine

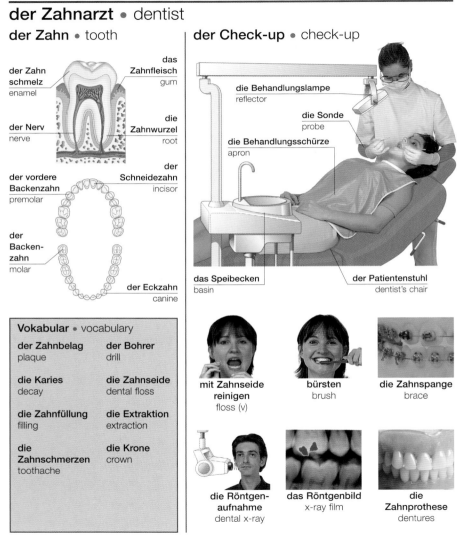

### Vokabular • vocabulary

| | |
|---|---|
| der Zahnbelag<br>plaque | der Bohrer<br>drill |
| die Karies<br>decay | die Zahnseide<br>dental floss |
| die Zahnfüllung<br>filling | die Extraktion<br>extraction |
| die Zahnschmerzen<br>toothache | die Krone<br>crown |

## der Check-up • check-up

die Behandlungslampe
reflector

die Sonde
probe

die Behandlungsschürze
apron

das Speibecken
basin

der Patientenstuhl
dentist's chair

mit Zahnseide reinigen
floss (v)

bürsten
brush

die Zahnspange
brace

die Röntgenaufnahme
dental x-ray

das Röntgenbild
x-ray film

die Zahnprothese
dentures

# der Augenoptiker • optician

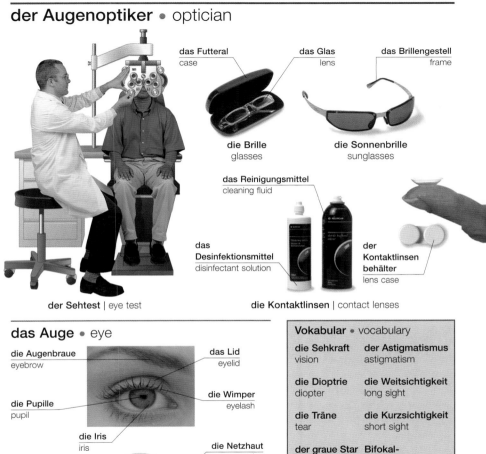

**das Futteral**
case

**das Glas**
lens

**das Brillengestell**
frame

**die Brille**
glasses

**die Sonnenbrille**
sunglasses

**das Reinigungsmittel**
cleaning fluid

**das Desinfektionsmittel**
disinfectant solution

**der Kontaktlinsen behälter**
lens case

**der Sehtest** | eye test

**die Kontaktlinsen** | contact lenses

## das Auge • eye

**die Augenbraue**
eyebrow

**das Lid**
eyelid

**die Pupille**
pupil

**die Wimper**
eyelash

**die Iris**
iris

**die Netzhaut**
retina

**die Linse**
lens

**der Sehnerv**
optic nerve

**die Hornhaut**
cornea

| **Vokabular** • vocabulary | |
|---|---|
| **die Sehkraft** vision | **der Astigmatismus** astigmatism |
| **die Dioptrie** diopter | **die Weitsichtigkeit** long sight |
| **die Träne** tear | **die Kurzsichtigkeit** short sight |
| **der graue Star** cataract | **Bifokal-** bifocal |

# die Schwangerschaft • pregnancy

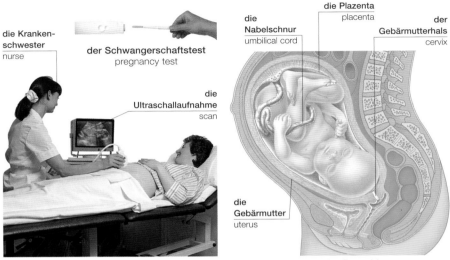

die Kranken-
schwester
nurse

der Schwangerschaftstest
pregnancy test

die
Ultraschallaufnahme
scan

die Plazenta
placenta

die
Nabelschnur
umbilical cord

der
Gebärmutterhals
cervix

die
Gebärmutter
uterus

**der Ultraschall** | ultrasound

**der Fetus** | foetus

| **Vokabular** • vocabulary | | | | | |
|---|---|---|---|---|---|
| **der Eisprung** ovulation | **vorgeburtlich** antenatal | **das Fruchtwasser** amniotic fluid | **die Erweiterung** dilation | **die Naht** stitches | **Steiß-** breech |
| **schwanger** pregnant | **der Embryo** embryo | **die Amniozentese** amniocentesis | **der Kaiserschnitt** caesarean section | **die Geburt** birth | **vorzeitig** premature |
| **die Empfängnis** conception | **die Gebärmutter** womb | **das Fruchtwasser geht ab** break waters (v) | **die Periduralanästhesie** epidural | **die Entbindung** delivery | **der Gynäkologe** gynaecologist |
| **schwanger** expectant | **das Trimester** trimester | **die Wehe** contraction | **der Dammschnitt** episiotomy | **die Fehlgeburt** miscarriage | **der Geburtshelfer** obstetrician |

# die Geburt • childbirth

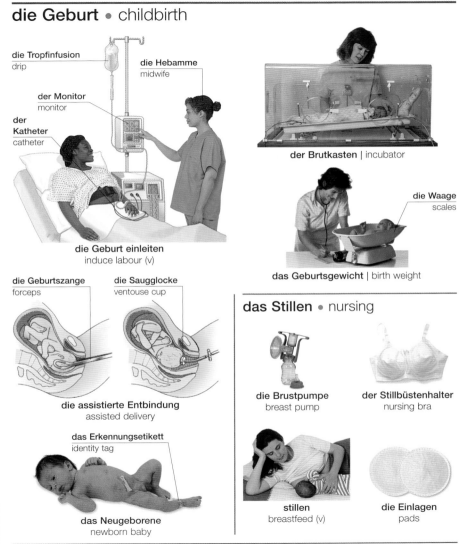

die Tropfinfusion
drip

die Hebamme
midwife

der Monitor
monitor

der Katheter
catheter

**die Geburt einleiten**
induce labour (v)

der Brutkasten | incubator

die Waage
scales

**das Geburtsgewicht** | birth weight

die Geburtszange
forceps

die Saugglocke
ventouse cup

**die assistierte Entbindung**
assisted delivery

das Erkennungsetikett
identity tag

**das Neugeborene**
newborn baby

## das Stillen • nursing

die Brustpumpe
breast pump

der Stillbüstenhalter
nursing bra

stillen
breastfeed (v)

die Einlagen
pads

# die Alternativtherapien • alternative therapy

der Lehrer
teacher

die Massage
massage

das Shiatsu
shiatsu

**das Yoga** | yoga

die Matte
mat

die Meditation
meditation

**die Chiropraktik**
chiropractic

**die Osteopathie**
osteopathy

**die Reflexzonenmassage**
reflexology

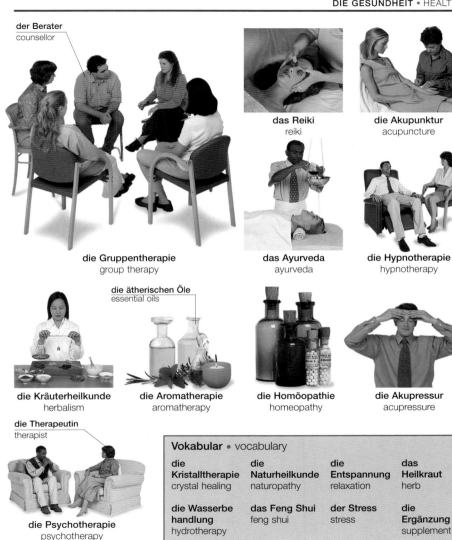

**der Berater**
counsellor

**die Gruppentherapie**
group therapy

**das Reiki**
reiki

**die Akupunktur**
acupuncture

**das Ayurveda**
ayurveda

**die Hypnotherapie**
hypnotherapy

**die ätherischen Öle**
essential oils

**die Kräuterheilkunde**
herbalism

**die Aromatherapie**
aromatherapy

**die Homöopathie**
homeopathy

**die Akupressur**
acupressure

**die Therapeutin**
therapist

**die Psychotherapie**
psychotherapy

**Vokabular** • vocabulary

| | | | |
|---|---|---|---|
| **die Kristalltherapie** crystal healing | **die Naturheilkunde** naturopathy | **die Entspannung** relaxation | **das Heilkraut** herb |
| **die Wasserbe handlung** hydrotherapy | **das Feng Shui** feng shui | **der Stress** stress | **die Ergänzung** supplement |

**das Haus**
home

# das Haus • house

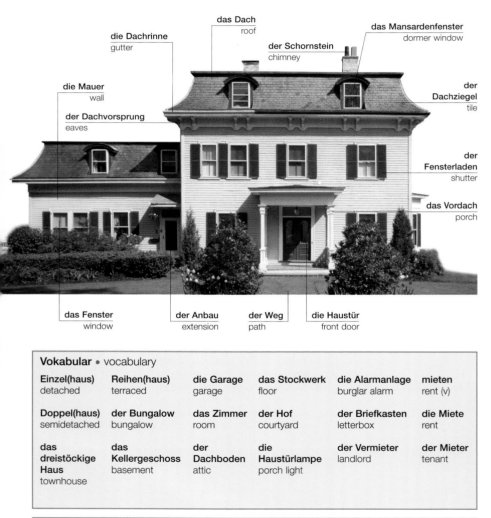

das Dach
roof

die Dachrinne
gutter

der Schornstein
chimney

das Mansardenfenster
dormer window

die Mauer
wall

der Dachvorsprung
eaves

der
Dachziegel
tile

der
Fensterladen
shutter

das Vordach
porch

das Fenster
window

der Anbau
extension

der Weg
path

die Haustür
front door

**Vokabular** • vocabulary

| | | | | | |
|---|---|---|---|---|---|
| **Einzel(haus)**<br>detached | **Reihen(haus)**<br>terraced | **die Garage**<br>garage | **das Stockwerk**<br>floor | **die Alarmanlage**<br>burglar alarm | **mieten**<br>rent (v) |
| **Doppel(haus)**<br>semidetached | **der Bungalow**<br>bungalow | **das Zimmer**<br>room | **der Hof**<br>courtyard | **der Briefkasten**<br>letterbox | **die Miete**<br>rent |
| **das dreistöckige Haus**<br>townhouse | **das Kellergeschoss**<br>basement | **der Dachboden**<br>attic | **die Haustürlampe**<br>porch light | **der Vermieter**<br>landlord | **der Mieter**<br>tenant |

# der Eingang • entrance

das Geländer
hand rail

der Treppen-absatz
landing

das Treppen-geländer
banister

die Treppe
staircase

die Diele
hallway

die Türklingel
doorbell

der Fußabtreter
doormat

der Türklopfer
door knocker

der Schlüssel
key

die Türkette
door chain

das Schloss
lock

der Türriegel
bolt

## die Wohnung • flat

der Balkon
balcony

der Wohnblock
block of flats

die Sprechanlage
intercom

der Fahrstuhl
lift

# die Hausanschlüsse • internal systems

der Flügel
blade

der Ventilator
fan

der Heizlüfter
convector heater

der Heizkörper
radiator

der Heizofen
heater

## die Elektrizität • electricity

der Glühfaden
filament

die Erdung
earthing

neutral
neutral

die Bajonettfassung
bayonet fitting

der Pol
pin

geladen
live

die Birne
light bulb

der Stecker
plug

die Leitung
wires

**Vokabular** • vocabulary

| | | | | |
|---|---|---|---|---|
| **die Spannung** voltage | **die Sicherung** fuse | **die Steckdose** socket | **der Gleichstrom** direct current | **der Transformator** transformer |
| **das Ampère** amp | **der Generator** generator | **der Schalter** switch | **der Stromzähler** electricity meter | **das Stromnetz** mains supply |
| **der Strom** power | **der Sicherungskasten** fuse box | **der Wechselstrom** alternating current | **der Stromausfall** power cut | |

# die Installation • plumbing

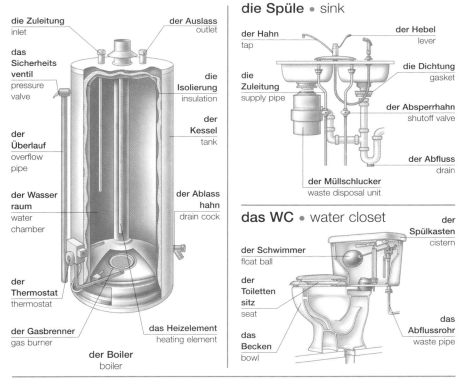

**die Zuleitung**
inlet

**der Auslass**
outlet

**das Sicherheits ventil**
pressure valve

**die Isolierung**
insulation

**der Überlauf**
overflow pipe

**der Kessel**
tank

**der Wasser raum**
water chamber

**der Ablass hahn**
drain cock

**der Thermostat**
thermostat

**der Gasbrenner**
gas burner

**das Heizelement**
heating element

**der Boiler**
boiler

## die Spüle • sink

**der Hahn**
tap

**der Hebel**
lever

**die Dichtung**
gasket

**die Zuleitung**
supply pipe

**der Absperrhahn**
shutoff valve

**der Abfluss**
drain

**der Müllschlucker**
waste disposal unit

## das WC • water closet

**der Spülkasten**
cistern

**der Schwimmer**
float ball

**der Toiletten sitz**
seat

**das Becken**
bowl

**das Abflussrohr**
waste pipe

# die Abfallentsorgung • waste disposal

**die Flasche**
bottle

**der Deckel**
lid

**der Trethebel**
pedal

**der Recyclingbehälter**
recycling bin

**der Abfalleimer**
rubbish bin

**die Abfallsortiereinheit**
sorting unit

**der Bio-Abfall**
organic waste

# das Wohnzimmer • living room

**das Gemälde**
painting

**der Bilderrahmen**
frame

**die Lampe**
lamp

**die Wandlampe**
wall light

**die Uhr**
clock

**die Decke**
ceiling

**die Vitrine**
cabinet

**das Sofa**
sofa

**das Sofakissen**
cushion

**der Couchtisch**
coffee table

**der Fußboden**
floor

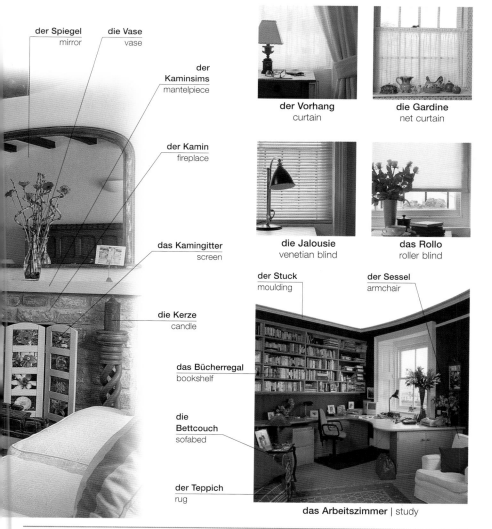

der Spiegel
mirror

die Vase
vase

der
**Kaminsims**
mantelpiece

der **Kamin**
fireplace

das **Kamingitter**
screen

die **Kerze**
candle

das **Bücherregal**
bookshelf

die
**Bettcouch**
sofabed

der **Teppich**
rug

**der Vorhang**
curtain

**die Gardine**
net curtain

**die Jalousie**
venetian blind

**das Rollo**
roller blind

der **Stuck**
moulding

der **Sessel**
armchair

**das Arbeitszimmer** | study

# das Esszimmer • dining room

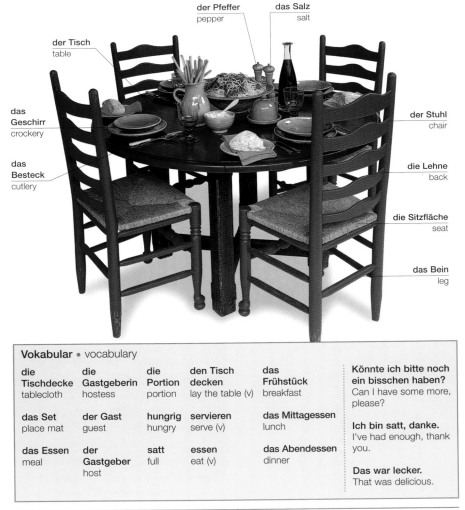

der Pfeffer
pepper

das Salz
salt

der Tisch
table

das
Geschirr
crockery

das
Besteck
cutlery

der Stuhl
chair

die Lehne
back

die Sitzfläche
seat

das Bein
leg

## Vokabular • vocabulary

| | | | | | |
|---|---|---|---|---|---|
| **die Tischdecke** tablecloth | **die Gastgeberin** hostess | **die Portion** portion | **den Tisch decken** lay the table (v) | **das Frühstück** breakfast | **Könnte ich bitte noch ein bisschen haben?** Can I have some more, please? |
| **das Set** place mat | **der Gast** guest | **hungrig** hungry | **servieren** serve (v) | **das Mittagessen** lunch | **Ich bin satt, danke.** I've had enough, thank you. |
| **das Essen** meal | **der Gastgeber** host | **satt** full | **essen** eat (v) | **das Abendessen** dinner | **Das war lecker.** That was delicious. |

# das Geschirr und das Besteck • crockery and cutlery

**der Teelöffel**
teaspoon

**der Becher**
mug

**die Kaffeetasse**
coffee cup

**die Teetasse**
teacup

**der Teller**
plate

**die Schüssel**
bowl

**das Weinglas**
wine glass

**das Wasserglas**
tumbler

**die Cafetière**
cafetière

**die Teekanne**
teapot

**das Kännchen**
jug

**der Eierbecher**
egg cup

**die Glaswaren**
glassware

**der Serviettenring**
napkin ring

**der Beilagenteller**
side plate

**der Essteller**
dinner plate

**der Suppenteller**
soup bowl

**der Suppenlöffel**
soup spoon

**die Gabel**
fork

**die Serviette**
napkin

**das Gedeck**
place setting

**der Löffel**
spoon

**das Messer**
knife

# die Küche • kitchen

der Dunstabzug
extractor

das Küchenregal
shelves

das
Glaskeramik
kochfeld
ceramic hob

der Spritzschutz
splashback

der Wasserhahn
tap

die
Arbeitsfläche
worktop

das
Spülbecken
sink

der Backofen
oven

die Schublade
drawer

der Küchen
schrank
cabinet

## die Küchengeräte • appliances

die
Mixerschüssel
mixing bowl

der Deckel
lid

das
Messer
blade

**die Mikrowelle**
microwave oven

**der Toaster**
toaster

**die
Küchenmaschine**
food processor

**der Mixer**
blender

**die Spülmaschine**
dishwasher

**der
Elektrokessel**
kettle

das
**Eisfach**
ice maker

der
**Kühlschrank**
refrigerator

**der Rost**
shelf

das
**Gefrierfach**
freezer

das
**Gemüsefach**
crisper

**der Gefrier-Kühlschrank** | fridge-freezer

| **Vokabular** • vocabulary | |
|---|---|
| **das Kochfeld**<br>hob | **einfrieren**<br>freeze (v) |
| **das Abtropfbrett**<br>draining board | **auftauen**<br>defrost (v) |
| **der Brenner**<br>burner | **dämpfen**<br>steam (v) |
| **der Mülleimer**<br>rubbish bin | **anbraten**<br>sauté (v) |

## das Kochen • cooking

**schälen**
peel (v)

**schneiden**
slice (v)

**reiben**
grate (v)

**gießen**
pour (v)

**verrühren**
mix (v)

**schlagen**
whisk (v)

**kochen**
boil (v)

**braten**
fry (v)

**ausrollen**
roll (v)

**rühren**
stir (v)

**köcheln lassen**
simmer (v)

**pochieren**
poach (v)

**backen**
bake (v)

**braten**
roast (v)

**grillen**
grill (v)

# die Küchengeräte • kitchenware

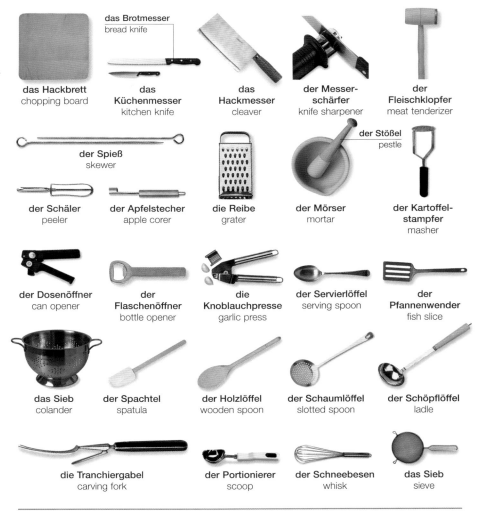

**das Brotmesser**
bread knife

**das Hackbrett**
chopping board

**das Küchenmesser**
kitchen knife

**das Hackmesser**
cleaver

**der Messerschärfer**
knife sharpener

**der Fleischklopfer**
meat tenderizer

**der Spieß**
skewer

**der Stößel**
pestle

**der Schäler**
peeler

**der Apfelstecher**
apple corer

**die Reibe**
grater

**der Mörser**
mortar

**der Kartoffelstampfer**
masher

**der Dosenöffner**
can opener

**der Flaschenöffner**
bottle opener

**die Knoblauchpresse**
garlic press

**der Servierlöffel**
serving spoon

**der Pfannenwender**
fish slice

**das Sieb**
colander

**der Spachtel**
spatula

**der Holzlöffel**
wooden spoon

**der Schaumlöffel**
slotted spoon

**der Schöpflöffel**
ladle

**die Tranchiergabel**
carving fork

**der Portionierer**
scoop

**der Schneebesen**
whisk

**das Sieb**
sieve

der Deckel
lid

kunststoffbeschichtet
non-stick

**die Bratpfanne**
frying pan

**der Kochtopf**
saucepan

**das Grillblech**
grill pan

**der Wok**
wok

**der Schmortopf**
earthenware dish

Glas-
glass

feuerfest
ovenproof

**die Rührschüssel**
mixing bowl

**die Souffléform**
soufflé dish

**die Auflaufform**
gratin dish

**das Auflaufförmchen**
ramekin

**die Kasserolle**
casserole dish

## das Kuchenbacken • baking cakes

**die Haushaltswaage**
scales

**der Messbecher**
measuring jug

**die Kuchenform**
cake tin

**die Pastetenform**
pie tin

**die Obstkuchen-form**
flan tin

**der Backpinsel**
pastry brush

**das Nudelholz**
rolling pin

**der Spritzbeutel**
piping bag

**die Törtchen-form**
muffin tray

**das Kuchenblech**
baking tray

**das Abkühlgitter**
cooling rack

**der Topfhandschuh**
oven glove

**die Schürze**
apron

# das Schlafzimmer • bedroom

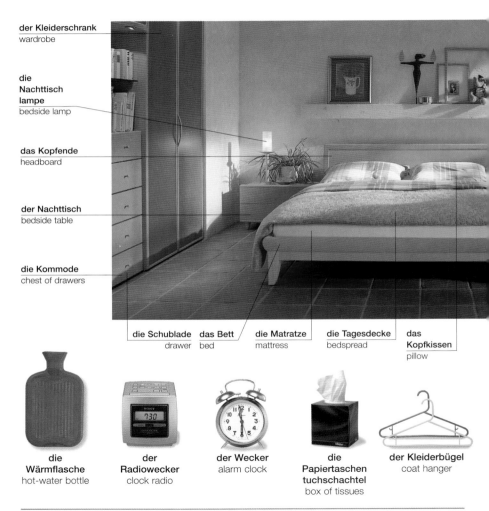

**der Kleiderschrank**
wardrobe

**die
Nachttisch
lampe**
bedside lamp

**das Kopfende**
headboard

**der Nachttisch**
bedside table

**die Kommode**
chest of drawers

**die Schublade** | **das Bett** | **die Matratze** | **die Tagesdecke** | **das Kopfkissen**
drawer | bed | mattress | bedspread | pillow

**die
Wärmflasche**
hot-water bottle

**der
Radiowecker**
clock radio

**der Wecker**
alarm clock

**die
Papiertaschen
tuchschachtel**
box of tissues

**der Kleiderbügel**
coat hanger

# die Bettwäsche • bed linen

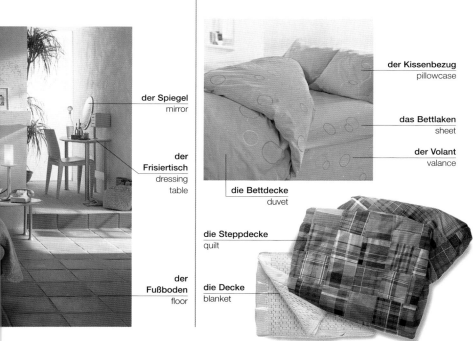

der Kissenbezug
pillowcase

das Bettlaken
sheet

der Volant
valance

der Spiegel
mirror

der
Frisiertisch
dressing
table

die Bettdecke
duvet

die Steppdecke
quilt

der
Fußboden
floor

die Decke
blanket

## Vokabular • vocabulary

| | | | | |
|---|---|---|---|---|
| **das Einzelbett**<br>single bed | **das Fußende**<br>footboard | **die Schlaflosigkeit**<br>insomnia | **aufwachen**<br>wake up (v) | **den Wecker stellen**<br>set the alarm (v) |
| **das Doppelbett**<br>double bed | **die Sprungfeder**<br>spring | **ins Bett gehen**<br>go to bed (v) | **aufstehen**<br>get up (v) | **schnarchen**<br>snore (v) |
| **die Heizdecke**<br>electric blanket | **der Teppich**<br>carpet | **einschlafen**<br>go to sleep (v) | **das Bett machen**<br>make the bed (v) | **der Einbauschrank**<br>built-in wardrobe |

# das Badezimmer • bathroom

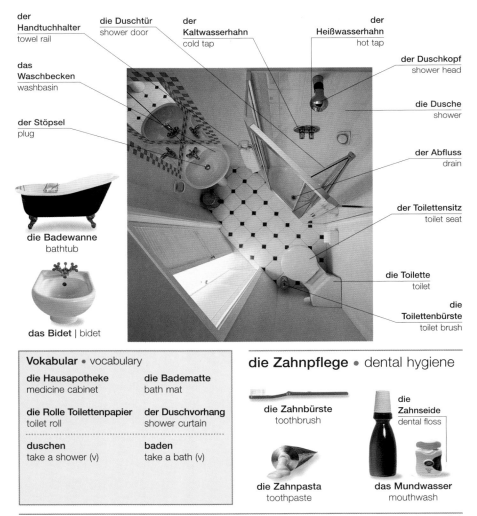

der
**Handtuchhalter**
towel rail

**die Duschtür**
shower door

der
**Kaltwasserhahn**
cold tap

der
**Heißwasserhahn**
hot tap

das
**Waschbecken**
washbasin

**der Duschkopf**
shower head

**die Dusche**
shower

**der Stöpsel**
plug

**der Abfluss**
drain

**der Toilettensitz**
toilet seat

**die Badewanne**
bathtub

**die Toilette**
toilet

**das Bidet** | bidet

die
**Toilettenbürste**
toilet brush

## Vokabular • vocabulary

| | |
|---|---|
| **die Hausapotheke**<br>medicine cabinet | **die Badematte**<br>bath mat |
| **die Rolle Toilettenpapier**<br>toilet roll | **der Duschvorhang**<br>shower curtain |
| **duschen**<br>take a shower (v) | **baden**<br>take a bath (v) |

## die Zahnpflege • dental hygiene

**die Zahnbürste**
toothbrush

die
**Zahnseide**
dental floss

**die Zahnpasta**
toothpaste

**das Mundwasser**
mouthwash

der
**Luffaschwamm**
loofah

**der Schwamm**
sponge

**der Bimsstein**
pumice stone

**die Rückenbürste**
back brush

**das Deo**
deodorant

die
**Seifenschale**
soap dish

das **Duschgel**
shower gel

**die Seife**
soap

**die Gesichtscreme**
face cream

**das Schaumbad**
bubble bath

**das Handtuch**
hand towel

das
**Badetuch**
bath towel

**die Handtücher**
towels

**die Körperlotion**
body lotion

**der Körperpuder**
talcum powder

**der Bademantel**
bathrobe

## das Rasieren • shaving

der
**Elektrorasierer**
electric razor

die
**Rasierklinge**
razor blade

**der Rasierschaum**
shaving foam

**der Einwegrasierer**
disposable razor

**das Rasierwasser**
aftershave

# das Kinderzimmer • nursery

## die Säuglingspflege • baby care

die Wundsalbe
nappy rash cream

das
Erfrischungstuch
wet wipe

der
Schwamm
sponge

die Babywanne
baby bath

das Töpfchen
potty

die Wickelmatte
changing mat

## das Schlafen • sleeping

das Laken
sheet

die Decke
blanket

das Mobile
mobile

die Gitterstäbe
bars

die Flauschdecke
fleece

das Bettzeug
bedding

der Kopfschutz
bumper

die Matratze
mattress

die Rassel
rattle

das Körbchen
moses basket

das Kinderbett | cot

# das Spielen • playing

**die Puppe**
doll

**das Kuscheltier**
soft toy

**das Puppenhaus**
doll's house

**das Spielhaus**
playhouse

**der Teddy**
teddy bear

**das Spielzeug**
toy

**der Spielzeugkorb**
toy basket

**der Ball**
ball

**der Laufstall**
playpen

# die Sicherheit • safety

**die Kindersicherung**
child lock

**die Babysprechanlage**
baby monitor

**das Treppengitter**
stair gate

# das Essen • eating

**der Kinderstuhl**
high chair

**der Sauger**
teat

**der Babybecher**
drinking cup

**die Babyflasche**
bottle

# das Ausgehen • going out

**der Sportwagen**
pushchair

**das Verdeck**
hood

**der Kinderwagen**
pram

**die Windel**
nappy

**das Tragebettchen**
carrycot

**die Babytasche**
changing bag

**die Babytrageschlinge**
baby sling

# der Allzweckraum • utility room

## die Wäsche • laundry

die saubere Wäsche
clean clothes

die schmutzige Wäsche
dirty washing

**der Wäschekorb**
laundry basket

**die Waschmaschine**
washing machine

**der Waschtrockner**
washer-dryer

**der Trockner**
tumble dryer

**der Wäschekorb**
linen basket

die Wäscheleine
clothes line

das Bügeleisen
iron

die Wäsche klammer
clothes peg

**trocknen**
dry (v)

**das Bügelbrett** | ironing board

---

**Vokabular** • vocabulary

| | | | |
|---|---|---|---|
| **füllen** load (v) | **schleudern** spin (v) | **bügeln** iron (v) | **Wie benutze ich die Waschmaschine?** How do I operate the washing machine? |
| **spülen** rinse (v) | **die Wäscheschleuder** spin dryer | **der Weichspüler** conditioner | **Welches Programm nehme ich für farbige/weiße Wäsche?** What is the setting for coloureds/whites? |

# die Reinigungsartikel • cleaning equipment

**der Saugschlauch**
suction hose

**der Handfeger**
brush

**die Müllschaufel**
dust pan

**das Reinigungsmittel**
bleach

**der Eimer**
bucket

**das Pulver**
powder

**die Flüssigkeit**
liquid

**das Staubtuch**
duster

**der Staubsauger**
vacuum cleaner

**der Mopp**
mop

**das Waschmittel**
detergent

**die Politur**
polish

# die Tätigkeiten • activities

**putzen**
clean (v)

**spülen**
wash (v)

**wischen**
wipe (v)

**schrubben**
scrub (v)

**kratzen**
scrape (v)

**der Besen**
broom

**fegen**
sweep (v)

**Staub wischen**
dust (v)

**polieren**
polish (v)

# die Heimwerkstatt • workshop

das Bohrfutter
chuck

der Bohrer
drill bit

die Batterie
battery pack

**die Stichsäge**
jigsaw

**der Bohrer mit
Batteriebetrieb**
rechargeable drill

**der Elektrobohrer**
electric drill

**die Leimpistole**
glue gun

die Zwinge
clamp

das Blatt
blade

**der Schraubstock**
vice

**die Schleifmaschine**
sander

**die Kreissäge**
circular saw

**die Werkbank**
workbench

der Holzleim
wood glue

das
Werkzeuggestell
tool rack

der Grundhobel
router

die Bohrwinde
bit brace

die Holzspäne
wood shavings

die
Verlängerungsschnur
extension lead

# die Fertigkeiten • techniques

**schneiden**
cut (v)

**sägen**
saw (v)

**bohren**
drill (v)

**hämmern**
hammer (v)

**hobeln**
plane (v)

**drechseln**
turn (v)

**schnitzen**
carve (v)

**der Lötzinn**
solder

**löten**
solder (v)

# die Materialien • materials

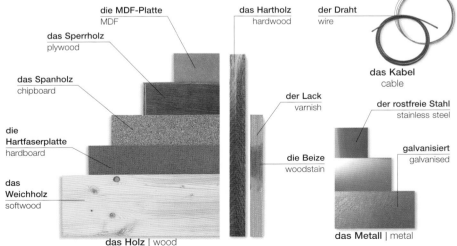

**die MDF-Platte**
MDF

**das Sperrholz**
plywood

**das Spanholz**
chipboard

**die Hartfaserplatte**
hardboard

**das Weichholz**
softwood

**das Hartholz**
hardwood

**der Lack**
varnish

**die Beize**
woodstain

**das Holz** | wood

**der Draht**
wire

**das Kabel**
cable

**der rostfreie Stahl**
stainless steel

**galvanisiert**
galvanised

**das Metall** | metal

# der Werkzeugkasten • toolbox

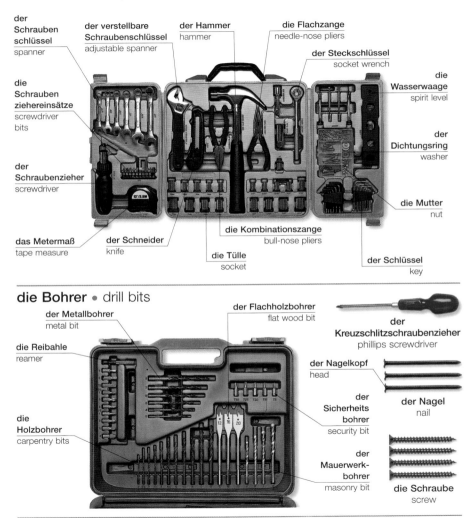

der Schrauben schlüssel
spanner

der verstellbare Schraubenschlüssel
adjustable spanner

der Hammer
hammer

die Flachzange
needle-nose pliers

der Steckschlüssel
socket wrench

die Wasserwaage
spirit level

die Schrauben ziehereinsätze
screwdriver bits

der Dichtungsring
washer

der Schraubenzieher
screwdriver

die Mutter
nut

das Metermaß
tape measure

der Schneider
knife

die Kombinationszange
bull-nose pliers

die Tülle
socket

der Schlüssel
key

# die Bohrer • drill bits

der Metallbohrer
metal bit

der Flachholzbohrer
flat wood bit

der Kreuzschlitzschraubenzieher
phillips screwdriver

die Reibahle
reamer

der Nagelkopf
head

die Holzbohrer
carpentry bits

der Sicherheits bohrer
security bit

der Nagel
nail

der Mauerwerk- bohrer
masonry bit

die Schraube
screw

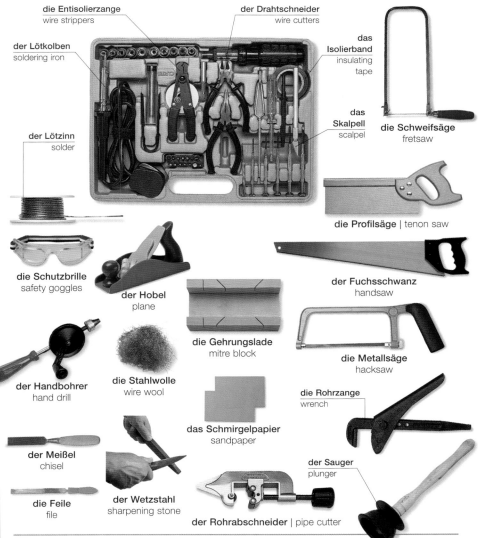

die Entisolierzange
wire strippers

der Drahtschneider
wire cutters

der Lötkolben
soldering iron

das
Isolierband
insulating
tape

der Lötzinn
solder

das
Skalpell
scalpel

die Schweifsäge
fretsaw

die Profilsäge | tenon saw

die Schutzbrille
safety goggles

der Hobel
plane

die Gehrungslade
mitre block

der Fuchsschwanz
handsaw

der Handbohrer
hand drill

die Stahlwolle
wire wool

die Metallsäge
hacksaw

der Meißel
chisel

das Schmirgelpapier
sandpaper

die Rohrzange
wrench

die Feile
file

der Wetzstahl
sharpening stone

der Sauger
plunger

der Rohrabschneider | pipe cutter

# das Tapezieren • decorating

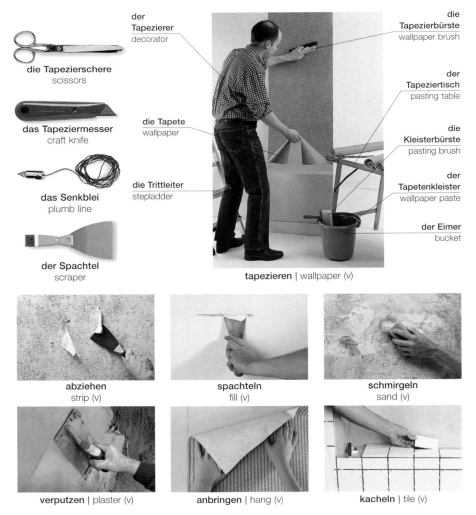

die Tapezierschere
scissors

das Tapeziermesser
craft knife

das Senkblei
plumb line

der Spachtel
scraper

der
Tapezierer
decorator

die Tapete
wallpaper

die Trittleiter
stepladder

die
Tapezierbürste
wallpaper brush

der
Tapeziertisch
pasting table

die
Kleisterbürste
pasting brush

der
Tapetenkleister
wallpaper paste

der Eimer
bucket

**tapezieren** | wallpaper (v)

**abziehen**
strip (v)

**spachteln**
fill (v)

**schmirgeln**
sand (v)

**verputzen** | plaster (v)

**anbringen** | hang (v)

**kacheln** | tile (v)

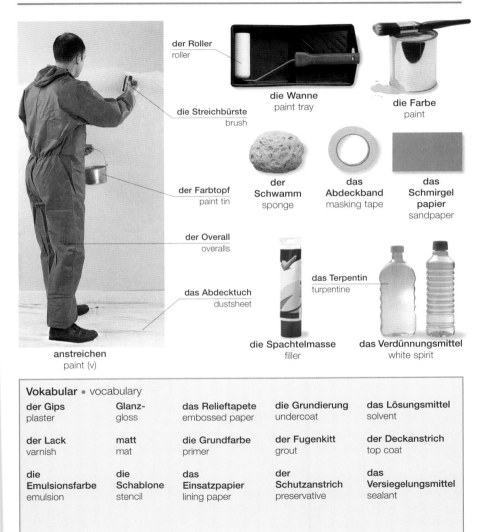

der Roller
roller

die Wanne
paint tray

die Farbe
paint

die Streichbürste
brush

der Schwamm
sponge

das Abdeckband
masking tape

das Schmirgel papier
sandpaper

der Farbtopf
paint tin

der Overall
overalls

das Terpentin
turpentine

das Abdecktuch
dustsheet

die Spachtelmasse
filler

das Verdünnungsmittel
white spirit

anstreichen
paint (v)

## Vokabular • vocabulary

| | | | | |
|---|---|---|---|---|
| der Gips<br>plaster | Glanz-<br>gloss | das Relieftapete<br>embossed paper | die Grundierung<br>undercoat | das Lösungsmittel<br>solvent |
| der Lack<br>varnish | matt<br>mat | die Grundfarbe<br>primer | der Fugenkitt<br>grout | der Deckanstrich<br>top coat |
| die Emulsionsfarbe<br>emulsion | die Schablone<br>stencil | das Einsatzpapier<br>lining paper | der Schutzanstrich<br>preservative | das Versiegelungsmittel<br>sealant |

# der Garten • garden

## die Gartentypen • garden styles

# die Garten ornamente •
garden features

**der Patio**
patio garden

**der Dachgarten**
roof garden

**die Blumenampel**
hanging basket

**der architektonische Garten** | formal garden

**der Steingarten**
rock garden

**der Hof**
courtyard

**das Spalier**
trellis

**der Bauerngarten**
cottage garden

**der Kräutergarten**
herb garden

**der Wassergarten**
water garden

**die Pergola**
pergola

die Platten
paving

der Weg
path

der Kompost
haufen
compost heap

das Tor
gate

das
Blumenbeet
flowerbed

der
Schuppen
shed

das
Gewächshaus
greenhouse

der Rasen
lawn

der Zaun
fence

der Teich
pond

die Hecke
hedge

der Bogen
arch

der
Gemüsegarten
vegetable
garden

die Staudenrabatte
herbaceous border

# der Boden
● soil

die Erde
topsoil

der Sand
sand

der Kalk
chalk

der Schlick
silt

der Lehm
clay

die Planken
decking

der Springbrunnen | fountain

# die Gartenpflanzen • garden plants

## die Pflanzenarten • types of plants

**einjährig**
annual

**zweijährig**
biennial

**mehrjährig**
perennial

**die Zwiebel**
bulb

**der Farn**
fern

**die Binse**
rush

**der Bambus**
bamboo

**das Unkraut**
weeds

**das Kraut**
herb

**die Wasserpflanze**
water plant

**der Baum**
tree

**der Laubbaum**
deciduous

**die Palme**
palm

**der Nadelbaum**
conifer

**immergrün**
evergreen

**der Formschnitt**
topiary

**die Alpenpflanze**
alpine

**die Fettpflanze**
succulent

**der Kaktus**
cactus

**die Topfpflanze**
potted plant

**die Schattenpflanze**
shade plant

die
**Kletterpflanze**
climber

der **Zierstrauch**
flowering shrub

der
**Bodendecker**
ground cover

**die Kriechpflanze**
creeper

**Zier-**
ornamental

**das Gras**
grass

# die Gartengeräte • garden tools

**der Laubrechen**
lawn rake

**die Komposterde**
compost

**die Samen**
seeds

**die Knochenasche**
bone meal

**der Kies**
gravel

**der Spaten**
spade

**die Gabel**
fork

**die Schere**
long-handled shears

**der Rechen**
rake

**die Hacke**
hoe

**der Grasfangsack**
grass bag

**der Motor**
motor

**der Griff**
handle

**der Gartenkorb**
trug

**der Schutz**
shield

**der Ständer**
stand

**der Schneider**
trimmer

**der Rasenmäher**
lawnmower

**der Schubkarren**
wheelbarrow

**die Handgabel**
hand fork

**die Rosenschere**
secateurs

**die Gartenhandschuhe**
gardening gloves

**die Pflanzschaufel**
trowel

**der Zwirn**
twine

**die Pflanzenschildchen**
labels

**das Messer**
blade

**der Setzkasten**
seed tray

**die Befestigungen**
twist ties

**die Ringbefestigungen**
ring ties

**die Heckenschere**
shears

**die Garten stöcke**
canes

**das Pestizid**
pesticide

**das Sieb**
sieve

**die Handsäge**
hand saw

**der Blumentopf**
plant pot

**die Gummistiefel**
rubber boots

## das Gießen • watering

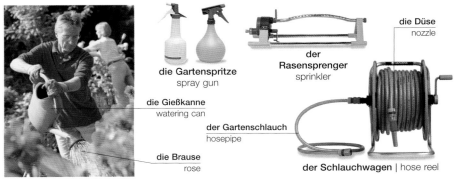

**die Gartenspritze**
spray gun

**der Rasensprenger**
sprinkler

**die Düse**
nozzle

**die Gießkanne**
watering can

**der Gartenschlauch**
hosepipe

**die Brause**
rose

**der Schlauchwagen** | hose reel

# die Gartenarbeit • gardening

der Rasen
lawn

das
Blumenbeet
flowerbed

der
Rasenmäher
lawnmower

die Hecke
hedge

die Stange
stake

**mähen** | mow (v)

**mit Rasen bedecken**
turf (v)

**stechen**
spike (v)

**harken**
rake (v)

**stutzen**
trim (v)

**graben**
dig (v)

**säen**
sow (v)

**mit Kopfdünger
düngen**
top dress (v)

**gießen**
water (v)

**ziehen**
train (v)

**köpfen**
deadhead (v)

**sprühen**
spray (v)

der Stock
cane

**pfropfen**
graft (v)

der Ableger
cutting

**vermehren**
propagate (v)

**beschneiden**
prune (v)

**hochbinden**
stake (v)

**umpflanzen**
transplant (v)

**jäten**
weed (v)

**mulchen**
mulch (v)

**ernten**
harvest (v)

**Vokabular** • vocabulary

| | | | | | | |
|---|---|---|---|---|---|---|
| **züchten** cultivate (v) | **gestalten** landscape (v) | **düngen** fertilize (v) | **sieben** sieve (v) | **biodynamisch** organic | **die Entwässerung** drainage | **der Dünger** fertilizer |
| **hegen** tend (v) | **eintopfen** pot up (v) | **pflücken** pick (v) | **auflockern** aerate (v) | **der Untergrund** subsoil | **der Unkrautver- nichter** weedkiller | **der Sämling** seedling |

**die Dienstleistungen**
services

# die Dienstleistungen • emergency services

## die Notdienste • ambulance

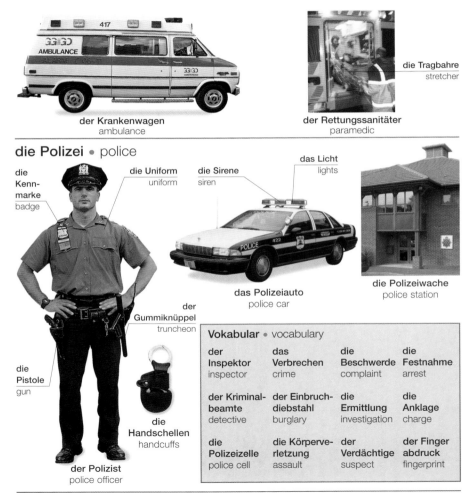

**der Krankenwagen**
ambulance

**die Tragbahre**
stretcher

**der Rettungssanitäter**
paramedic

## die Polizei • police

die Kenn-marke
badge

**die Uniform**
uniform

**die Sirene**
siren

**das Licht**
lights

**das Polizeiauto**
police car

**die Polizeiwache**
police station

der Gummiknüppel
truncheon

die Pistole
gun

**die Handschellen**
handcuffs

**der Polizist**
police officer

### Vokabular • vocabulary

| | | | |
|---|---|---|---|
| **der Inspektor**<br>inspector | **das Verbrechen**<br>crime | **die Beschwerde**<br>complaint | **die Festnahme**<br>arrest |
| **der Kriminal-beamte**<br>detective | **der Einbruch-diebstahl**<br>burglary | **die Ermittlung**<br>investigation | **die Anklage**<br>charge |
| **die Polizeizelle**<br>police cell | **die Körperve-rletzung**<br>assault | **der Verdächtige**<br>suspect | **der Finger abdruck**<br>fingerprint |

# die Feuerwehr • fire brigade

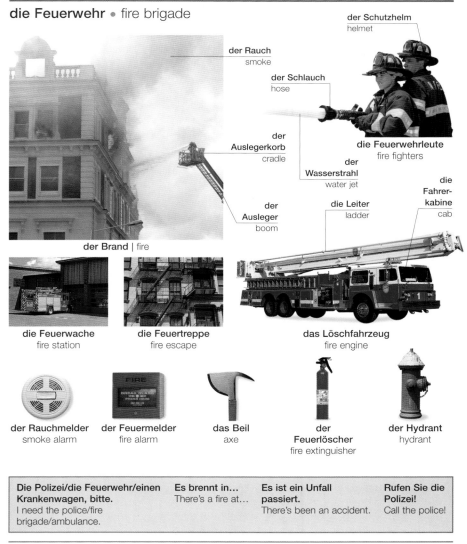

der Schutzhelm
helmet

der Rauch
smoke

der Schlauch
hose

der
Auslegerkorb
cradle

die Feuerwehrleute
fire fighters

der
Wasserstrahl
water jet

der
Ausleger
boom

die
Fahrer-
kabine
cab

die Leiter
ladder

der Brand | fire

die Feuerwache
fire station

die Feuertreppe
fire escape

das Löschfahrzeug
fire engine

der Rauchmelder
smoke alarm

der Feuermelder
fire alarm

das Beil
axe

der
Feuerlöscher
fire extinguisher

der Hydrant
hydrant

| | | | |
|---|---|---|---|
| **Die Polizei/die Feuerwehr/einen Krankenwagen, bitte.** I need the police/fire brigade/ambulance. | **Es brennt in…** There's a fire at… | **Es ist ein Unfall passiert.** There's been an accident. | **Rufen Sie die Polizei!** Call the police! |

# die Bank • bank

der Kunde
customer

die Broschüren
leaflets

der Schalter
window

der Schalter
counter

der Kassierer
cashier

die Einzahlungs
scheine
paying-in slips

die EC-Karte
debit card

der
Abschnitt
stub

die
Kontonummer
account number

die
Unterschrift
signature

der Betrag
amount

der Filialleiter
bank manager

die Kreditkarte
credit card

das Scheckheft
chequebook

der Scheck
cheque

---

## Vokabular • vocabulary

| | | | | |
|---|---|---|---|---|
| **die Steuer**<br>tax | **die Hypothek**<br>mortgage | **die Zahlung**<br>payment | **einzahlen**<br>pay in (v) | **das Girokonto**<br>current account |
| **das Darlehen**<br>loan | **der Zinssatz**<br>interest rate | **der Einzugsauftrag**<br>direct debit | **die Bankgebühr**<br>bank charge | **das Sparkonto**<br>savings account |
| **die Spareinlagen**<br>savings | **die Kontoüberziehung**<br>overdraft | **das Abhebungsformular**<br>withdrawal slip | **die Banküberweisung**<br>bank transfer | **der PIN-Kode**<br>pin number |

---

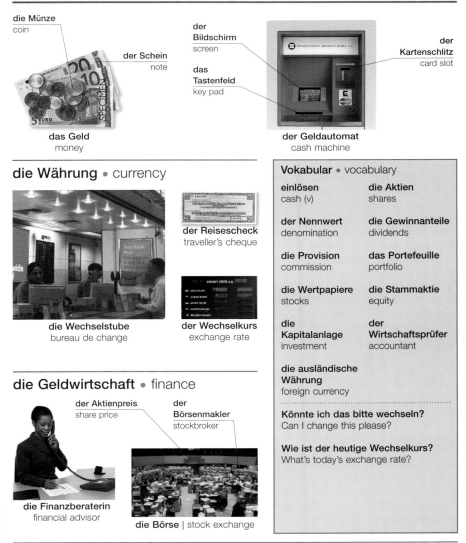

die Münze
coin

der Schein
note

der
Bildschirm
screen

das
Tastenfeld
key pad

der
Kartenschlitz
card slot

das Geld
money

der Geldautomat
cash machine

## die Währung • currency

der Reisescheck
traveller's cheque

die Wechselstube
bureau de change

der Wechselkurs
exchange rate

## die Geldwirtschaft • finance

der Aktienpreis
share price

der
Börsenmakler
stockbroker

die Finanzberaterin
financial advisor

die Börse | stock exchange

**Vokabular • vocabulary**

| | |
|---|---|
| einlösen<br>cash (v) | die Aktien<br>shares |
| der Nennwert<br>denomination | die Gewinnanteile<br>dividends |
| die Provision<br>commission | das Portefeuille<br>portfolio |
| die Wertpapiere<br>stocks | die Stammaktie<br>equity |
| die<br>Kapitalanlage<br>investment | der<br>Wirtschaftsprüfer<br>accountant |
| die ausländische<br>Währung<br>foreign currency | |

**Könnte ich das bitte wechseln?**
Can I change this please?

**Wie ist der heutige Wechselkurs?**
What's today's exchange rate?

# die Kommunikation • communications

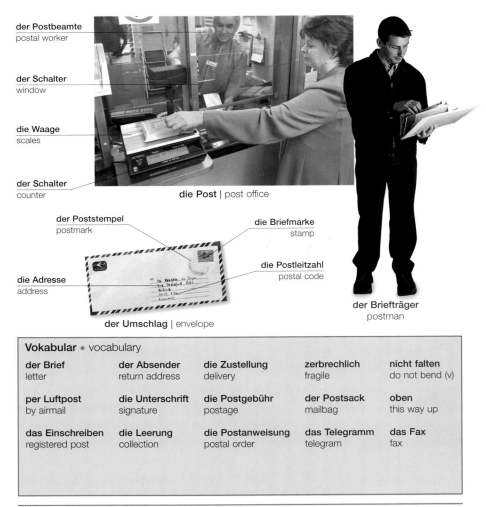

**der Postbeamte**
postal worker

**der Schalter**
window

**die Waage**
scales

**der Schalter**
counter

**die Post** | post office

**der Poststempel**
postmark

**die Briefmarke**
stamp

**die Postleitzahl**
postal code

**die Adresse**
address

**der Umschlag** | envelope

**der Briefträger**
postman

---

**Vokabular** • vocabulary

| | | | | |
|---|---|---|---|---|
| **der Brief**<br>letter | **der Absender**<br>return address | **die Zustellung**<br>delivery | **zerbrechlich**<br>fragile | **nicht falten**<br>do not bend (v) |
| **per Luftpost**<br>by airmail | **die Unterschrift**<br>signature | **die Postgebühr**<br>postage | **der Postsack**<br>mailbag | **oben**<br>this way up |
| **das Einschreiben**<br>registered post | **die Leerung**<br>collection | **die Postanweisung**<br>postal order | **das Telegramm**<br>telegram | **das Fax**<br>fax |

---

**der Briefkasten**
postbox

**der Hausbriefkasten**
letterbox

**das Paket**
parcel

**der Kurierdienst**
courier

## das Telefon • telephone

**der Hörer**
handset

**die Basis**
base station

**das schnurlose Telefon**
cordless phone

**der Anrufbeantworter**
answering machine

**das Fernsehtelefon**
video phone

**die Telefonzelle**
telephone box

**das Tastenfeld**
keypad

**das Handy**
mobile phone

**der Hörer**
receiver

**die Münzrückgabe**
coin return

**der Münzfern-sprecher**
coin phone

**das Kartentelefon**
card phone

---

### Vokabular • vocabulary

| | | | |
|---|---|---|---|
| **abheben** answer (v) | **die Auskunft** directory enquiries | **besetzt** engaged/busy | **Können Sie mir die Nummer für…geben?** Can you give me the number for…? |
| **wählen** dial (v) | **die SMS** text message | **unterbrochen** disconnected | **Was ist die Vorwahl für…?** What is the dialling code for…? |
| **das R-Gespräch** reverse charge call | **die Sprachmit-teilung** voice message | **die Vermit-tlung** operator | |

---

# das Hotel • hotel
## die Empfangshalle • lobby

der Gast
guest

der Zimmerschlüssel
room key

die Nachrichten
messages

das Fach
pigeonhole

die
Empfangsdame
receptionist

das
Gästebuch
register

der Schalter
counter

**der Empfang** | reception

das
Gepäck
luggage

der Kofferkuli
trolley

**der Hoteldiener**
porter

**der Fahrstuhl**
lift

**die Zimmernummer**
room number

## die Zimmer • rooms

**das Einzelzimmer**
single room

**das Doppelzimmer**
double room

**das Zweibettzimmer**
twin room

**das
Privatbadezimmer**
private bathroom

# die Dienstleistungen • services

**die Zimmerreinigung**
maid service

**der Wäschedienst**
laundry service

**das Frühstückstablett**
breakfast tray

**der Zimmerservice** | room service

**die Minibar**
mini bar

**das Restaurant**
restaurant

**der Fitnessraum**
gym

**das Schwimmbad**
swimming pool

---

**Vokabular** • vocabulary

**die Vollpension**
full board

**die Halbpension**
half board

**die Übernachtung mit Frühstück**
bed and breakfast

**Haben Sie ein Zimmer frei?**
Do you have any vacancies?

**Ich möchte ein Einzelzimmer.**
I'd like a single room.

**Ich habe ein Zimmer reserviert.**
I have a reservation.

**Ich möchte ein Zimmer für drei Nächte.**
I'd like a room for three nights.

**Was kostet das Zimmer pro Nacht?**
What is the charge per night?

**Wann muss ich das Zimmer räumen?**
When do I have to vacate the room?

---

**der Einkauf**
shopping

# das Einkaufszentrum • shopping centre

das Atrium
atrium

das Schild
sign

der
Fahrstuhl
lift

die zweite
Etage
second floor

die erste
Etage
first floor

die Rolltreppe
escalator

das
Erdgeschoss
ground floor

der Kunde
customer

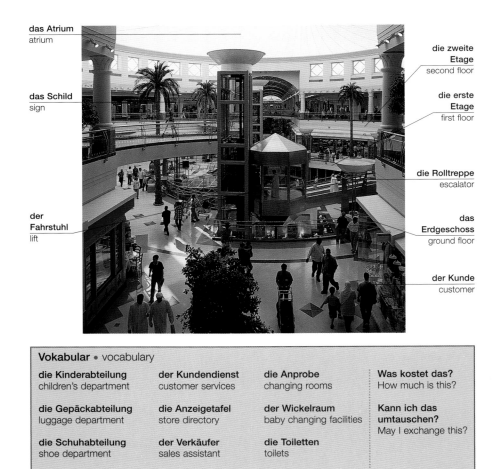

## Vokabular • vocabulary

**die Kinderabteilung**
children's department

**die Gepäckabteilung**
luggage department

**die Schuhabteilung**
shoe department

**der Kundendienst**
customer services

**die Anzeigetafel**
store directory

**der Verkäufer**
sales assistant

**die Anprobe**
changing rooms

**der Wickelraum**
baby changing facilities

**die Toiletten**
toilets

**Was kostet das?**
How much is this?

**Kann ich das
umtauschen?**
May I exchange this?

# das Kaufhaus • department store

**die Herrenbekleidung**
men's wear

**die Damenoberbekleidung**
women's wear

**die Damenwäsche**
lingerie

**die Parfümerie**
perfumery

**die Schönheitspflege**
beauty

**die Wäsche**
linen

**die Möbel**
home furnishings

**die Kurzwaren**
haberdashery

**die Küchengeräte**
kitchenware

**das Porzellan**
china

**die Elektroartikel**
electrical goods

**die Lampen**
lighting

**die Sportartikel**
sports

**die Spielwaren**
toys

**die Schreibwaren**
stationery

**die Lebensmittelabteilung**
food hall

# der Supermarkt • supermarket

**der Gang**
aisle

**das Warenregal**
shelf

**das Laufband**
conveyer belt

**der Kassierer**
cashier

**die Angebote**
offers

**die Kasse** | checkout

**der Kunde**
customer

**die Kasse**
till

**die Einkaufstasche**
shopping bag

**die Lebensmittel**
groceries

**der Henkel**
handle

7 80863 185779

**der Strichkode**
bar code

**der Einkaufswagen**
trolley

**der Einkaufskorb**
basket

**der Scanner**
scanner

**die Backwaren**
bakery

**die Milchprodukte**
dairy

**die Getreideflocken**
cereals

**die Konserven**
tinned food

**die Süßwaren**
confectionery

**das Gemüse**
vegetables

**das Obst**
fruit

**das Fleisch und das Geflügel**
meat and poultry

**der Fisch**
fish

**die Feinkost**
deli

**die Gefrierware**
frozen food

**die Fertiggerichte**
convenience food

**die Getränke**
drinks

**die Haushaltswaren**
household products

**die Toilettenartikel**
toiletries

**die Babyprodukte**
baby products

**die Elektroartikel**
electrical goods

**das Tierfutter**
pet food

**die Zeitschriften** | magazines

# die Apotheke • chemist

**die Zahnpflege**
dental care

**die Monats-hygiene**
feminine hygiene

**die Deos**
deodorants

**die Vitamintabletten**
vitamins

**die Apotheke**
dispensary

**der Apotheker**
pharmacist

**das Hustenmedikament**
cough medicine

**das Kräuterheilmittel**
herbal remedies

**die Hautpflege**
skin care

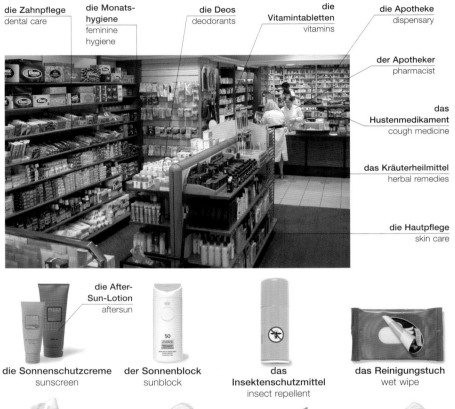

**die After-Sun-Lotion**
aftersun

**die Sonnenschutzcreme**
sunscreen

**der Sonnenblock**
sunblock

**das Insektenschutzmittel**
insect repellent

**das Reinigungstuch**
wet wipe

**das Papiertaschentuch**
tissue

**die Damenbinde**
sanitary towel

**der Tampon**
tampon

**die Slipeinlage**
panty liner

der Messlöffel
measuring spoon

die Gebrauchs-
anweisung
instructions

**die Kapsel**
capsule

**die Pille**
pill

**der Saft**
syrup

**der Inhalierstift**
inhaler

**die Creme**
cream

**die Salbe**
ointment

**das Gel**
gel

**das Zäpfchen**
suppository

der Tropfer
dropper

die Nadel
needle

**die Tropfen**
drops

**die Spritze**
syringe

**der Spray**
spray

**der Puder**
powder

**Vokabular** • vocabulary

| | | | | |
|---|---|---|---|---|
| **das Eisen**<br>iron | **das Multivitaminmittel**<br>multivitamins | **Wegwerf-**<br>disposable | **das Medikament**<br>medicine | **das Schmerzmittel**<br>painkiller |
| **das Kalzium**<br>calcium | **die Nebenwirkungen**<br>side-effects | **löslich**<br>soluble | **der Durchfall**<br>diarrhoea | **das Beruhigungsmittel**<br>sedative |
| **das Insulin**<br>insulin | **das Verfallsdatum**<br>expiry date | **die Dosierung**<br>dosage | **die Halspastille**<br>throat lozenge | **die Schlaftablette**<br>sleeping pill |
| **das Magnesium**<br>magnesium | **die Reisekrankheitstabletten**<br>travel sickness pills | **die Verordnung**<br>medication | **das Abführmittel**<br>laxative | **der Entzündungshemmer**<br>anti-inflammatory |

# das Blumengeschäft • florist

**die Blumen**
flowers

**die Gladiole**
gladiolus

**die Lilie**
lily

**die Iris**
iris

**die Margerite**
daisy

**die Akazie**
acacia

**die Chrysantheme**
chrysanthemum

**die Nelke**
carnation

**das Schleierkraut**
gypsophila

**die Topfpflanze**
pot plant

**die Levkoje**
stocks

**die Gerbera**
gerbera

**die Blätter**
foliage

**die Rose**
rose

**die Freesie**
freesia

die **Blumenvase**
vase

die **Orchidee**
orchid

die **Pfingstrose**
peony

## die **Blumenarrangements** • arrangements

das **Band**
ribbon

das **Bukett**
bouquet

die **Trockenblumen**
dried flowers

der **Strauß**
bunch

der **Stengel**
stem

die **Osterglocke**
daffodil

die **Knospe**
bud

das **Ein
wickelpapier**
wrapping

die **Tulpe** | tulip

das **Duftsträußchen** | pot-pourri

der **Kranz** | wreath

die
**Blumengirlande**
garland

**Ich möchte einen Strauß…,
bitte.**
Can I have a bunch of…
please.

**Können Sie die Blumen
bitte einwickeln?**
Can I have them wrapped?

**Kann ich eine Nachricht
mitschicken?**
Can I attach a message?

**Wie lange halten sie?**
How long will these last?

**Duften sie?**
Are they fragrant?

**Können Sie die Blumen
an… schicken?**
Can you send them to….?

# der Zeitungshändler • newsagent

**die Zigaretten**
cigarettes

**das Päckchen Zigaretten**
packet of cigarettes

**die Streichhölzer**
matches

**die Lottoscheine**
lottery tickets

die
**Briefmarken**
stamps

**die Postkarte**
postcard

**das Comicheft**
comic

**die Zeitschrift**
magazine

**die Zeitung**
newspaper

## das Rauchen • smoking

**der Stiel**
stem

**der Kopf**
bowl

**der Tabak**
tobacco

**das Feuerzeug**
lighter

**die Pfeife**
pipe

**die Zigarre**
cigar

# der Konditor • confectioner

die Schachtel Pralinen
box of chocolates

die **Nascherei**
snack bar

die **Chips**
crisps

**das Süßwarengeschäft** | sweet shop

# die Süßwaren • confectionery

die **Praline**
chocolate

die **Tafel Schokolade**
chocolate bar

die **Bonbons**
sweets

der **Lutscher**
lollipop

das **Toffee**
toffee

der **Nugat**
nougat

das **Marshmallow**
marshmallow

das **Pfefferminz**
mint

der **Kaugummi**
chewing gum

der **Geleebonbon**
jellybean

der **Fruchtgummi**
fruit gum

die **Lakritze**
licquorice

# andere Geschäfte • other shops

**die Bäckerei**
baker's

**die Konditorei**
cake shop

**die Metzgerei**
butcher's

**das Fischgeschäft**
fishmonger's

**der Gemüseladen**
greengrocer's

**das Lebensmittelgeschäft**
grocer's

**das Schuhgeschäft**
shoe shop

**die Eisenwaren-handlung**
hardware shop

**der Antiquitätenladen**
antiques shop

**der Geschenkartikel-laden**
gift shop

**das Reisebüro**
travel agent's

**das Juweliergeschäft**
jeweller's

**der Buchladen**
book shop

**das Plattengeschäft**
record shop

**die Weinhandlung**
off licence

**die Tierhandlung**
pet shop

**das Möbelgeschäft**
furniture shop

**die Boutique**
boutique

**Vokabular** • vocabulary

| | |
|---|---|
| **das Gartencenter** garden centre | **das Fotogeschäft** camera shop |
| **die Reinigung** dry cleaner's | **das Reformhaus** health food shop |
| **der Waschsalon** launderette | **die Kunsthandlung** art shop |
| **der Immobilienmakler** estate agent's | **der Gebrauchtwarenhändler** second-hand shop |

**die Schneiderei**
tailor's

**der Frisiersalon**
hairdresser's

**der Markt** | market

**die Nahrungsmittel**
food

# das Fleisch • meat

**das Lamm**
lamb

**der Metzger**
butcher

**der Fleischerhaken**
meat hook

**die Waage**
scales

**der Messerschärfer**
knife sharpener

**der Speck**
bacon

**die Würstchen**
sausages

**die Leber**
liver

## Vokabular • vocabulary

| | | | | |
|---|---|---|---|---|
| **das Rindfleisch**<br>beef | **das Wild**<br>venison | **die Zunge**<br>tongue | **aus Freilandhaltung**<br>free range | **das rote Fleisch**<br>red meat |
| **das Kalbfleisch**<br>veal | **das Kaninchen**<br>rabbit | **gepökelt**<br>cured | **biologisch kontrolliert**<br>organic | **das magere Fleisch**<br>lean meat |
| **das Schweinefleisch**<br>pork | **die Innereien**<br>offal | **geräuchert**<br>smoked | **das weiße Fleisch**<br>white meat | **das gekochte Fleisch**<br>cooked meat |

# die Fleischsorten • cuts

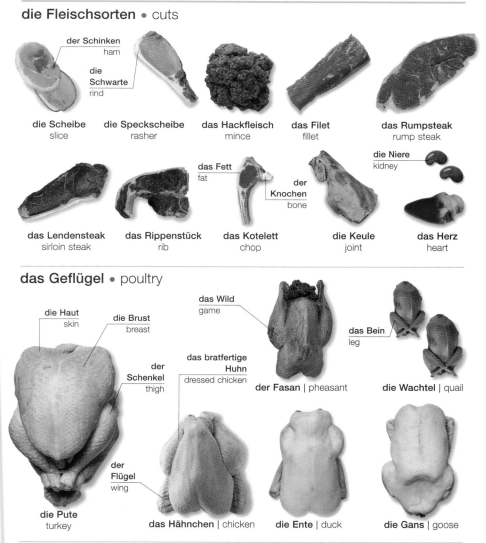

**der Schinken**
ham

**die Schwarte**
rind

**die Scheibe**
slice

**die Speckscheibe**
rasher

**das Hackfleisch**
mince

**das Filet**
fillet

**das Rumpsteak**
rump steak

**die Niere**
kidney

**das Fett**
fat

**der Knochen**
bone

**das Lendensteak**
sirloin steak

**das Rippenstück**
rib

**das Kotelett**
chop

**die Keule**
joint

**das Herz**
heart

# das Geflügel • poultry

**das Wild**
game

**die Haut**
skin

**die Brust**
breast

**das Bein**
leg

**der Schenkel**
thigh

**das bratfertige Huhn**
dressed chicken

**der Fasan** | pheasant

**die Wachtel** | quail

**der Flügel**
wing

**die Pute**
turkey

**das Hähnchen** | chicken

**die Ente** | duck

**die Gans** | goose

# der Fisch • fish

die geschälten
**Garnelen**
peeled prawns

**das Eis**
ice

die rote
**Meeräsche**
red mullet

die **Heilbuttfilets**
halibut fillets

die
**Regenbogenforelle**
rainbow trout

die
**Rochenflügel**
skate wings

**das Fischgeschäft**
fishmonger's

**die Quappe**
monkfish

**die Makrele**
mackerel

**die Forelle**
trout

**der Schwertfisch**
swordfish

**die Seezunge**
Dover sole

**die Rotzunge**
lemon sole

**der Schellfisch**
haddock

**die Sardine**
sardine

**der Rochen**
skate

**der Weißfisch**
whiting

**der Seebarsch**
sea bass

**der Lachs** | salmon

**der Kabeljau**
cod

**der Seebrassen**
sea bream

**der Tunfisch**
tuna

# die Meeresfrüchte • seafood

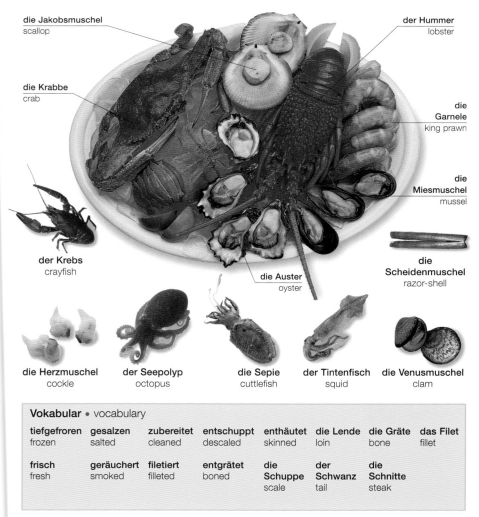

die Jakobsmuschel
scallop

der Hummer
lobster

die Krabbe
crab

die
Garnele
king prawn

die
Miesmuschel
mussel

der Krebs
crayfish

die Auster
oyster

die
Scheidenmuschel
razor-shell

die Herzmuschel
cockle

der Seepolyp
octopus

die Sepie
cuttlefish

der Tintenfisch
squid

die Venusmuschel
clam

## Vokabular • vocabulary

| tiefgefroren | gesalzen | zubereitet | entschuppt | enthäutet | die Lende | die Gräte | das Filet |
|---|---|---|---|---|---|---|---|
| frozen | salted | cleaned | descaled | skinned | loin | bone | fillet |
| | | | | | | | |
| frisch | geräuchert | filetiert | entgrätet | die | der | die | |
| fresh | smoked | filleted | boned | Schuppe | Schwanz | Schnitte | |
| | | | | scale | tail | steak | |

# das Gemüse 1 • vegetables 1

der Samen
seed

**die dicke Bohne**
broad bean

**die Stangenbohne**
runner bean

**die grüne Bohne**
French bean

**die grüne Erbse**
garden pea

die Schote
pod

**die
Sojabohnensprosse**
bean sprout

**der Bambus**
bamboo

**die Okra**
okra

**der Mais**
sweetcorn

**der Chicorée**
chicory

**der Fenchel**
fennel

**die Palmherzen**
palm hearts

**der
Stangensellerie**
celery

---

**Vokabular • vocabulary**

| | | | | |
|---|---|---|---|---|
| **das Blatt**<br>leaf | **das Röschen**<br>floret | **die Spitze**<br>tip | **biodynamisch**<br>organic | **Verkaufen Sie Biogemüse?**<br>Do you sell organic vegetables? |
| **der Strunk**<br>stalk | **der Kern**<br>kernel | **das Herz**<br>heart | **die Plastiktüte**<br>plastic bag | **Werden sie in dieser Gegend angebaut?**<br>Are these grown locally? |

---

**die Rauke**
rocket

**die Brunnenkresse**
watercress

**der Radicchio**
radicchio

**der Rosenkohl**
brussel sprout

**der Mangold**
swiss chard

**der Grünkohl**
kale

**der Garten-Sauerampfer**
sorrel

**die Endivie**
endive

**der Löwenzahn**
dandelion

**der Spinat**
spinach

**der Kohlrabi**
kohlrabi

**der Chinakohl**
pak-choi

**der Salat**
lettuce

**der Brokkoli**
broccoli

**der Kohl**
cabbage

**der Frühkohl**
spring greens

# das Gemüse 2 • vegetables 2

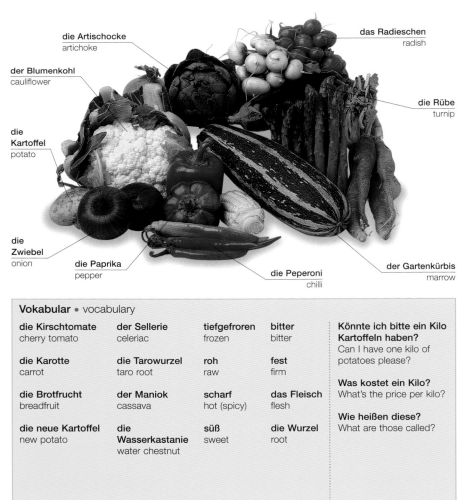

**die Artischocke**
artichoke

**das Radieschen**
radish

**der Blumenkohl**
cauliflower

**die Rübe**
turnip

**die Kartoffel**
potato

**die Zwiebel**
onion

**die Paprika**
pepper

**die Peperoni**
chilli

**der Gartenkürbis**
marrow

## Vokabular • vocabulary

| | | | | |
|---|---|---|---|---|
| **die Kirschtomate**<br>cherry tomato | **der Sellerie**<br>celeriac | **tiefgefroren**<br>frozen | **bitter**<br>bitter | **Könnte ich bitte ein Kilo Kartoffeln haben?**<br>Can I have one kilo of potatoes please? |
| **die Karotte**<br>carrot | **die Tarowurzel**<br>taro root | **roh**<br>raw | **fest**<br>firm | |
| **die Brotfrucht**<br>breadfruit | **der Maniok**<br>cassava | **scharf**<br>hot (spicy) | **das Fleisch**<br>flesh | **Was kostet ein Kilo?**<br>What's the price per kilo? |
| **die neue Kartoffel**<br>new potato | **die Wasserkastanie**<br>water chestnut | **süß**<br>sweet | **die Wurzel**<br>root | **Wie heißen diese?**<br>What are those called? |

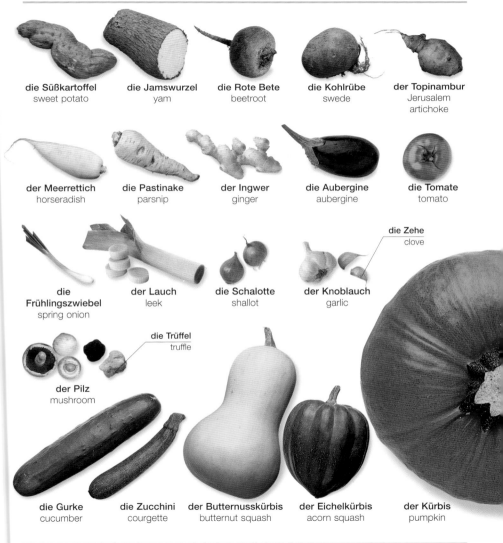

**die Süßkartoffel**
sweet potato

**die Jamswurzel**
yam

**die Rote Bete**
beetroot

**die Kohlrübe**
swede

**der Topinambur**
Jerusalem
artichoke

**der Meerrettich**
horseradish

**die Pastinake**
parsnip

**der Ingwer**
ginger

**die Aubergine**
aubergine

**die Tomate**
tomato

**die
Frühlingszwiebel**
spring onion

**der Lauch**
leek

**die Schalotte**
shallot

**der Knoblauch**
garlic

**die Zehe**
clove

**die Trüffel**
truffle

**der Pilz**
mushroom

**die Gurke**
cucumber

**die Zucchini**
courgette

**der Butternusskürbis**
butternut squash

**der Eichelkürbis**
acorn squash

**der Kürbis**
pumpkin

# das Obst 1 • fruit 1

## die Zitrusfrüchte • citrus fruit

## das Steinobst • stoned fruit

**die Orange**
orange

**die Klementine**
clementine

**der Pfirsich**
peach

**die Nektarine**
nectarine

**die weiße Haut**
pith

**die Tangelo**
ugli fruit

**die Grapefruit**
grapefruit

**die Aprikose**
apricot

**die Pflaume**
plum

**die Kirsche**
cherry

**der Schnitz**
segment

**die Mandarine**
tangerine

**die Satsuma**
satsuma

**der Apfel**
apple

**die Birne**
pear

**die Schale**
zest

**die Limone**
lime

**die Zitrone**
lemon

**die Kumquat**
kumquat

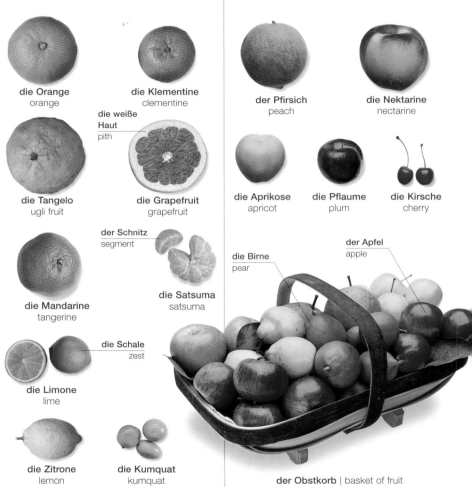

**der Obstkorb** | basket of fruit

# das Beerenobst und die Melonen • berries and melons

**die Erdbeere**
strawberry

**die Himbeere**
raspberry

**die Melone**
melon

**die Weintrauben**
grapes

**die Brombeere**
blackberry

**die Johannisbeere**
redcurrant

**die Schale**
rind

**die Preiselbeere**
cranberry

**die schwarze Johannisbeere**
blackcurrant

**der Kern**
seed

**das Fruchtfleisch**
flesh

**die Heidelbeere**
blueberry

**die weiße Johannisbeere**
white currant

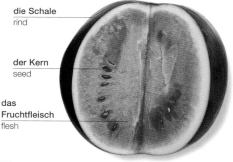

**die Wassermelone**
watermelon

**die Loganbeere**
loganberry

**die Stachelbeere**
gooseberry

## Vokabular • vocabulary

| | | | | |
|---|---|---|---|---|
| **saftig** juicy | **sauer** sour | **knackig** crisp | **kernlos** seedless | **Sind sie reif?** Are they ripe? |
| **die Faser** fibre | **frisch** fresh | **faul** rotten | **der Saft** juice | **Könnte ich eine probieren?** Can I try one? |
| **süß** sweet | **der Rhabarber** rhubarb | **das Fruchtmark** pulp | **das Kerngehäuse** core | **Wie lange halten sie sich?** How long will they keep? |

# das Obst 2 • fruit 2

**die Mango**
mango

**die Avocado**
avocado

**der Pfirsich**
peach

**die Kiwi**
kiwifruit

**die Ananas**
pineapple

**die Papaya**
papaya

**die Litschi**
lychee

**die Kapstachelbeere**
cape gooseberry

**der Kern**
pip

**die Schale**
skin

**die Quitte**
quince

**die Passionsfrucht**
passion fruit

**die Banane**
banana

**die Guave**
guava

**der Granatapfel**
pomegranate

**die Kaki**
persimmon

**die Feijoa**
feijoa

**die Kaktusfeige**
prickly pear

**die Sternfrucht**
starfruit

**die Mangostane**
mangosteen

# die Nüsse und das Dörrobst • nuts and dried fruit

**die Piniennuss**
pine nut

**die Pistazie**
pistachio

**die Cashewnuss**
cashewnut

**die Erdnuss**
peanut

**die Haselnuss**
hazelnut

**die Paranuss**
brazilnut

**die Pecannuss**
pecan

**die Mandel**
almond

**die Walnuss**
walnut

**die Esskastanie**
chestnut

**die Macadamianuss**
macadamia

**die Feige**
fig

**die Dattel**
date

**die Backpflaume**
prune

**die Schale**
shell

**die Sultanine**
sultana

**die Rosine**
raisin

**die Korinthe**
currant

das
**Fruchtfleisch**
flesh

**die Kokosnuss**
coconut

## Vokabular • vocabulary

| | | | | | | |
|---|---|---|---|---|---|---|
| **grün** green | **hart** hard | **der Kern** kernel | **gesalzen** salted | **geröstet** roasted | **die Südfrüchte** tropical fruit | **geschält** shelled |
| **reif** ripe | **weich** soft | **getrocknet** desiccated | **roh** raw | **Saison-** seasonal | **die kandierten Früchte** candied fruit | **ganz** whole |

# die Getreidearten und die Hülsenfrüchte •
## grains and pulses

### das Getreide • grains

**der Weizen**
wheat

**der Hafer**
oats

**die Gerste**
barley

**die Hirse**
millet

**der Mais**
corn

**die Reismelde**
quinoa

**Vokabular** • vocabulary

| | | |
|---|---|---|
| **trocken**<br>dry | **frisch**<br>fresh | **Vollkorn**<br>wholegrain |
| **die Hülse**<br>husk | **aromatisch**<br>fragranced | **Langkorn**<br>long-grain |
| **der Kern**<br>kernel | **einweichen**<br>soak (v) | **Rundkorn**<br>short-grain |
| **der Samen**<br>seed | **die Getreideflocken**<br>cereal | **leicht zu kochen**<br>easy cook |

### der Reis • rice

### die verarbeiteten Getreidearten •
processed grains

**der weiße Reis**
white rice

**der Naturreis**
brown rice

**der Kuskus**
couscous

**der Weizenschrot**
cracked wheat

**der Wasserreis**
wild rice

**der Milchreis**
pudding rice

**der Grieß**
semolina

**die Kleie**
bran

# die Bohnen und die Erbsen • beans and peas

**die Mondbohnen**
butter beans

**die weißen Bohnen**
haricot beans

**die roten Bohnen**
red kidney beans

**die Adzuki-bohnen**
aduki beans

**die Saubohnen**
broad beans

**die Sojabohnen**
soya beans

**die Teparybohnen**
black-eyed beans

**die Pintobohnen**
pinto beans

**die Mungbohnen**
mung beans

**die französischen Bohnen**
flageolet beans

**die braunen Linsen**
brown lentils

**die roten Linsen**
red lentils

**die grünen Erbsen**
green peas

**die Kichererbsen**
chick peas

**die getrockneten Erbsen**
split peas

# die Körner • seeds

**der Kürbiskern**
pumpkin seed

**das Senfkorn**
mustard seed

**der Kümmel**
caraway

**das Sesamkorn**
sesame seed

**der Sonnenblumenkern**
sunflower seed

# die Kräuter und Gewürze • herbs and spices

## die Gewürze • spices

**die Vanille**
vanilla

**die Muskatnuss**
nutmeg

**die Muskatblüte**
mace

**die Kurkuma**
turmeric

**der Kreuzkümmel**
cumin

**die Kräutermischung**
bouquet garni

**der Piment**
allspice

**das Pfefferkorn**
peppercorn

**der Bockshornklee**
fenugreek

**der Chili**
chilli

**ganz**
whole

**zerstoßen**
crushed

**der Safran**
saffron

**der Kardamom**
cardamom

**das Currypulver**
curry powder

**gemahlen**
ground

**der Paprika**
paprika

**geraspelt**
flakes

**der Knoblauch**
garlic

# die Kräuter • herbs

**die Stangen**
sticks

**der Zimt**
cinnamon

**das Zitronengras**
lemon grass

**die Gewürznelke**
cloves

**der Sternanis**
star anise

**der Ingwer**
ginger

**der Fenchel**
fennel

**die Fenchelsamen**
fennel seeds

**der Schnittlauch**
chives

**der Estragon**
tarragon

**der Oregano**
oregano

**die Minze**
mint

**der Majoran**
marjoram

**der Koriander**
coriander

**das Lorbeerblatt**
bay leaf

**der Thymian**
thyme

**das Basilikum**
basil

**der Dill**
dill

**die Petersilie**
parsley

**der Salbei**
sage

**der Rosmarin**
rosemary

# die Nahrungsmittel in Flaschen • bottled foods

der Korken
cork

das
Sonnenblumenöl
sunflower oil

das Walnussöl
walnut oil

das Traubenkernöl
grapeseed oil

das
Mandelöl
almond oil

das
Sesamöl
sesame
seed oil

das Haselnussöl
hazelnut oil

das Olivenöl
olive oil

die Kräuter
herbs

das
aromatische Öl
flavoured oil

die Öle
oils

# der süße Aufstrich • sweet spreads

das Glas
jar

die Honigwabe
honeycomb

der feste Honig
set honey

der
Zitronenaufstrich
lemon curd

die
Himbeerkonfitüre
raspberry jam

die
Orangenmarmelade
marmalade

der flüssige
Honig
clear honey

der Ahornsirup
maple syrup

# die Würzen • condiments and spreads

**der Apfelweinessig**
cider vinegar

**der Gewürzessig**
balsamic vinegar

**die Flasche**
bottle

**die Majonäse**
mayonnaise

**der englische Senf**
English mustard

**der Ketchup**
ketchup

**der französische Senf**
French mustard

**das Chutney**
chutney

**der Malzessig**
malt vinegar

**der Weinessig**
wine vinegar

**der Essig**
vinegar

**die Soße**
sauce

**der grobe Senf**
wholegrain mustard

**das Einmachglas**
sealed jar

**die Erdnussbutter**
peanut butter

**der Schokoladenaufstrich**
chocolate spread

**das eingemachte Obst**
preserved fruit

## Vokabular • vocabulary

**das Pflanzenöl**
vegetable oil

**das Rapsöl**
rapeseed oil

**das Maiskeimöl**
corn oil

**das kaltgepresste Öl**
cold-pressed oil

**das Erdnussöl**
groundnut oil

# die Milchprodukte • dairy produce

## der Käse • cheese

die Rinde
rind

der mittelharte Käse
semi-hard cheese

der geriebene Käse
grated cheese

der Hartkäse
hard cheese

der halbfeste Käse
semi-soft cheese

der Hüttenkäse
cottage cheese

der Rahmkäse
cream cheese

der Blauschimmelkäse
blue cheese

der Weichkäse
soft cheese

**der Frischkäse** | fresh cheese

## die Milch • milk

die Vollmilch
whole milk

die Halbfettmilch
semi-skimmed milk

die Magermilch
skimmed milk

die Milchtüte
milk carton

die Ziegenmilch
goat's milk

die Kondensmilch
condensed milk

**die Kuhmilch** | cow's milk

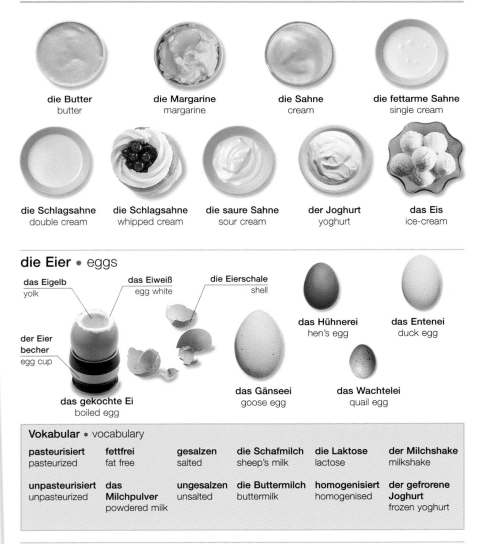

**die Butter**
butter

**die Margarine**
margarine

**die Sahne**
cream

**die fettarme Sahne**
single cream

**die Schlagsahne**
double cream

**die Schlagsahne**
whipped cream

**die saure Sahne**
sour cream

**der Joghurt**
yoghurt

**das Eis**
ice-cream

# die Eier • eggs

**das Eigelb**
yolk

**das Eiweiß**
egg white

**die Eierschale**
shell

**der Eier becher**
egg cup

**das Hühnerei**
hen's egg

**das Entenei**
duck egg

**das gekochte Ei**
boiled egg

**das Gänseei**
goose egg

**das Wachtelei**
quail egg

**Vokabular** • vocabulary

| | | | | | |
|---|---|---|---|---|---|
| **pasteurisiert** pasteurized | **fettfrei** fat free | **gesalzen** salted | **die Schafmilch** sheep's milk | **die Laktose** lactose | **der Milchshake** milkshake |
| **unpasteurisiert** unpasteurized | **das Milchpulver** powdered milk | **ungesalzen** unsalted | **die Buttermilch** buttermilk | **homogenisiert** homogenised | **der gefrorene Joghurt** frozen yoghurt |

# das Brot und das Mehl • breads and flours

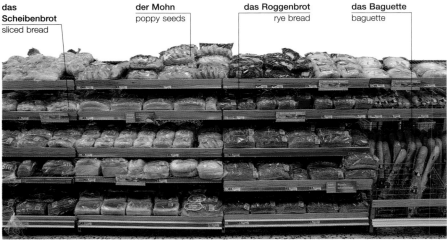

das
**Scheibenbrot**
sliced bread

der **Mohn**
poppy seeds

das **Roggenbrot**
rye bread

das **Baguette**
baguette

die **Bäckerei** | bakery

## Brot backen • making bread

**das Weizenmehl**
white flour

**das Roggenmehl**
brown flour

**das Vollkornmehl**
wholemeal flour

**die Hefe**
yeast

der **Teig**
dough

**sieben** | sift (v)

**verrühren** | mix (v)

**backen** | bake (v)

**die Kruste**
crust

**das Weißbrot**
white bread

**der Laib**
loaf

**das Graubrot**
brown bread

**das Vollkornbrot**
wholemeal bread

**die Scheibe**
slice

**das Mehrkornbrot**
granary bread

**das Maisbrot**
corn bread

**das Sodabrot**
soda bread

**das Sauerteigbrot**
sourdough bread

**das Fladenbrot**
flatbread

**das Hefebrötchen**
bagel

**das weiche Brötchen**
bap

**das Brötchen**
roll

**das Rosinenbrot**
fruit bread

**das Körnerbrot**
seeded bread

**der Naan**
naan bread

**das Pitabrot**
pitta bread

**das Knäckebrot**
crispbread

**Vokabular • vocabulary**

| | | | | |
|---|---|---|---|---|
| **das angereicherte Mehl**<br>strong flour | **das Paniermehl**<br>breadcrumbs | **gehen lassen**<br>prove (v) | **aufgehen**<br>rise (v) | **der Brotschneider**<br>slicer |
| **das Mehl mit Backpulver**<br>self-raising flour | **das Mehl ohne Backpulver**<br>plain flour | **glasieren**<br>glaze (v) | **die Flöte**<br>flute | **der Bäcker**<br>baker |

# Kuchen und Nachspeisen • cakes and desserts

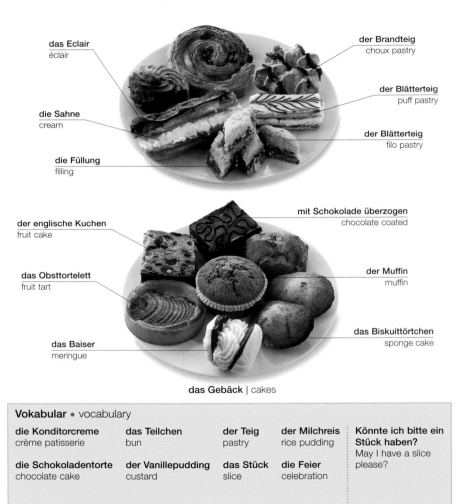

**das Eclair**
éclair

**der Brandteig**
choux pastry

**die Sahne**
cream

**der Blätterteig**
puff pastry

**die Füllung**
filling

**der Blätterteig**
filo pastry

**der englische Kuchen**
fruit cake

**mit Schokolade überzogen**
chocolate coated

**das Obsttortelett**
fruit tart

**der Muffin**
muffin

**das Baiser**
meringue

**das Biskuittörtchen**
sponge cake

**das Gebäck** | cakes

## Vokabular • vocabulary

| | | | | |
|---|---|---|---|---|
| **die Konditorcreme**<br>crème patisserie | **das Teilchen**<br>bun | **der Teig**<br>pastry | **der Milchreis**<br>rice pudding | **Könnte ich bitte ein Stück haben?**<br>May I have a slice please? |
| **die Schokoladentorte**<br>chocolate cake | **der Vanillepudding**<br>custard | **das Stück**<br>slice | **die Feier**<br>celebration | |

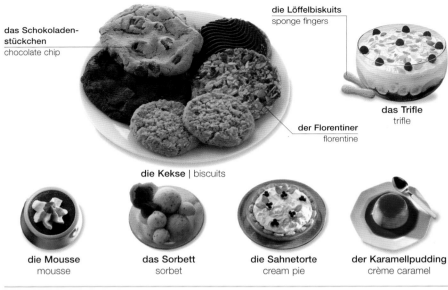

**das Schokoladen-
stückchen**
chocolate chip

**die Löffelbiskuits**
sponge fingers

**das Trifle**
trifle

**der Florentiner**
florentine

**die Kekse** | biscuits

**die Mousse**
mousse

**das Sorbett**
sorbet

**die Sahnetorte**
cream pie

**der Karamellpudding**
crème caramel

# die festlichen Kuchen • celebration cakes

**der obere Kuchenteil**
top tier

**das Band**
ribbon

**der untere
Kuchenteil**
bottom tier

**der
Zuckerguss**
icing

**das
Marzipan**
marzipan

**die Hochzeitstorte** | wedding cake

**die
Dekoration**
decoration

**die
Geburtstagskerzen**
birthday candles

**ausblasen**
blow out (v)

**der Geburtstagskuchen** | birthday cake

# die Feinkost • delicatessen

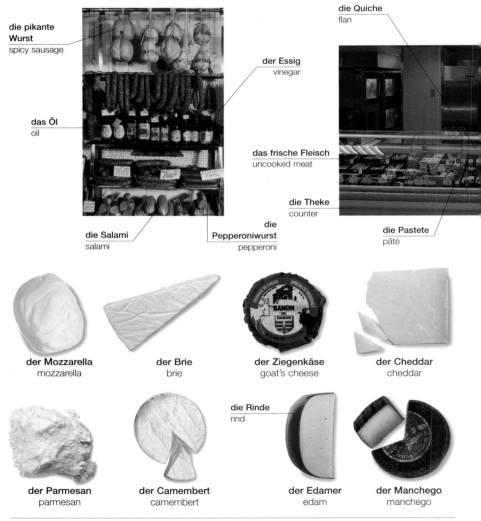

die pikante Wurst
spicy sausage

der Essig
vinegar

das Öl
oil

die Quiche
flan

das frische Fleisch
uncooked meat

die Theke
counter

die Salami
salami

die Pepperoniwurst
pepperoni

die Pastete
pâté

**der Mozzarella**
mozzarella

**der Brie**
brie

**der Ziegenkäse**
goat's cheese

**der Cheddar**
cheddar

**der Parmesan**
parmesan

**der Camembert**
camembert

die Rinde
rind

**der Edamer**
edam

**der Manchego**
manchego

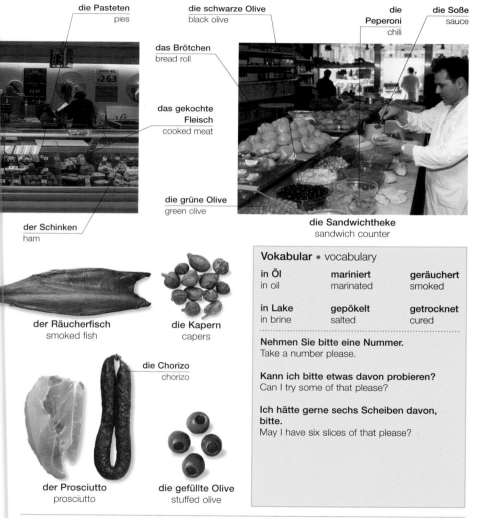

**die Pasteten**
pies

**die schwarze Olive**
black olive

**die
Peperoni**
chili

**die Soße**
sauce

**das Brötchen**
bread roll

**das gekochte
Fleisch**
cooked meat

**die grüne Olive**
green olive

**die Sandwichtheke**
sandwich counter

**der Schinken**
ham

**der Räucherfisch**
smoked fish

**die Kapern**
capers

**die Chorizo**
chorizo

**der Prosciutto**
prosciutto

**die gefüllte Olive**
stuffed olive

**Vokabular** • vocabulary

| | | |
|---|---|---|
| **in Öl**<br>in oil | **mariniert**<br>marinated | **geräuchert**<br>smoked |
| **in Lake**<br>in brine | **gepökelt**<br>salted | **getrocknet**<br>cured |

**Nehmen Sie bitte eine Nummer.**
Take a number please.

**Kann ich bitte etwas davon probieren?**
Can I try some of that please?

**Ich hätte gerne sechs Scheiben davon,
bitte.**
May I have six slices of that please?

# die Getränke • drinks

## das Wasser • water

das
**Flaschenwasser**
bottled water

**mit
Kohlensäure**
sparkling

**das Leitungswasser**
tap water

**ohne
Kohlensäure**
still

**das Tonicwater**
tonic water

**das Mineralwasser**
mineral water

**das Sodawasser**
soda water

## die heißen Getränke • hot drinks

**der Teebeutel**
teabag

**die Teeblätter**
loose leaf tea

**der Tee**
tea

**die Bohnen**
beans

**der gemahlene
Kaffee**
ground coffee

**der Kaffee**
coffee

**die heiße
Schokolade**
hot chocolate

**das Malzgetränk**
malted drink

## die alkoholfreien Getränke • soft drinks

**der Strohhalm**
straw

**der Tomatensaft**
tomato juice

**der Traubensaft**
grape juice

**die Limonade**
lemonade

**die Orangeade**
orangeade

**die Cola**
cola

# die alkoholischen Getränke • alcoholic drinks

**der Gin**
gin

die Dose
can

**das Bier**
beer

**der Apfelwein**
cider

**das halbdunkle Bier**
bitter

**der Stout**
stout

**der Wodka**
vodka

**der Whisky**
whisky

**der Rum**
rum

**der Weinbrand**
brandy

**der Portwein**
port

trocken
dry

**der Sherry**
sherry

**der Campari**
campari

rosé
rosé

weiß
white

rot
red

**der Likör**
liqueur

**der Tequila**
tequila

**der Champagner**
champagne

**der Wein**
wine

# auswärts essen
eating out

# das Café • café

**die Markise**
awning

**die Speisekarte**
menu

das Straßencafé | pavement café

**der Sonnenschirm**
umbrella

**das Terrassencafé**
terrace café

**der Kellner**
waiter

**die Kaffeemaschine**
coffee machine

**der Tisch**
table

die Snackbar | snack bar

# der Kaffee • coffee

**der Kaffee mit Milch**
white coffee

**der schwarze Kaffee**
black coffee

**das Kakaopulver**
cocoa powder

**der Schaum**
froth

**der Filterkaffee**
filter coffee

**der Espresso**
espresso

**der Cappuccino**
cappuccino

**der Eiskaffee**
iced coffee

# der Tee • tea

**der Kräutertee**
herbal tea

**der Kamillentee**
camomile tea

**der grüne Tee**
green tea

**der Tee mit Milch**
tea with milk

**der schwarze Tee**
black tea

**der Tee mit Zitrone**
tea with lemon

**der Pfefferminztee**
mint tea

**der Eistee**
iced tea

## die Säfte und Milchshakes • juices and milkshakes

**der Schokoladenmilchshake**
chocolate milkshake

**der Erdbeermilchshake**
strawberry milkshake

**der Orangensaft**
orange juice

**der Apfelsaft**
apple juice

**der Ananassaft**
pineapple juice

**der Tomatensaft**
tomato juice

**der Kaffeemilchshake**
coffee milkshake

## das Essen • food

**das Graubrot**
brown bread

**die Kugel**
scoop

**der getoastete Sandwich**
toasted sandwich

**der Salat**
salad

**das Eis**
ice cream

**das Gebäck**
pastry

# die Bar • bar

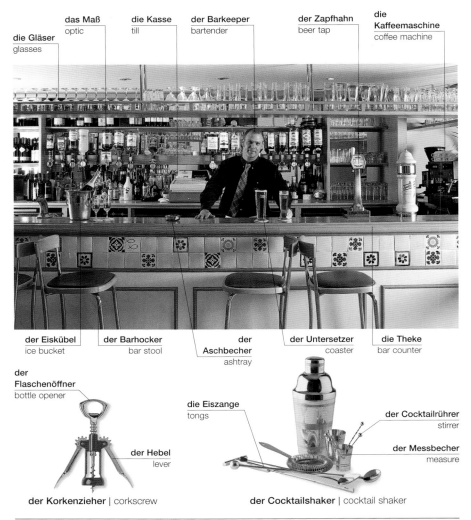

**die Gläser**
glasses

**das Maß**
optic

**die Kasse**
till

**der Barkeeper**
bartender

**der Zapfhahn**
beer tap

**die Kaffeemaschine**
coffee machine

**der Eiskübel**
ice bucket

**der Barhocker**
bar stool

**der Aschbecher**
ashtray

**der Untersetzer**
coaster

**die Theke**
bar counter

**der Flaschenöffner**
bottle opener

**der Hebel**
lever

**der Korkenzieher** | corkscrew

**die Eiszange**
tongs

**der Cocktailrührer**
stirrer

**der Messbecher**
measure

**der Cocktailshaker** | cocktail shaker

der Krug
pitcher

der Eiswürfel
ice cube

**der Gin Tonic**
gin and tonic

**der Scotch mit Wasser**
scotch and water

**der Rum mit Cola**
rum and coke

**der Wodka mit Orangensaft**
vodka and orange

**der Martini**
martini

**der Cocktail**
cocktail

**der Wein**
wine

**das Bier** | beer

einfach
single

doppelt
double

Eis und Zitrone
ice and lemon

**ein Schuss**
a shot

**das Maß**
measure

**ohne Eis**
without ice

**mit Eis**
with ice

# die Knabbereien • bar snacks

die
Cashewnüsse
cashewnuts

die
Erdnüsse
peanuts

die Mandeln
almonds

**die Kartoffelchips** | crisps

**die Nüsse** | nuts

**die Oliven** | olives

# das Restaurant • restaurant

**der Nicht-raucherbereich**
non-smoking section

**die Serviette**
napkin

**der Hilfskoch**
commis chef

**das Gedeck**
table setting

**der Küchenchef**
chef

**die Küche**
kitchen

**das Glas**
glass

**das Tablett**
tray

**der Kellner**
waiter

**Vokabular • vocabulary**

| | | | | | |
|---|---|---|---|---|---|
| **das Abendmenü** evening menu | **die Spezialitäten** specials | **der Preis** price | **das Trinkgeld** tip | **das Buffet** buffet | **der Kunde** customer |
| **die Weinkarte** wine list | **à la carte** à la carte | **die Quittung** receipt | **ohne Bedienung** service not included | **die Bar** bar | **das Salz** salt |
| **das Mittagsmenü** lunch menu | **der Dessertwagen** sweet trolley | **die Rechnung** bill | **Bedienung inbegriffen** service included | **der Raucherbereich** smoking section | **der Pfeffer** pepper |

die Speisekarte
menu

die Kinderportion
child's meal

bestellen
order (v)

bezahlen
pay (v)

# die Gänge • courses

der Aperitif
apéritif

die Vorspeise
starter

die Suppe
soup

das Hauptgericht
main course

die Beilage
side order

die Gabel
fork

der Kaffeelöffel
coffee spoon

der Nachtisch | dessert

der Kaffee | coffee

---

**Ein Tisch für zwei Personen bitte.**
A table for two please.

**Könnte ich bitte die Speisekarte/Weinliste sehen?**
Can I see the menu/winelist please?

**Gibt es ein Festpreismenü?**
Is there a fixed price menu?

**Haben Sie vegetarische Gerichte?**
Do you have any vegetarian dishes?

**Könnte ich die Rechnung/Quittung haben?**
Could I have the bill/a receipt please?

**Könnten wir getrennt zahlen?**
Can we pay separately?

**Wo sind die Toiletten bitte ?**
Where are the toilets, please?

---

# der Schnellimbiss • fast food

**der Strohhalm**
straw

**der Hamburger**
burger

**das alkoholfreie Getränk**
soft drink

**die Pommes frites**
french fries

**die Papierserviette**
paper napkin

**das Tablett**
tray

**der Hamburger mit Pommes frites**
burger meal

**die Pizza**
pizza

**die Preisliste**
price list

**das Dosengetränk**
canned drink

**die Lieferung ins Haus**
home delivery

**der Imbissstand**
street stall

das
**Brötchen**
bun

der Senf · die Wurst
mustard · sausage

**der Hamburger**
hamburger

**der Chickenburger**
chicken burger

**der vegetarische
Hamburger**
veggie burger

**das Hot Dog**
hot dog

**der Sandwich**
sandwich

**der Klubsandwich**
club sandwich

**das belegte Brot**
open sandwich

die Füllung
filling

**das gefüllte
Fladenbrot**
wrap

die Soße
sauce

salzig
savoury

süß
sweet

**der Kebab**
kebab

**die Hähnchenstückchen**
chicken nuggets

**die Crêpes** | crêpes

der Pizzabelag
topping

**der Bratfisch mit
Pommes frites**
fish and chips

**die Rippen**
ribs

**das gebratene Hähnchen**
fried chicken

**die Pizza**
pizza

# das Frühstück • breakfast

**die Milch** milk

**die Getreideflocken** cereal

**die Konfitüre** jam

**das Dörrobst** dried fruit

**der Schinken** ham

**der Käse** cheese

**das Knäckebrot** crispbread

**das Frühstücksbuffet** breakfast buffet

**die Orangenmarmelade** marmalade

**die Pastete** pâté

**die Butter** butter

**der Obstsaft** fruit juice

**der Kaffee** coffee

**die Schokolade** hot chocolate

**das Croissant** croissant

**der Tee** tea

**der Frühstückstisch** | breakfast table

**die Getränke** | drinks

**die Brioche**
brioche

**das Brot**
bread

die Tomate
tomato

die Blutwurst
black pudding

der Toast
toast

das
Würstchen
sausage

das Spiegelei
fried egg

der Frühstücks
speck
bacon

**das englische Frühstück**
English breakfast

das Eigelb
yolk

**die Räucherheringe**
kippers

**das in Ei gebratene Brot**
french toast

**das gekochte Ei**
boiled egg

**das Rührei**
scrambled eggs

die Sahne
cream

der Früchtejoghurt
fruit yoghurt

**die Pfannkuchen**
pancakes

**die Waffeln**
waffles

**der Porridge**
porridge

**das Obst**
fresh fruit

# die Hauptmahlzeit • dinner

**die Suppe** | soup

**die Brühe** | broth

**der Eintopf** | stew

**das Curry** | curry

**der Braten**
roast

**die Pastete**
pie

**das Soufflé**
soufflé

**der Schaschlik**
kebab

**die Fleischklöße**
meatballs

**das Omelett**
omelette

**die Nudeln**
noodles

**das Schnellbratgericht**
stir fry

**die Nudeln** | pasta

**der Reis**
rice

**der gemischte Salat**
mixed salad

**der grüne Salat**
green salad

**die Salatsoße**
dressing

# die Zubereitung • techniques

**gefüllt** | stuffed

**in Soße** | in sauce

**gegrillt** | grilled

**mariniert** | marinated

**pochiert** | poached

**püriert** | mashed

**gebacken** | baked

**kurzgebraten** | pan fried

**gebraten**
fried

**eingelegt**
pickled

**geräuchert**
smoked

**frittiert**
deep fried

**in Saft**
in syrup

**angemacht**
dressed

**gedämpft**
steamed

**getrocknet**
cured

**das Lernen**
study

# die Schule • school

die Lehrerin
teacher

die Tafel
blackboard

das Klassenzimmer | classroom

der Schuljunge
schoolboy

der Schüler
pupil

die Schuluniform
school uniform

das Pult
desk

die Schultasche
school bag

die Kreide
chalk

das Schulmädchen
schoolgirl

---

**Vokabular • vocabulary**

| | | |
|---|---|---|
| die Literatur<br>literature | die Kunst<br>art | die Physik<br>physics |
| die Sprachen<br>languages | die Musik<br>music | die Chemie<br>chemistry |
| die Erdkunde<br>geography | die Mathematik<br>maths | die Biologie<br>biology |
| die Geschichte<br>history | die Naturwissenschaft<br>science | der Sport<br>physical education |

## die Aktivitäten • activities

lesen | read (v)

schreiben | write (v)

buchstabieren
spell (v)

zeichnen
draw (v)

**die Feder**
nib

**der Buntstift**
colouring pencil

**der Spitzer**
pencil
sharpener

**der Overheadprojektor**
overhead projector

**der Füller**
pen

**der Bleistift**
pencil

**das Heft**
notebook

**der Radiergummi**
rubber

**das Schulbuch** | textbook

**das Federmäppchen**
pencil case

**das Lineal**
ruler

**fragen**
question (v)

**antworten**
answer (v)

**diskutieren**
discuss (v)

**lernen**
learn (v)

**Vokabular** • vocabulary

| | | |
|---|---|---|
| **der Schulleiter** head teacher | **die Antwort** answer | **die Note** grade |
| **die Stunde** lesson | **der Aufsatz** essay | **die Klasse** year |
| **die Frage** question | **die Prüfung** examination | **das Lexikon** encyclopedia |
| **Notizen machen** take notes (v) | **die Hausaufgabe** homework | **das Wörterbuch** dictionary |

# die Mathematik • maths

## die Formen • shapes

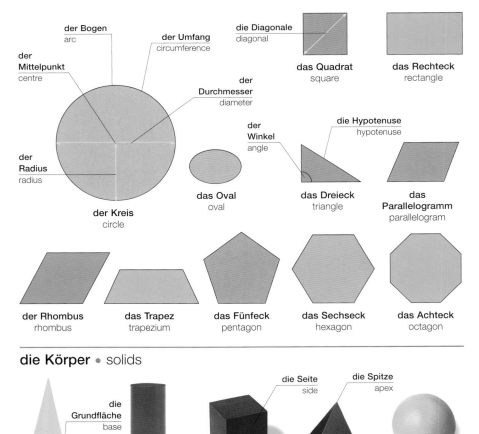

**der Bogen**
arc

**der Umfang**
circumference

**der Mittelpunkt**
centre

**die Diagonale**
diagonal

**der Durchmesser**
diameter

**das Quadrat**
square

**das Rechteck**
rectangle

**der Radius**
radius

**der Winkel**
angle

**die Hypotenuse**
hypotenuse

**das Oval**
oval

**der Kreis**
circle

**das Dreieck**
triangle

**das Parallelogramm**
parallelogram

**der Rhombus**
rhombus

**das Trapez**
trapezium

**das Fünfeck**
pentagon

**das Sechseck**
hexagon

**das Achteck**
octagon

## die Körper • solids

**die Seite**
side

**die Spitze**
apex

**die Grundfläche**
base

**der Kegel**
cone

**der Zylinder**
cylinder

**der Würfel**
cube

**die Pyramide**
pyramid

**die Kugel**
sphere

# die Linien • lines

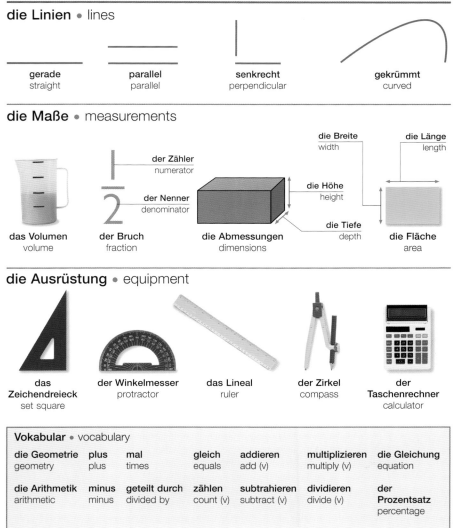

**gerade**
straight

**parallel**
parallel

**senkrecht**
perpendicular

**gekrümmt**
curved

# die Maße • measurements

**das Volumen**
volume

**der Bruch**
fraction

**der Zähler**
numerator

**der Nenner**
denominator

**die Abmessungen**
dimensions

**die Breite**
width

**die Länge**
length

**die Höhe**
height

**die Tiefe**
depth

**die Fläche**
area

# die Ausrüstung • equipment

**das Zeichendreieck**
set square

**der Winkelmesser**
protractor

**das Lineal**
ruler

**der Zirkel**
compass

**der Taschenrechner**
calculator

---

**Vokabular • vocabulary**

| | | | | | | |
|---|---|---|---|---|---|---|
| **die Geometrie** geometry | **plus** plus | **mal** times | **gleich** equals | **addieren** add (v) | **multiplizieren** multiply (v) | **die Gleichung** equation |
| **die Arithmetik** arithmetic | **minus** minus | **geteilt durch** divided by | **zählen** count (v) | **subtrahieren** subtract (v) | **dividieren** divide (v) | **der Prozentsatz** percentage |

---

# die Wissenschaft • science

**das Labor**
laboratory

**die Laborwaage**
scales

das
**Gewicht**
weight

**die Federwaage**
spring balance

**der Tiegel**
crucible

der
**Bunsenbrenner**
bunsen burner

**der Dreifuß**
tripod

**die Glasflasche**
glass bottle

**das Stativ**
lamp stand

**das Reagenzglas**
test tube

**das Gestell**
rack

**der Trichter**
funnel

**die Klammer**
clamp

**der Stöpsel**
stopper

**der Zeitmesser**
timer

**der Kolben**
flask

**die Petrischale**
petri dish

**der Versuch** | experiment

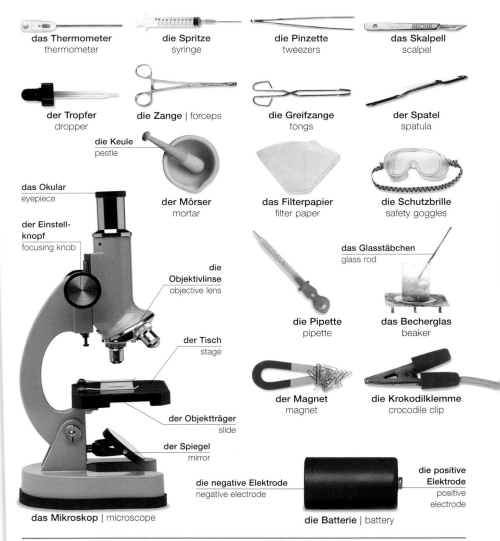

**das Thermometer**
thermometer

**die Spritze**
syringe

**die Pinzette**
tweezers

**das Skalpell**
scalpel

**der Tropfer**
dropper

**die Zange** | forceps

**die Greifzange**
tongs

**der Spatel**
spatula

**die Keule**
pestle

**der Mörser**
mortar

**das Filterpapier**
filter paper

**die Schutzbrille**
safety goggles

**das Okular**
eyepiece

**der Einstell-knopf**
focusing knob

**die Objektivlinse**
objective lens

**das Glasstäbchen**
glass rod

**der Tisch**
stage

**die Pipette**
pipette

**das Becherglas**
beaker

**der Objektträger**
slide

**der Spiegel**
mirror

**der Magnet**
magnet

**die Krokodilklemme**
crocodile clip

**die negative Elektrode**
negative electrode

**die positive Elektrode**
positive electrode

**das Mikroskop** | microscope

**die Batterie** | battery

# die Hochschule • college

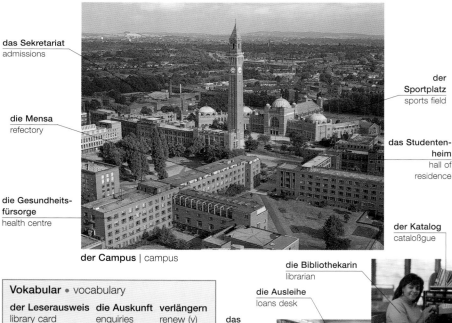

das Sekretariat
admissions

die Mensa
refectory

die Gesundheits-
fürsorge
health centre

der
Sportplatz
sports field

das Studenten-
heim
hall of
residence

der Campus | campus

der Katalog
cataloßgue

die Bibliothekarin
librarian

die Ausleihe
loans desk

das
Bücher
regal
bookshelf

das
Periodikum
periodical

die
Zeitschrift
journal

die Bibliothek | library

## Vokabular • vocabulary

| der Leserausweis | die Auskunft | verlängern |
|---|---|---|
| library card | enquiries | renew (v) |
| der Lesesaal | ausleihen | das Buch |
| reading room | borrow (v) | book |
| die Literaturliste | vorbestellen | der Titel |
| reading list | reserve (v) | title |
| das | die | der Gang |
| Rückgabedatum | Ausleihe | aisle |
| return date | loan | |

**der Student**
undergraduate

**der Dozent**
lecturer

**die Graduierte**
graduate

**die Robe**
robe

**der Hörsaal**
lecture theatre

**die Graduierungsfeier**
graduation ceremony

# die Fachhochschulen • schools

**das Model**
model

**die Kunsthochschule**
art college

**die Musikhochschule**
music school

**die Tanzakademie**
dance academy

**Vokabular** • vocabulary

| | | | | |
|---|---|---|---|---|
| **das Stipendium**<br>scholarship | **die Forschung**<br>research | **die Examensarbeit**<br>dissertation | **die Medizin**<br>medicine | **die Philosophie**<br>philosophy |
| **postgraduiert**<br>postgraduate | **der Magister**<br>masters | **der Fachbereich**<br>department | **die Zoologie**<br>zoology | **die Politologie**<br>politics |
| **das Diplom**<br>diploma | **die Promotion**<br>doctorate | **der Maschinenbau**<br>engineering | **die Physik**<br>physics | **die Literatur**<br>literature |
| **der akademische Grad**<br>degree | **die Dissertation**<br>thesis | **die Kunstgeschichte**<br>history of art | **die Rechtswissenschaft**<br>law | |
| | | | **die Wirtschaftswissenschaft**<br>economics | |

**die Arbeit**
work

# das Büro 1 • office 1
## das Büro • office

**der Bildschirm**
monitor

**der Stifthalter**
desktop organizer

**der Ordner**
file

**die Ablage für Eingänge**
in-tray

**die Ablage für Ausgänge**
out-tray

**der Computer**
computer

**die Tastatur**
keyboard

**das Telefon**
telephone

**das Notizbuch**
notebook

**das Schild**
label

**der Schreibtisch**
desk

**der Papierkorb**
wastebasket

**der Drehstuhl**
swivel chair

**das Schreibtischschränkchen**
drawer unit

**die Schublade**
drawer

**der Aktenschrank**
filing cabinet

---

# die Büroausstattung • office equipment

**der Papierbehälter**
paper tray

**die Papierführung**
paper guide

**das Fax**
fax

**der Drucker** | printer

**das Faxgerät** | fax machine

### Vokabular • vocabulary

**drucken**
print (v)

**vergrößern**
enlarge (v)

**kopieren**
copy (v)

**verkleinern**
reduce (v)

**Ich möchte fotokopieren.**
I need to make some copies.

---

# der Bürobedarf • office supplies

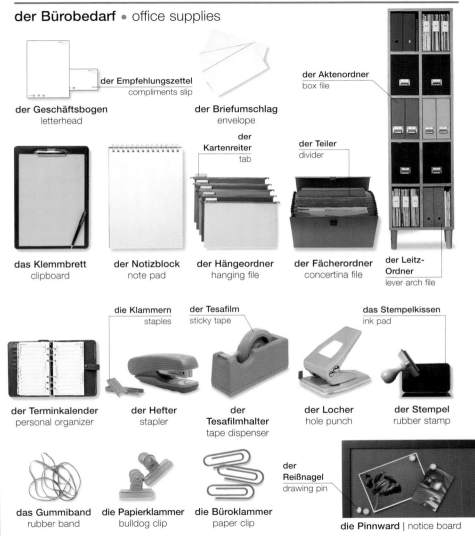

**der Empfehlungszettel**
compliments slip

**der Geschäftsbogen**
letterhead

**der Briefumschlag**
envelope

**der Aktenordner**
box file

**der Kartenreiter**
tab

**der Teiler**
divider

**das Klemmbrett**
clipboard

**der Notizblock**
note pad

**der Hängeordner**
hanging file

**der Fächerordner**
concertina file

**der Leitz-Ordner**
lever arch file

**die Klammern**
staples

**der Tesafilm**
sticky tape

**das Stempelkissen**
ink pad

**der Terminkalender**
personal organizer

**der Hefter**
stapler

**der Tesafilmhalter**
tape dispenser

**der Locher**
hole punch

**der Stempel**
rubber stamp

**das Gummiband**
rubber band

**die Papierklammer**
bulldog clip

**die Büroklammer**
paper clip

**der Reißnagel**
drawing pin

**die Pinnward** | notice board

# das Büro 2 • office 2

**das Flipchart**
flipchart

**das Protokoll**
minutes

**das Gestell**
easel

**der Bericht**
report

**der Manager**
manager

**das Angebot**
proposal

**der leitende Angestellte**
executive

**die Sitzung** | meeting

---

**Vokabular** • vocabulary

**der Sitzungsraum**
meeting room

**teilnehmen**
attend (v)

**die Tagesordnung**
agenda

**den Vorsitz führen**
chair (v)

**Um wieviel Uhr ist die Sitzung?**
What time is the meeting?

**Was sind Ihre Geschäftszeiten?**
What are your office hours?

**der Projektor**
projector

**der Sprecher**
speaker

**die Präsentation** | presentation

---

# das Geschäft • business

**der Laptop**
laptop

**die Notizen**
notes

**der Geschäftsmann**
businessman

**die Geschäftsfrau**
businesswoman

**das Arbeitsessen**
business lunch

**die Geschäftsreise**
business trip

**der Kunde**
client

**der Termin**
appointment

**der Palmtop**
palmtop

**der Terminkalender** | diary

**der Generaldirektor**
managing director

**das Geschäftsabkommen**
business deal

---

## Vokabular • vocabulary

| | | | |
|---|---|---|---|
| **die Firma**<br>company | **das Personal**<br>staff | **die Buchhaltung**<br>accounts department | **die Rechtsabteilung**<br>legal department |
| **die Zentrale**<br>head office | **die Lohnliste**<br>payroll | **die Marketingabteilung**<br>marketing department | **die Kundendienstabteilung**<br>customer service department |
| **die Zweigstelle**<br>branch | **das Gehalt**<br>salary | **die Verkaufsabteilung**<br>sales department | **die Personalabteilung**<br>personnel department |

---

# der Computer • computer

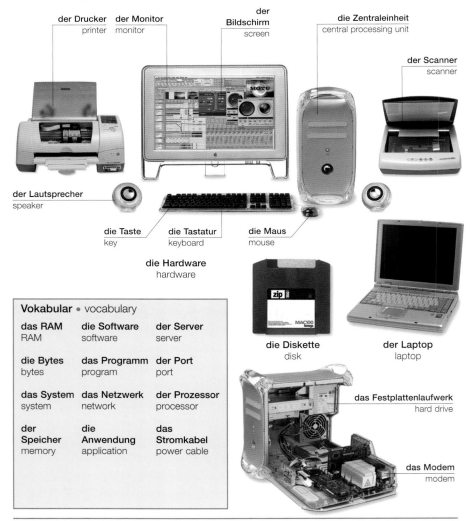

der Drucker
printer

der Monitor
monitor

der
Bildschirm
screen

die Zentraleinheit
central processing unit

der Scanner
scanner

der Lautsprecher
speaker

die Taste
key

die Tastatur
keyboard

die Maus
mouse

**die Hardware**
hardware

**Vokabular** • vocabulary

| | | |
|---|---|---|
| **das RAM**<br>RAM | **die Software**<br>software | **der Server**<br>server |
| **die Bytes**<br>bytes | **das Programm**<br>program | **der Port**<br>port |
| **das System**<br>system | **das Netzwerk**<br>network | **der Prozessor**<br>processor |
| **der Speicher**<br>memory | **die Anwendung**<br>application | **das Stromkabel**<br>power cable |

**die Diskette**
disk

**der Laptop**
laptop

das Festplattenlaufwerk
hard drive

das Modem
modem

# das Desktop • desktop

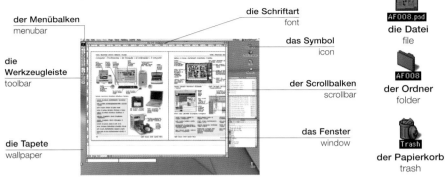

**die Schriftart**
font

**das Symbol**
icon

**der Menübalken**
menubar

**die Werkzeugleiste**
toolbar

**der Scrollbalken**
scrollbar

**die Tapete**
wallpaper

**das Fenster**
window

**die Datei**
file

**der Ordner**
folder

**der Papierkorb**
trash

---

# das Internet • internet

**der Browser**
browser

**die Inbox**
inbox

**die Web-Site**
website

**browsen**
browse (v)

# die E-Mail • email

**die E-Mail-Adresse**
email address

---

**Vokabular** • vocabulary

| | | | | | |
|---|---|---|---|---|---|
| **verbinden**<br>connect (v) | **der Serviceprovider**<br>service provider | **einloggen**<br>log on (v) | **herunterladen**<br>download (v) | **senden**<br>send (v) | **sichern**<br>save (v) |
| **installieren**<br>instal (v) | **das E-Mail-Konto**<br>email account | **online**<br>on-line | **der Anhang**<br>attachment | **erhalten**<br>receive (v) | **suchen**<br>search (v) |

# die Medien • media

## das Fernsehstudio • television studio

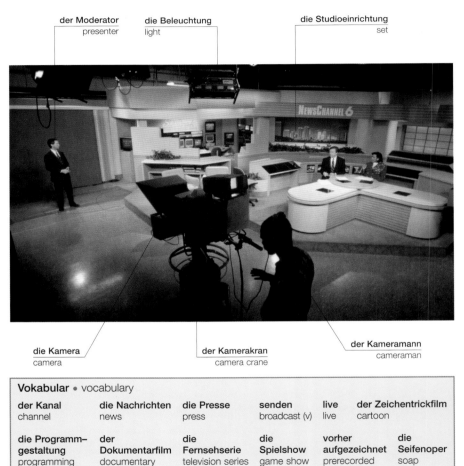

der Moderator
presenter

die Beleuchtung
light

die Studioeinrichtung
set

die Kamera
camera

der Kamerakran
camera crane

der Kameramann
cameraman

---

**Vokabular** • vocabulary

| | | | | | |
|---|---|---|---|---|---|
| **der Kanal**<br>channel | **die Nachrichten**<br>news | **die Presse**<br>press | **senden**<br>broadcast (v) | **live**<br>live | **der Zeichentrickfilm**<br>cartoon |
| **die Programm–gestaltung**<br>programming | **der Dokumentarfilm**<br>documentary | **die Fernsehserie**<br>television series | **die Spielshow**<br>game show | **vorher aufgezeichnet**<br>prerecorded | **die Seifenoper**<br>soap |

---

**der Interviewer**
interviewer

**die Reporterin**
reporter

**der Teleprompter**
autocue

**die Nachrichtensprecherin**
newsreader

**die Schauspieler**
actors

**der Mikrophongalgen**
sound boom

**die Klappe**
clapper board

**das Set**
film set

## das Radio • radio

das **Mischpult**
mixing desk

das **Mikrophon**
microphone

der **Tonmeister**
sound technician

**das Tonstudio** | recording studio

### Vokabular • vocabulary

| | |
|---|---|
| **der DJ**<br>DJ | **die Kurzwelle**<br>short wave |
| **die Sendung**<br>broadcast | **die Mittelwelle**<br>medium wave |
| **die Wellenlänge**<br>wavelength | **die Frequenz**<br>frequency |
| **die Langwelle**<br>long wave | **die Lautstärke**<br>volume |
| **die Rundfunkstation**<br>radio station | **einstellen**<br>tune (v) |

# das Recht • law

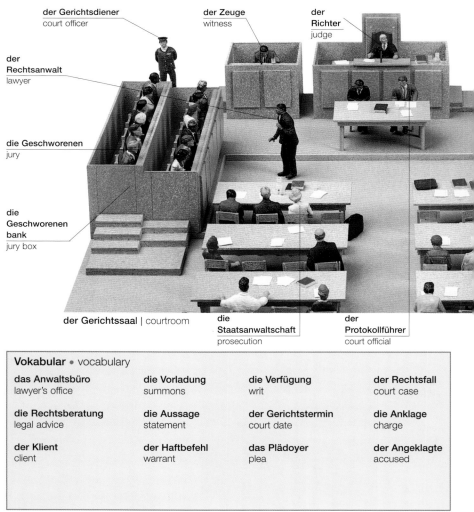

**der Gerichtsdiener**
court officer

**der Zeuge**
witness

**der Richter**
judge

**der Rechtsanwalt**
lawyer

**die Geschworenen**
jury

**die Geschworenen bank**
jury box

**der Gerichtssaal** | courtroom

**die Staatsanwaltschaft**
prosecution

**der Protokollführer**
court official

## Vokabular • vocabulary

**das Anwaltsbüro**
lawyer's office

**die Vorladung**
summons

**die Verfügung**
writ

**der Rechtsfall**
court case

**die Rechtsberatung**
legal advice

**die Aussage**
statement

**der Gerichtstermin**
court date

**die Anklage**
charge

**der Klient**
client

**der Haftbefehl**
warrant

**das Plädoyer**
plea

**der Angeklagte**
accused

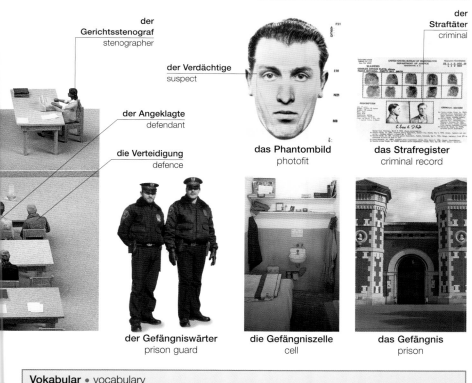

**der Gerichtsstenograf**
stenographer

**der Verdächtige**
suspect

**der Angeklagte**
defendant

**die Verteidigung**
defence

**der Straftäter**
criminal

**das Phantombild**
photofit

**das Strafregister**
criminal record

**der Gefängniswärter**
prison guard

**die Gefängniszelle**
cell

**das Gefängnis**
prison

---

## Vokabular • vocabulary

| | | | |
|---|---|---|---|
| **das Beweismittel**<br>evidence | **schuldig**<br>guilty | **die Kaution**<br>bail | **Ich möchte mit einem Anwalt sprechen.**<br>I want to see a lawyer. |
| **das Urteil**<br>verdict | **freigesprochen**<br>acquitted | **die Berufung**<br>appeal | **Wo ist das Gericht?**<br>Where is the courthouse? |
| **unschuldig**<br>innocent | **das Strafmaß**<br>sentence | **die Haftentlassung auf Bewährung**<br>parole | **Kann ich die Kaution leisten?**<br>Can I post bail? |

---

# der Bauernhof 1 • farm 1

**der Bauer**
farmer

das Ackerland
farmland

der Hof
farmyard

das
Nebengebäude
outbuilding

das
**Bauernhaus**
farmhouse

das Feld
field

die
**Scheune**
barn

der Gemüse-
garten
vegetable plot

die Hecke
hedge

das Tor
gate

der Zaun
fence

die Weide
pasture

das Vieh
livestock

der Kultivator
cultivator

**der Traktor** | tractor

**der Mähdrescher** | combine harvester

# die landwirtschaftlichen Betriebe • types of farm

die Feldfrucht
crop

**der Ackerbaubetrieb**
arable farm

**der Betrieb für
Milchproduktion**
dairy farm

die Herde
flock

**die Schaffarm**
sheep farm

**die Hühnerfarm**
poultry farm

**die Schweinefarm**
pig farm

**die Fischzucht**
fish farm

**der Obstanbau**
fruit farm

der Weinstock
vine

**der Weinberg**
vineyard

# die Tätigkeiten • actions

die
Furche
furrow

**pflügen**
plough (v)

**säen**
sow (v)

**melken**
milk (v)

**füttern**
feed (v)

**bewässern** | water (v)

**ernten** | harvest (v)

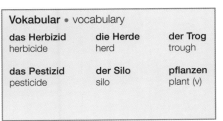

---

**Vokabular** • vocabulary

| | | |
|---|---|---|
| **das Herbizid** herbicide | **die Herde** herd | **der Trog** trough |
| **das Pestizid** pesticide | **der Silo** silo | **pflanzen** plant (v) |

# der Bauernhof 2 • farm 2

## die Feldfrüchte • crops

**der Weizen**
wheat

**der Mais**
corn

**die Gerste**
barley

**der Raps**
rapeseed

**die Sonnenblume**
sunflower

der Ballen
bale

**das Heu**
hay

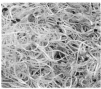

**die Luzerne**
alfalfa

**der Tabak**
tobacco

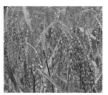

**der Reis**
rice

**der Tee**
tea

**der Kaffee**
coffee

**der Flachs**
flax

**das Zuckerrohr**
sugarcane

**die Baumwolle**
cotton

**die Vogelscheuche**
scarecrow

# das Vieh • livestock

**das Ferkel**
piglet

**das Kalb**
calf

**das Schwein**
pig

**die Kuh**
cow

**der Stier**
bull

**das Schaf**
sheep

**das Zicklein**
kid

**das Fohlen**
foal

**das Lamm**
lamb

**die Ziege**
goat

**das Pferd**
horse

**der Esel**
donkey

**das Küken**
chick

**das Entenküken**
duckling

**das Huhn**
chicken

**der Hahn**
cockerel

**der Truthahn**
turkey

**die Ente**
duck

**der Stall**
stable

**der Pferch**
pen

**der Hühnerstall**
chicken coop

**der Schweinestall**
pigsty

# der Bau • construction

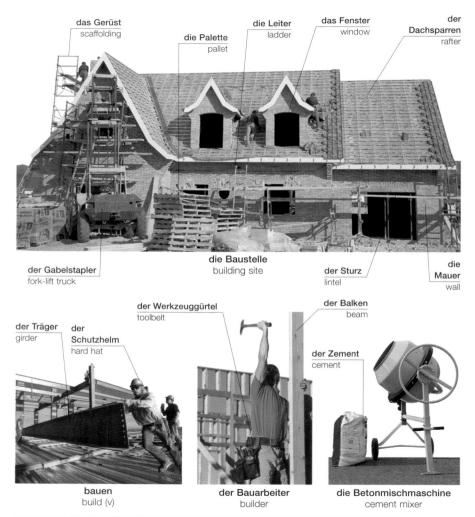

das Gerüst
scaffolding

die Palette
pallet

die Leiter
ladder

das Fenster
window

der
Dachsparren
rafter

der Gabelstapler
fork-lift truck

die Baustelle
building site

der Sturz
lintel

die
Mauer
wall

der Werkzeuggürtel
toolbelt

der Balken
beam

der Träger
girder

der
Schutzhelm
hard hat

der Zement
cement

bauen
build (v)

der Bauarbeiter
builder

die Betonmischmaschine
cement mixer

# das Material • materials

**der Ziegelstein**
brick

**das Bauholz**
timber

**der Dachziegel**
roof tile

**der Betonblock**
concrete block

# die Werkzeuge • tools

 der Mörtel
mortar

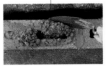

**die Kelle**
trowel

**die Wasserwaage**
spirit level

der Stiel
handle

**der Vorschlaghammer**
sledgehammer

**die Spitzhacke**
pickaxe

**die Schaufel**
shovel

# die Maschinen • machinery

**die Walze**
roller

**der Kipper**
dumper truck

die Stütze
support

der Haken
hook

**der Kran | crane**

# die Straßenarbeiten • roadworks

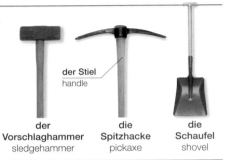

der Asphalt
tarmac

der Leitkegel
cone

**der Pressluftbohrer**
pneumatic drill

**der Neubelag**
resurfacing

**der Bagger**
mechanical digger

# die Berufe 1 • occupations 1

**der Schreiner**
carpenter

**der Elektriker**
electrician

**der Klempner**
plumber

**der Bauhandwerker**
builder

**der Gärtner**
gardener

der **Staubsauger**
vacuum cleaner

**der Gebäudereiniger**
cleaner

**der Mechaniker**
mechanic

**der Metzger**
butcher

die **Schere**
scissors

**die Fischhändlerin**
fishmonger

**der Gemüsehändler**
greengrocer

**die Floristin**
florist

**der Friseur**
hairdresser

**der Friseur**
barber

**der Juwelier**
jeweller

**die Verkäuferin**
shop assistant

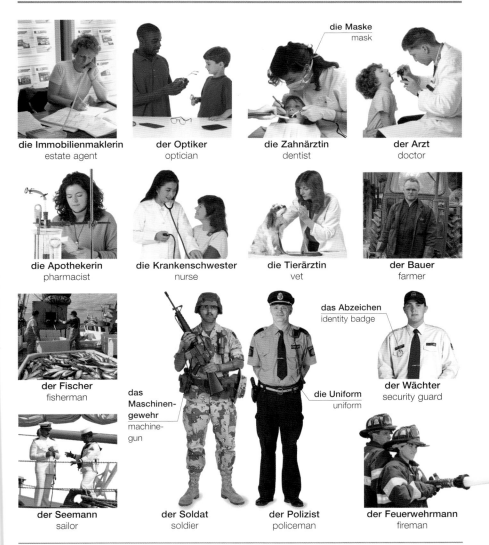

**die Immobilienmaklerin**
estate agent

**der Optiker**
optician

**die Maske**
mask

**die Zahnärztin**
dentist

**der Arzt**
doctor

**die Apothekerin**
pharmacist

**die Krankenschwester**
nurse

**die Tierärztin**
vet

**der Bauer**
farmer

**der Fischer**
fisherman

**das Maschinen-gewehr**
machine-gun

**das Abzeichen**
identity badge

**die Uniform**
uniform

**der Wächter**
security guard

**der Seemann**
sailor

**der Soldat**
soldier

**der Polizist**
policeman

**der Feuerwehrmann**
fireman

# die Berufe 2 • occupations 2

**der Rechtsanwalt**
lawyer

**der Wirtschaftsprüfer**
accountant

das Modell
model

**der Architekt**
architect

**der Wissenschaftler**
scientist

**die Lehrerin**
teacher

**der Bibliothekar**
librarian

**die Empfangsdame**
receptionist

die
Posttasche
mailbag

**der Briefträger**
postman

**der Busfahrer**
bus driver

**der Lastwagenfahrer**
lorry driver

**der Taxifahrer**
taxi driver

**der Pilot**
pilot

**die Flugbegleiterin**
air stewardess

**die Reisebürokauffrau**
travel agent

die
Kochmütze
chef's hat

**der Koch**
chef

das
Ballett
röckchen
tutu

**der Musiker**
musician

**die Tänzerin**
dancer

**der Schauspieler**
actor

**die Sängerin**
singer

**die Kellnerin**
waitress

**der Barkeeper**
barman

**der Sportler**
sportsman

**der Bildhauer**
sculptor

**die Malerin**
painter

**der Fotograf**
photographer

**der Nachrichtensprecher**
newsreader

die Notizen
notes

**der Journalist**
journalist

**die Redakteurin**
editor

**die Designerin**
designer

**die Damenschneiderin**
seamstress

**der Schneider**
tailor

**der Verkehr**
transport

# die Straßen • roads

**die Autobahn**
motorway

**die Mautstelle**
toll booth

**die Straßen-markierungen**
road markings

**die Zufahrtsstraße**
slip road

**Einbahn-**
one-way

**die Verkehrsinsel**
divider

**die Kreuzung**
junction

**die Verkehrs-ampel**
traffic light

**der Lastwagen**
lorry

**die rechte Spur**
inside lane

**die mittlere Spur**
middle lane

**die Überholspur**
outside lane

**die Ausfahrt**
exit ramp

**der Verkehr**
traffic

**die Überführung**
flyover

**der Seitenstreifen**
hard shoulder

**der Mittelstreifen**
central reservation

**die Unterführung**
underpass

**die Notrufsäule**
emergency phone

**der Behindertenparkplatz**
disabled parking

**der Verkehrsstau**
traffic jam

**der Fußgängerüberweg**
pedestrian crossing

**die Landkarte**
map

**die Parkuhr**
parking meter

**der Verkehrspolizist**
traffic policeman

### Vokabular • vocabulary

**parken**
park (v)

**überholen**
overtake (v)

**rückwärts fahren**
reverse (v)

**fahren**
drive (v)

**abschleppen**
tow away (v)

**die Umleitung**
diversion

**die Leitplanke**
crash barrier

**die Straßenbaustelle**
roadworks

**die Schnellstraße**
dual carriageway

**der Kreisverkehr**
roundabout

**Ist dies die Straße nach...?**
Is this the road to...?

**Wo kann ich parken?**
Where can I park?

# die Verkehrsschilder • road signs

**keine Einfahrt**
no entry

**die Geschwindig-keitsbegrenzung**
speed limit

**Gefahr**
hazard

**Halten verboten**
no stopping

**rechts abbiegen verboten**
no right turn

# der Bus • bus

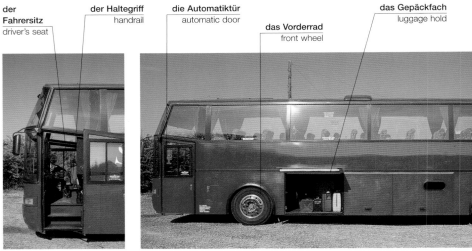

der **Fahrersitz**
driver's seat

der **Haltegriff**
handrail

die **Automatiktür**
automatic door

das **Vorderrad**
front wheel

das **Gepäckfach**
luggage hold

die **Tür** | door

der **Reisebus** | coach

## die Bustypen • types of buses

die **Liniennummer**
route number

der **Fahrer**
driver

der **Doppeldecker**
double-decker bus

die **Straßenbahn**
tram

der **Obus**
trolley bus

der **Schulbus** | school bus

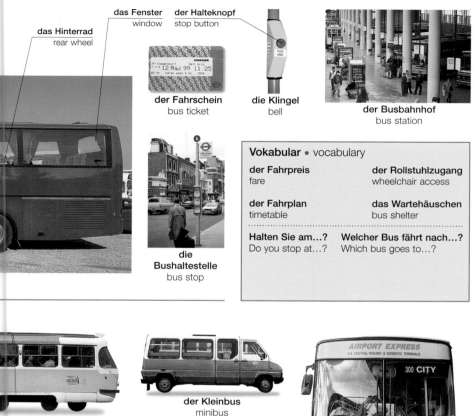

das Hinterrad
rear wheel

das Fenster
window

der Halteknopf
stop button

**der Fahrschein**
bus ticket

**die Klingel**
bell

**der Busbahnhof**
bus station

**die
Bushaltestelle**
bus stop

---

**Vokabular** • vocabulary

**der Fahrpreis**
fare

**der Rollstuhlzugang**
wheelchair access

**der Fahrplan**
timetable

**das Wartehäuschen**
bus shelter

**Halten Sie am…?**
Do you stop at…?

**Welcher Bus fährt nach…?**
Which bus goes to…?

---

**der Kleinbus**
minibus

This is an official London Sightseeing Bus.

LONDON PRIDE

**der Touristenbus** | tourist bus

AIRPORT EXPRESS
VIA CENTRAL RAILWAY & DOMESTIC TERMINALS

300 CITY

AIRPORT EXPRESS

**der Zubringer** | shuttle bus

# das Auto 1 • car 1

## das Äußere • exterior

**der Rückspiegel**
rearview mirror

**der Scheibenwischer**
windscreen wiper

**die Autotür**
door

**der Seitenspiegel**
wing mirror

**die Windschutz scheibe**
windscreen

**der Kofferraum**
boot

**die Motorhaube**
bonnet

**der Blinker**
indicator

**die Stoßstange**
bumper

**das Nummernschild**
licence plate

**der Scheinwerfer**
headlight

**das Rad**
wheel

**der Reifen**
tyre

**das Gepäck**
luggage

**der Dachgepäckträger**
roofrack

**die Hecktür**
tailgate

**der Sicherheitsgurt**
seat belt

**der Kindersitz**
child seat

# die Wagentypen • types

**der Kleinwagen**
small car

**die Fließhecklimousine**
hatchback

**die Limousine**
saloon

**der Kombiwagen**
estate

**das Kabriolett**
convertible

**das Sportkabriolett**
sports car

**die Großraum-
limousine**
people carrier

**der Geländewagen**
four-wheel drive

**das Vorkriegsmodell**
vintage

**die verlängerte Limousine**
limousine

# die Tankstelle • petrol station

**die Zapfsäule**
petrol pump

**der Benzinpreis**
price

*Chevron*

1.79
1.89
1.99

**der Tankstellenplatz**
forecourt

**das
Druckluftgerät**
air supply

**Vokabular** • vocabulary

| | | |
|---|---|---|
| **das Benzin** petrol | **verbleit** leaded | **die Autowaschanlage** car wash |
| **bleifrei** unleaded | **das Öl** oil | **das Frostschutzmittel** antifreeze |
| **die Werkstatt** garage | **der Diesel** diesel | **die Scheibenwasch anlage** screenwash |

**Voll tanken, bitte.**
Fill the tank, please.

# das Auto 2 · car 2

## die Innenausstattung · interior

der Rücksitz
back seat

die Armstütze
armrest

die Kopfstütze
headrest

die
Türverriegelung
door lock

der Türgriff
handle

**Vokabular** · vocabulary

| | | | | |
|---|---|---|---|---|
| **zweitürig** | **viertürig** | **die Zündung** | **die Bremse** | **das Gaspedal** |
| two-door | four-door | ignition | brake | accelerator |
| **dreitürig** | **mit Handschaltung** | **mit Automatik** | **die Kupplung** | **die Klimaanlage** |
| three-door | manual | automatic | clutch | air conditioning |

**Wie komme ich nach...?**
Can you tell me the way to...?

**Wo ist hier ein Parkplatz?**
Where is the car park?

**Kann ich hier parken?**
Can I park here?

# die Armaturen • controls

**das Lenkrad** steering wheel

**die Hupe** horn

**das Armaturenbrett** dashboard

**die Warnlichter** hazard lights

**das GPS-System** satellite navigation

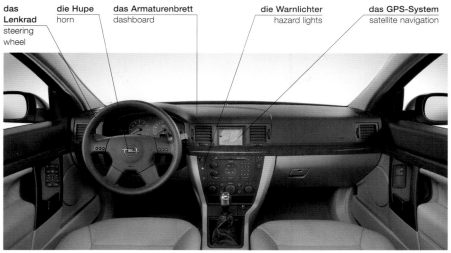

die Linkssteuerung | left-hand drive

**die Temperaturanzeige** temperature gauge

**der Drehzahlmesser** rev counter

**der Tachometer** speedometer

**die Kraftstoffanzeige** fuel gauge

**die Autostereoanlage** car stereo

**der Lichtschalter** lights switch

**der Heizungsregler** heater controls

**der Kilometerzähler** odometer

**der Airbag** air bag

**der Schalthebel** gearstick

die Rechtssteuerung | right-hand drive

# das Auto 3 • car 3

## die Mechanik • mechanics

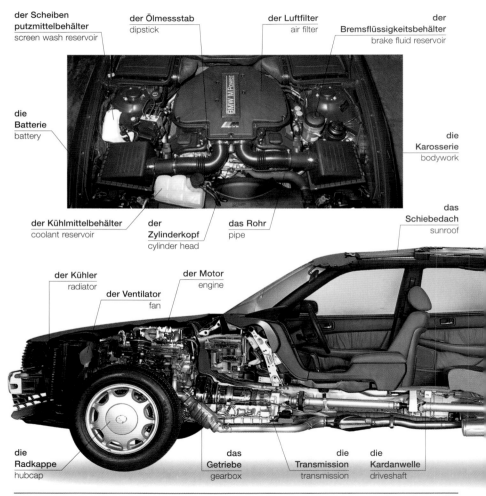

der Scheiben
putzmittelbehälter
screen wash reservoir

der Ölmessstab
dipstick

der Luftfilter
air filter

der
Bremsflüssigkeitsbehälter
brake fluid reservoir

die
Batterie
battery

die
Karosserie
bodywork

der Kühlmittelbehälter
coolant reservoir

der
Zylinderkopf
cylinder head

das Rohr
pipe

das
Schiebedach
sunroof

der Kühler
radiator

der Motor
engine

der Ventilator
fan

die
Radkappe
hubcap

das
Getriebe
gearbox

die
Transmission
transmission

die
Kardanwelle
driveshaft

# die Reifenpanne • puncture

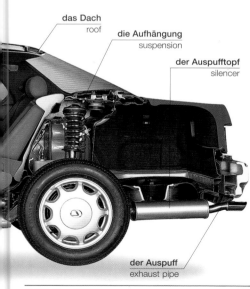

das Ersatzrad
spare tyre

der Radschlüssel
wrench

die Radmuttern
wheel nuts

der
Wagenheber
jack

**ein Rad wechseln**
change a wheel (v)

das Dach
roof

die Aufhängung
suspension

der Auspufftopf
silencer

der Auspuff
exhaust pipe

## Vokabular • vocabulary

**der Autounfall**
car accident

**die Panne**
breakdown

**die Versicherung**
insurance

**der Abschleppwagen**
tow truck

**der Mechaniker**
mechanic

**der Reifendruck**
tyre pressure

**der Sicherungskasten**
fuse box

**die Zündkerze**
spark plug

**der Keilriemen**
fan belt

**der Benzintank**
petrol tank

**der Nockenriemen**
cam belt

**der Turbolader**
turbocharger

**der Verteiler**
distributor

**die Einstellung**
timing

**das Chassis**
chassis

**die Handbremse**
handbrake

**die Lichtmaschine**
alternator

**Ich habe eine Panne.**
I've broken down.

**Mein Auto springt nicht an.**
My car won't start.

# das Motorrad • motorbike

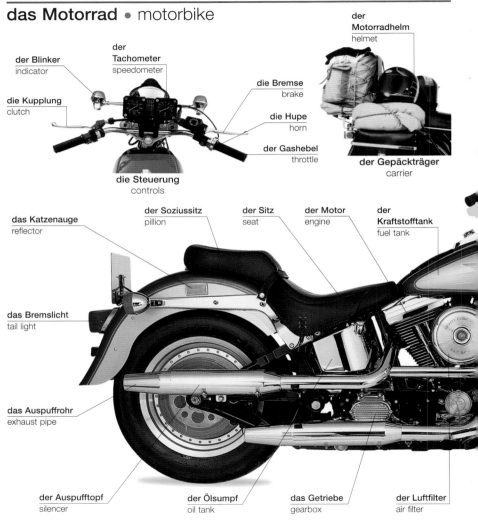

der Motorradhelm
helmet

der Blinker
indicator

der Tachometer
speedometer

die Bremse
brake

die Kupplung
clutch

die Hupe
horn

der Gashebel
throttle

die Steuerung
controls

der Gepäckträger
carrier

das Katzenauge
reflector

der Soziussitz
pillion

der Sitz
seat

der Motor
engine

der Kraftstofftank
fuel tank

das Bremslicht
tail light

das Auspuffrohr
exhaust pipe

der Auspufftopf
silencer

der Ölsumpf
oil tank

das Getriebe
gearbox

der Luftfilter
air filter

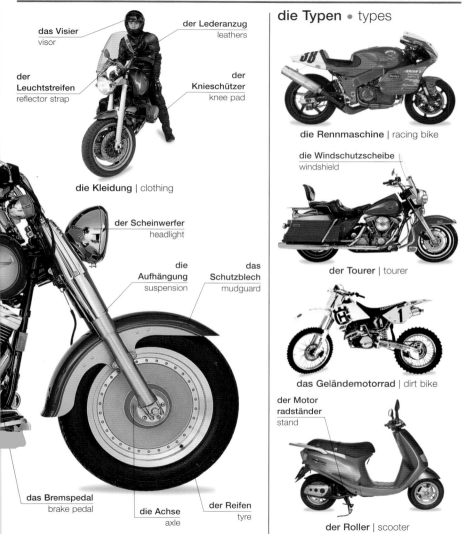

das Visier
visor

der Lederanzug
leathers

der
Leuchtstreifen
reflector strap

der
Knieschützer
knee pad

**die Kleidung** | clothing

der Scheinwerfer
headlight

die
Aufhängung
suspension

das
Schutzblech
mudguard

das Bremspedal
brake pedal

die Achse
axle

der Reifen
tyre

# die Typen • types

**die Rennmaschine** | racing bike

die Windschutzscheibe
windshield

**der Tourer** | tourer

**das Geländemotorrad** | dirt bike

der Motor
radständer
stand

**der Roller** | scooter

# das Fahrrad • bicycle

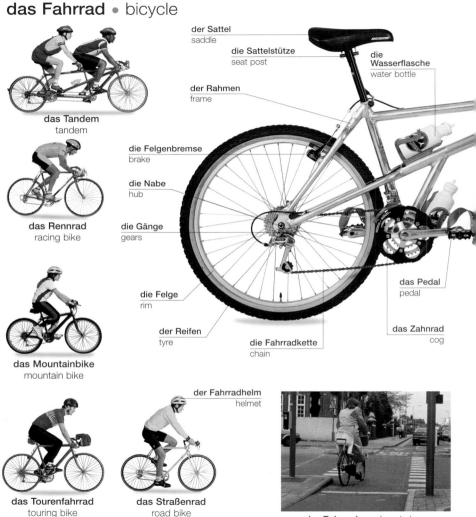

**das Tandem**
tandem

**das Rennrad**
racing bike

**das Mountainbike**
mountain bike

**das Tourenfahrrad**
touring bike

**das Straßenrad**
road bike

**der Sattel**
saddle

**die Sattelstütze**
seat post

**die Wasserflasche**
water bottle

**der Rahmen**
frame

**die Felgenbremse**
brake

**die Nabe**
hub

**die Gänge**
gears

**die Felge**
rim

**der Reifen**
tyre

**die Fahrradkette**
chain

**das Pedal**
pedal

**das Zahnrad**
cog

**der Fahrradhelm**
helmet

**der Fahrradweg** | cycle lane

die Stange
crossbar

die Lenkstange
handlebar

der Schalthebel
gear lever

der Bremsgriff
brake lever

der Reifenschlüssel
tyre lever

der Flicken
patch

**der Reparaturkasten** | repair kit

die Gabel
fork

die Speiche
spoke

der Schlüssel
key

die Luftpumpe
pump

das Fahrradschloss
lock

das Rad
wheel

das Ventil
valve

das Reifenprofil
tread

der Schlauch
inner tube

der Kindersitz
child seat

---

**Vokabular** • vocabulary

| | | | | | |
|---|---|---|---|---|---|
| das Rücklicht<br>rear light | die Stützräder<br>stabilisers | das Kabel<br>cable | der Korb<br>basket | der Riemen<br>toe strap | bremsen<br>brake (v) |
| die<br>Fahrradlampe<br>lamp | der<br>Fahrradständer<br>kickstand | die<br>Bremsbacke<br>brake block | die<br>Reifenpanne<br>puncture | der<br>Rennbügel<br>toe clip | schalten<br>change<br>gear (v) |
| der<br>Rückstrahler<br>reflector | der<br>Fahrradständer<br>bike rack | das<br>Kettenzahnrad<br>sprocket | der Dynamo<br>dynamo | treten<br>pedal (v) | Rad fahren<br>cycle (v) |

---

# der Zug • train

der
**Wagen**
carriage

der
**Bahnsteig**
platform

der
**Kofferkuli**
trolley

die
**Gleisnummer**
platform number

der **Pendler**
commuter

**der Bahnhof** | train station

# die Zugtypen • types of train

**die Dampflokomotive**
steam train

die
**Lokomotive**
engine

der **Führerstand**
driver's cab

die **Schiene**
rail

**die Diesellokomotive** | diesel train

**die Elektrolokomotive**
electric train

**der Hochgeschwindigkeitszug**
high-speed train

**die Einschienenbahn**
monorail

**die U-Bahn**
underground train

**die Straßenbahn**
tram

**der Güterzug**
freight train

die **Gepäckablage**
luggage rack

das **Zugfenster**
window

das **Gleis**
track

die **Tür**     der **Sitz**
door     seat

die **Eingangssperre**
ticket barrier

das **Abteil**
compartment

der **Lautsprecher**
public address system

der
**Fahrplan**
timetable

41213
KUPONG 7.00 kr
Typ 1105
Serie 964

die **Fahrkarte**
ticket

der **Speisewagen** | dining car

das **Schlafabteil**
sleeping compartment

die **Bahnhofshalle** | concourse

**Vokabular** • vocabulary

das **Bahnnetz**
rail network

der **Intercity**
inter-city train

die **Stoßzeit**
rush hour

der **U-Bahnplan**
underground map

die **Verspätung**
delay

der **Fahrpreis**
fare

der **Fahrkartenschalter**
ticket office

der **Schaffner**
ticket inspector

**umsteigen**
change (v)

die **stromführende
Schiene**
live rail

das **Signal**
signal

der **Nothebel**
emergency lever

# das Flugzeug • aircraft

## das Verkehrsflugzeug • airliner

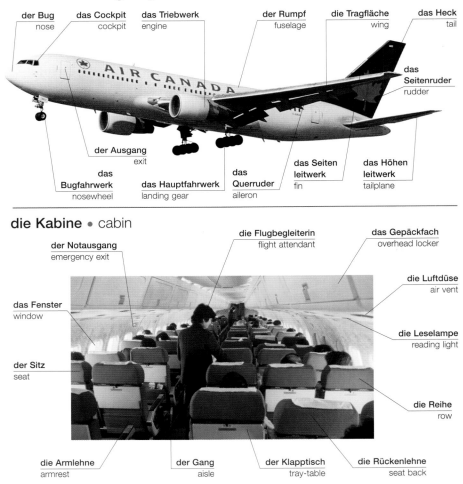

**der Bug**
nose

**das Cockpit**
cockpit

**das Triebwerk**
engine

**der Rumpf**
fuselage

**die Tragfläche**
wing

**das Heck**
tail

**das Seitenruder**
rudder

**der Ausgang**
exit

**das Bugfahrwerk**
nosewheel

**das Hauptfahrwerk**
landing gear

**das Querruder**
aileron

**das Seiten leitwerk**
fin

**das Höhen leitwerk**
tailplane

# die Kabine • cabin

**der Notausgang**
emergency exit

**die Flugbegleiterin**
flight attendant

**das Gepäckfach**
overhead locker

**die Luftdüse**
air vent

**das Fenster**
window

**die Leselampe**
reading light

**der Sitz**
seat

**die Reihe**
row

**die Armlehne**
armrest

**der Gang**
aisle

**der Klapptisch**
tray-table

**die Rückenlehne**
seat back

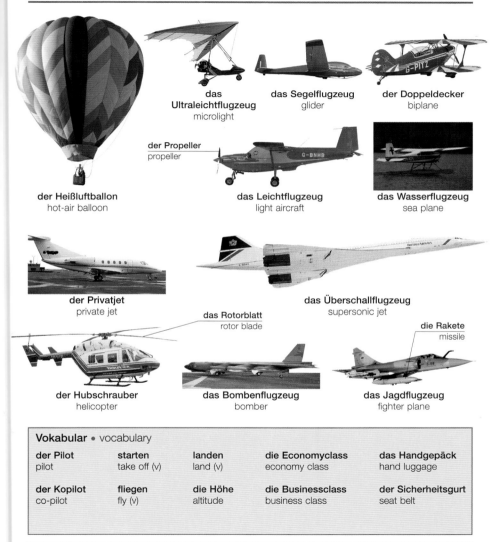

**das Ultraleichtflugzeug**
microlight

**das Segelflugzeug**
glider

**der Doppeldecker**
biplane

**der Propeller**
propeller

**der Heißluftballon**
hot-air balloon

**das Leichtflugzeug**
light aircraft

**das Wasserflugzeug**
sea plane

**der Privatjet**
private jet

**das Überschallflugzeug**
supersonic jet

**das Rotorblatt**
rotor blade

**die Rakete**
missile

**der Hubschrauber**
helicopter

**das Bombenflugzeug**
bomber

**das Jagdflugzeug**
fighter plane

**Vokabular • vocabulary**

| | | | | |
|---|---|---|---|---|
| **der Pilot** pilot | **starten** take off (v) | **landen** land (v) | **die Economyclass** economy class | **das Handgepäck** hand luggage |
| **der Kopilot** co-pilot | **fliegen** fly (v) | **die Höhe** altitude | **die Businessclass** business class | **der Sicherheitsgurt** seat belt |

# der Flughafen • airport

das Vorfeld
apron

der
Gepäckanhänger
baggage trailer

der Terminal
terminal

das Versorgungsfahrzeug
service vehicle

die Fluggastbrücke
walkway

**das Verkehrsflugzeug** | airliner

## Vokabular • vocabulary

| | | | |
|---|---|---|---|
| **das Gepäckband**<br>carousel | **die Flugnummer**<br>flight number | **die Start- und Landebahn**<br>runway | **der Urlaub**<br>holiday |
| **der Auslandsflug**<br>international flight | **die Passkontrolle**<br>immigration | **die Sicherheitsvorkehrungen**<br>security | **einen Flug buchen**<br>book a flight (v) |
| **der Inlandsflug**<br>domestic flight | **der Zoll**<br>customs | **die Gepäckröntgenmaschine**<br>X-ray machine | **einchecken**<br>check in (v) |
| **die Flugverbindung**<br>connection | **das Übergepäck**<br>excess baggage | **der Urlaubsprospekt**<br>holiday brochure | **der Kontrollturm**<br>control tower |

das **Handgepäck**
hand luggage

das **Gepäck**
luggage

der **Kofferkuli**
trolley

**der Abfertigungsschalter**
check-in desk

das **Visum**
visa

**der Pass** | passport

die **Bordkarte**
boarding pass

**die Passkontrolle**
passport control

**das Flugticket**
ticket

die **Gatenummer**
gate number

der **Abflug**
departures

**die Abflughalle**
departure lounge

das **Reiseziel**
destination

die **Ankunft**
arrivals

**die Fluginformationsanzeige**
information screen

**der Duty-free-Shop**
duty-free shop

**die Gepäckausgabe**
baggage reclaim

**der Taxistand**
taxi rank

**der Autoverleih**
car hire

# das Schiff • ship

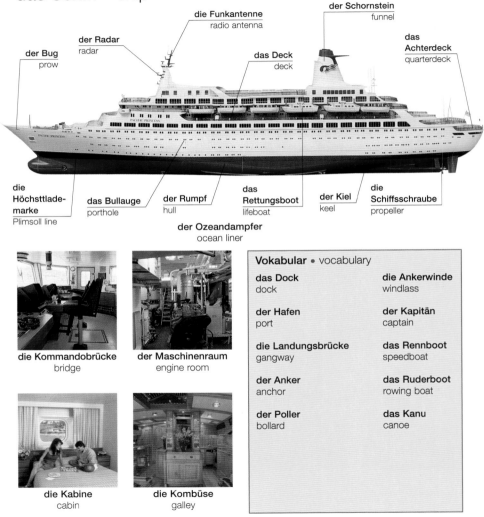

die Funkantenne
radio antenna

der Schornstein
funnel

der Radar
radar

das Deck
deck

das
Achterdeck
quarterdeck

der Bug
prow

die
Höchsttlade-
marke
Plimsoll line

das Bullauge
porthole

der Rumpf
hull

das
Rettungsboot
lifeboat

der Kiel
keel

die
Schiffsschraube
propeller

**der Ozeandampfer**
ocean liner

**die Kommandobrücke**
bridge

**der Maschinenraum**
engine room

**die Kabine**
cabin

**die Kombüse**
galley

**Vokabular** • vocabulary

| | |
|---|---|
| **das Dock**<br>dock | **die Ankerwinde**<br>windlass |
| **der Hafen**<br>port | **der Kapitän**<br>captain |
| **die Landungsbrücke**<br>gangway | **das Rennboot**<br>speedboat |
| **der Anker**<br>anchor | **das Ruderboot**<br>rowing boat |
| **der Poller**<br>bollard | **das Kanu**<br>canoe |

# andere Schiffe • other ships

**die Fähre**
ferry

der
**Außenbordmotor**
outboard motor

**das Schlauchboot**
inflatable dinghy

**das Tragflügelboot**
hydrofoil

**die Jacht**
yacht

**der Katamaran**
catamaran

**der Schleppdampfer**
tug boat

**das Luftkissenboot**
hovercraft

**das Containerschiff**
container ship

**die Takelung**
rigging

**das Segelboot**
sailboat

der
**Frachtraum**
hold

**das Frachtschiff**
freighter

**der Öltanker**
oil tanker

**der Flugzeugträger**
aircraft carrier

**das Kriegsschiff**
battleship

der
**Kommandoturm**
conning tower

**das U-Boot**
submarine

# der Hafen • port

**das Warenlager**
warehouse

**der Kran**
crane

**der Gabelstapler**
fork-lift truck

**die Zufahrtßsstraße**
access road

**das Zollamt**
customs house

**das Dock**
dock

**der Container**
container

**der Kai**
quay

**die Fracht**
cargo

**der Containerhafen** | container port

**der Fährterminal**
ferry terminal

**die Fähre**
ferry

**der Fahrkartenschalter**
ticket office

**der Passagier**
passenger

**der Passagierhafen** | passenger port

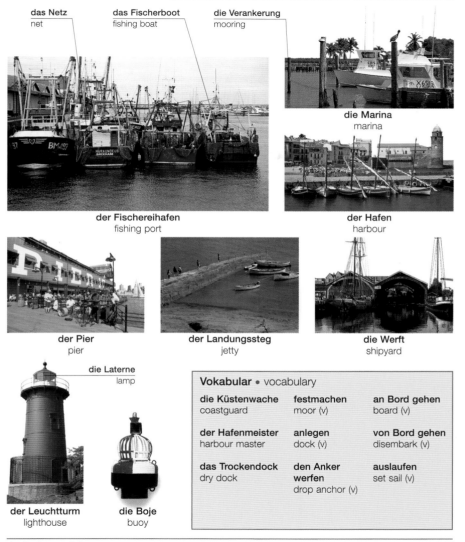

**das Netz**
net

**das Fischerboot**
fishing boat

**die Verankerung**
mooring

**die Marina**
marina

**der Fischereihafen**
fishing port

**der Hafen**
harbour

**der Pier**
pier

**der Landungssteg**
jetty

**die Werft**
shipyard

**die Laterne**
lamp

**der Leuchtturm**
lighthouse

**die Boje**
buoy

**Vokabular** • vocabulary

| | | |
|---|---|---|
| **die Küstenwache** coastguard | **festmachen** moor (v) | **an Bord gehen** board (v) |
| **der Hafenmeister** harbour master | **anlegen** dock (v) | **von Bord gehen** disembark (v) |
| **das Trockendock** dry dock | **den Anker werfen** drop anchor (v) | **auslaufen** set sail (v) |

**der Sport**
sports

# der Football • American football

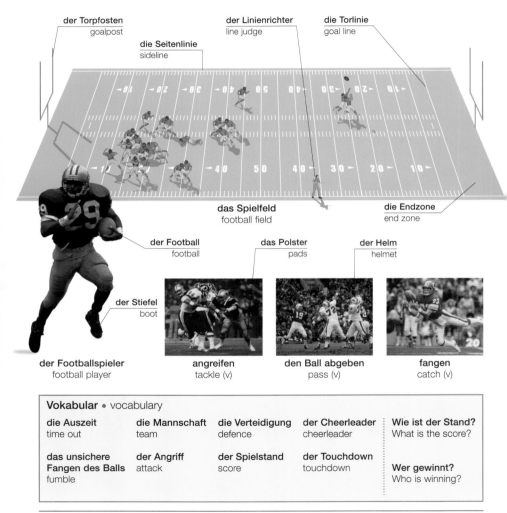

der Torpfosten
goalpost

der Linienrichter
line judge

die Torlinie
goal line

die Seitenlinie
sideline

das Spielfeld
football field

die Endzone
end zone

der Football
football

das Polster
pads

der Helm
helmet

der Stiefel
boot

der Footballspieler
football player

**angreifen**
tackle (v)

**den Ball abgeben**
pass (v)

**fangen**
catch (v)

**Vokabular • vocabulary**

| | | | | |
|---|---|---|---|---|
| **die Auszeit** time out | **die Mannschaft** team | **die Verteidigung** defence | **der Cheerleader** cheerleader | **Wie ist der Stand?** What is the score? |
| **das unsichere Fangen des Balls** fumble | **der Angriff** attack | **der Spielstand** score | **der Touchdown** touchdown | **Wer gewinnt?** Who is winning? |

# das Rugby • rugby

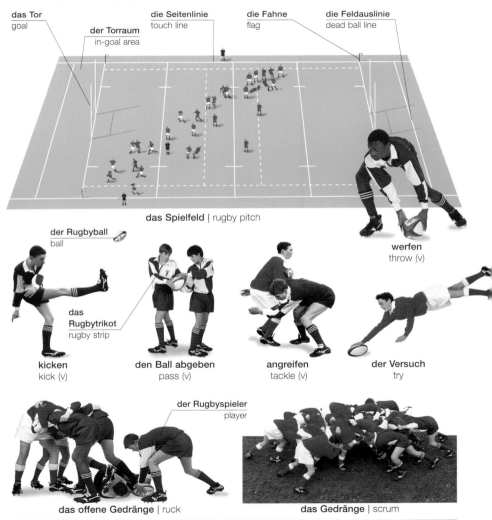

das Tor
goal

der Torraum
in-goal area

die Seitenlinie
touch line

die Fahne
flag

die Feldauslinie
dead ball line

**das Spielfeld** | rugby pitch

**werfen**
throw (v)

der Rugbyball
ball

das
Rugbytrikot
rugby strip

**kicken**
kick (v)

**den Ball abgeben**
pass (v)

**angreifen**
tackle (v)

**der Versuch**
try

der Rugbyspieler
player

**das offene Gedränge** | ruck

**das Gedränge** | scrum

# der Fußball • soccer

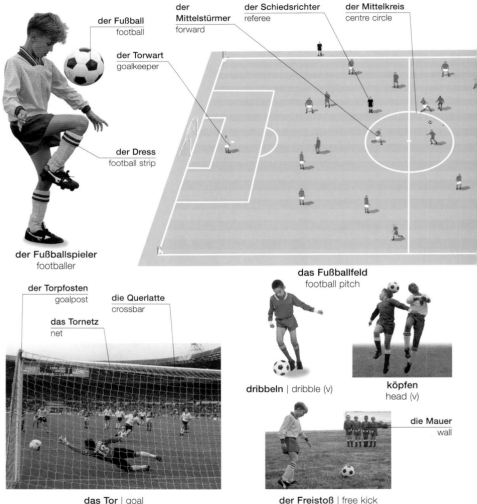

**der Fußball**
football

**der Torwart**
goalkeeper

**der**
**Mittelstürmer**
forward

**der Schiedsrichter**
referee

**der Mittelkreis**
centre circle

**der Dress**
football strip

**der Fußballspieler**
footballer

**das Fußballfeld**
football pitch

**der Torpfosten**
goalpost

**die Querlatte**
crossbar

**das Tornetz**
net

**das Tor** | goal

**dribbeln** | dribble (v)

**köpfen**
head (v)

**die Mauer**
wall

**der Freistoß** | free kick

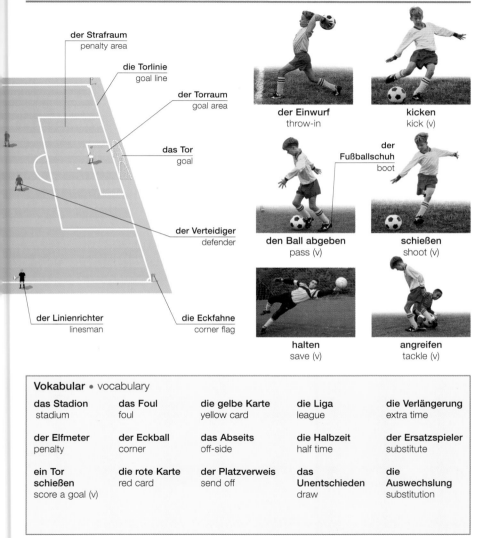

der Strafraum
penalty area

die Torlinie
goal line

der Torraum
goal area

das Tor
goal

der Verteidiger
defender

der Linienrichter
linesman

die Eckfahne
corner flag

der Einwurf
throw-in

kicken
kick (v)

der Fußballschuh
boot

den Ball abgeben
pass (v)

schießen
shoot (v)

halten
save (v)

angreifen
tackle (v)

**Vokabular • vocabulary**

| | | | | |
|---|---|---|---|---|
| das Stadion<br>stadium | das Foul<br>foul | die gelbe Karte<br>yellow card | die Liga<br>league | die Verlängerung<br>extra time |
| der Elfmeter<br>penalty | der Eckball<br>corner | das Abseits<br>off-side | die Halbzeit<br>half time | der Ersatzspieler<br>substitute |
| ein Tor schießen<br>score a goal (v) | die rote Karte<br>red card | der Platzverweis<br>send off | das Unentschieden<br>draw | die Auswechslung<br>substitution |

# das Hockey • hockey

## das Eishockey • ice hockey

die Verteidigungszone
defending zone

die neutrale
Zone
neutral zone

der Torwart
goalkeeper

die Torlinie
goal line

die Angriffszone
attack zone

das Tor
goal

der
Anspielkreis
face-off circle

der Mittelkreis
centre circle

der Handschuh
glove

das Polster
pad

die Eisfläche
ice hockey rink

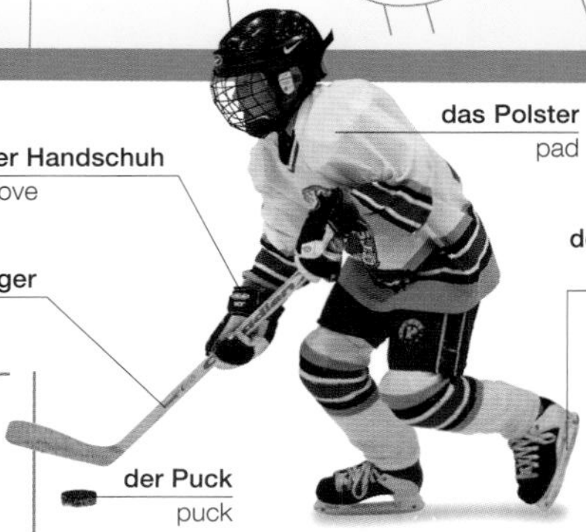

der Schläger
stick

der Schlitt
schuh
ice-skate

der Puck
puck

## das Hockey • field hockey

der Hockeyschläger
hockey stick

der
Hockeyball
ball

**der Eishockeyspieler** | ice hockey player

**Schlittschuh laufen**
skate (v)

**schlagen**
hit (v)

# das Kricket • cricket

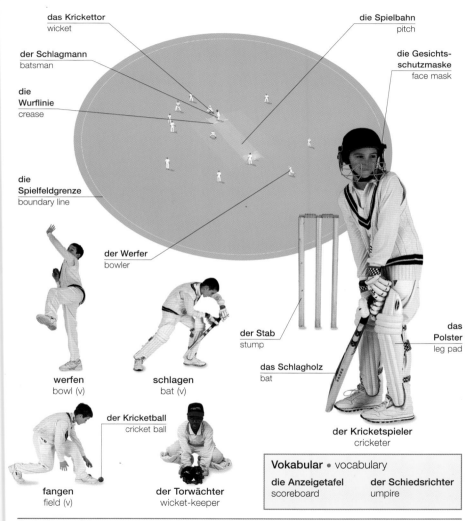

das Krickettor
wicket

die Spielbahn
pitch

der Schlagmann
batsman

die Gesichts-
schutzmaske
face mask

die
Wurflinie
crease

die
Spielfeldgrenze
boundary line

der Werfer
bowler

**werfen**
bowl (v)

**schlagen**
bat (v)

der Stab
stump

das
Polster
leg pad

das Schlagholz
bat

**fangen**
field (v)

der Kricketball
cricket ball

**der Torwächter**
wicket-keeper

**der Kricketspieler**
cricketer

**Vokabular** • vocabulary

| die Anzeigetafel | der Schiedsrichter |
|---|---|
| scoreboard | umpire |

# der Basketball • basketball

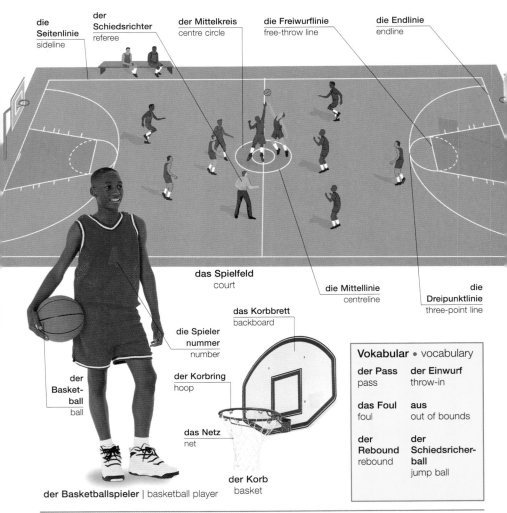

die **Seitenlinie**
sideline

der **Schiedsrichter**
referee

der **Mittelkreis**
centre circle

die **Freiwurflinie**
free-throw line

die **Endlinie**
endline

das **Spielfeld**
court

die **Mittellinie**
centreline

die **Dreipunktlinie**
three-point line

die **Spieler nummer**
number

das **Korbbrett**
backboard

der **Basket-ball**
ball

der **Korbring**
hoop

das **Netz**
net

der **Korb**
basket

**der Basketballspieler** | basketball player

| **Vokabular** • vocabulary | |
|---|---|
| der **Pass** pass | der **Einwurf** throw-in |
| das **Foul** foul | **aus** out of bounds |
| der **Rebound** rebound | der **Schiedsricher-ball** jump ball |

# die Aktionen • actions

**werfen**
throw (v)

**fangen**
catch (v)

**schießen**
shoot (v)

**springen**
jump (v)

**decken**
mark (v)

**blocken**
block (v)

**springen lassen**
bounce (v)

**einen Dunk spielen**
dunk (v)

# der Volleyball • volleyball

**blocken**
block (v)

**das Netz**
net

**baggern**
dig (v)

**der Schiedsrichter**
referee

**der Knieschützer**
knee support

**das Spielfeld** | court

# der Baseball • baseball

## das Spielfeld • field

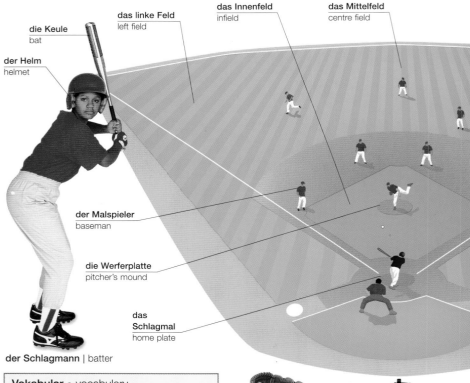

**das linke Feld**
left field

**das Innenfeld**
infield

**das Mittelfeld**
centre field

**die Keule**
bat

**der Helm**
helmet

**der Malspieler**
baseman

**die Werferplatte**
pitcher's mound

**das Schlagmal**
home plate

**der Schlagmann** | batter

---

**Vokabular** • vocabulary

| | | |
|---|---|---|
| **das Inning** inning | **aus** out | **der Schlagfehler** strike |
| **der Lauf** run | **in Sicherheit** safe | **der ungültige Schlag** foul ball |

**der Baseball**
ball

**der Handschuh**
mitt

**die Schutzmaske**
mask

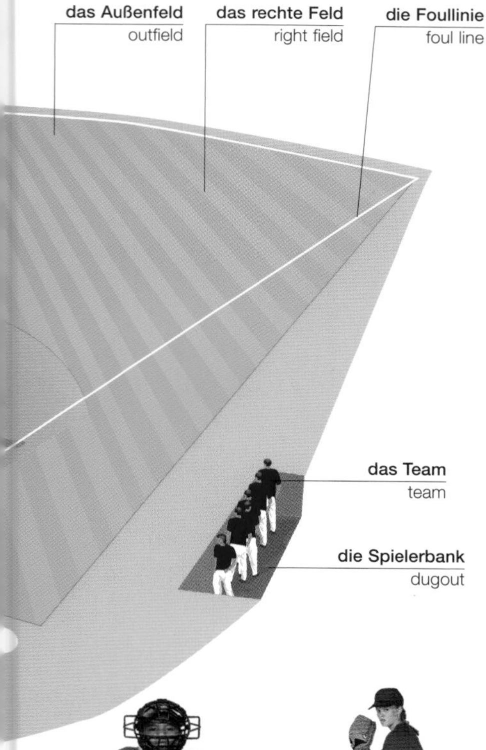

das Außenfeld
outfield

das rechte Feld
right field

die Foullinie
foul line

das Team
team

die Spielerbank
dugout

der Fänger
catcher

der Werfer
pitcher

## die Aktionen • actions

**werfen** | throw (v)

**fangen** | catch (v)

**rennen**
run (v)

**als Fänger spielen**
field (v)

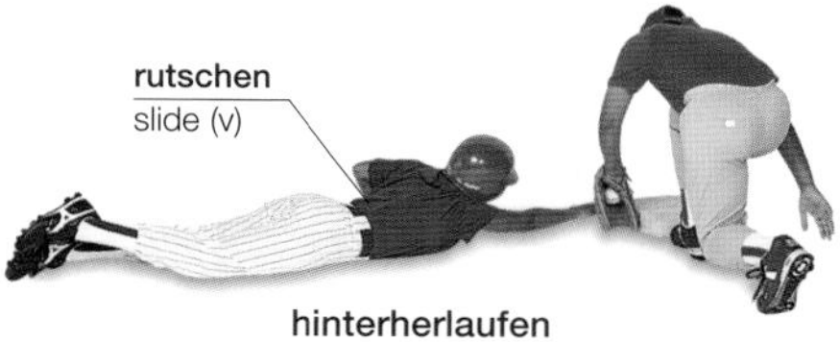

rutschen
slide (v)

**hinterherlaufen**
tag (v)

werfen
pitch (v)

schlagen
bat (v)

der
Schieds
richter
umpire

**spielen** | play (v)

# das Tennis • tennis

der Griff
handle

der Kopf
head

die Saite
string

der Schiedsrichter
umpire

die Grundlinie
baseline

der Tennis-
schläger
racquet

die Aufschlaglinie
service line

die Seitenlinie
sideline

der Tennisball
ball

das
Schweißband
wristband

**der Tennisplatz** | tennis court

| **Vokabular** • vocabulary | | | | | |
|---|---|---|---|---|---|
| **das Einzel**<br>singles | **der Satz**<br>set | **der Einstand**<br>deuce | **der Fehler**<br>fault | **der Slice**<br>slice | **der Spin**<br>spin |
| **das Doppel**<br>doubles | **das Match**<br>match | **der Vorteil**<br>advantage | **das Ass**<br>ace | **Netz!**<br>let! | **der Linienrichter**<br>linesman |
| **das Spiel**<br>game | **der Tiebreak**<br>tiebreak | **null**<br>love | **der Stoppball**<br>dropshot | **der**<br>**Ballwechsel**<br>rally | **die**<br>**Meisterschaft**<br>championship |

**das Netz**
net

**der Schmetterball**
smash

**der Balljunge**
ballboy

**aufschlagen**
serve (v)

**die Tennisschuhe**
tennis shoes

**der Tennisspieler**
player

## die Schläge • strokes

**der Aufschlag**
serve

**der Volley**
volley

**der Return**
return

**der Lob**
lob

**die Vorhand**
forehand

**die Rückhand**
backhand

## die Schlägerspiele • racquet games

**der Federball**
shuttlecock

**der Tischtennisschläger**
bat

**das Badminton**
badminton

**das Tischtennis**
table tennis

**das Squash**
squash

**das Racquetball**
racquetball

# das Golf • golf

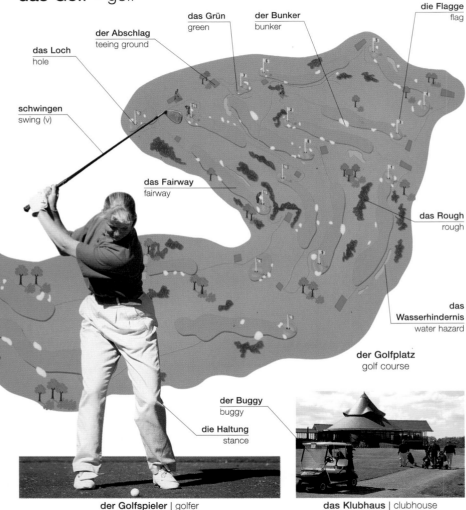

**das Loch**
hole

**der Abschlag**
teeing ground

**das Grün**
green

**der Bunker**
bunker

**die Flagge**
flag

**schwingen**
swing (v)

**das Fairway**
fairway

**das Rough**
rough

**das Wasserhindernis**
water hazard

**der Golfplatz**
golf course

**der Buggy**
buggy

**die Haltung**
stance

**der Golfspieler** | golfer

**das Klubhaus** | clubhouse

# die Ausrüstung • equipment

**der Golfball**
golf ball

**das Tee**
tee

**der Schirm**
umbrella

**die Golftasche**
golf bag

**die Spikes**
spikes

**der Handschuh**
glove

**der Caddie**
golf trolley

**der Golfschuh**
golf shoe

# die Golf-schläger • golf clubs

**das Holz**
wood

**der Putter**
putter

**das Eisen**
iron

**das Wedge**
wedge

# die Aktionen • actions

**vom Abschlag spielen**
tee-off (v)

**driven**
drive (v)

**einlochen**
putt (v)

**chippen**
chip (v)

---

**Vokabular** • vocabulary

| | | | | | |
|---|---|---|---|---|---|
| **das Par** par | **über Par** over par | **das Golfturnier** tournament | **der Caddie** caddy | **der Schlag** stroke | **die Spielbahn** line of play |
| **unter Par** under par | **das Hole-in-One** hole in one | **das Handicap** handicap | **die Zuschauer** spectators | **der Übungsschwung** practice swing | **der Durchschwung** backswing |

---

# die Leichtathletik • athletics

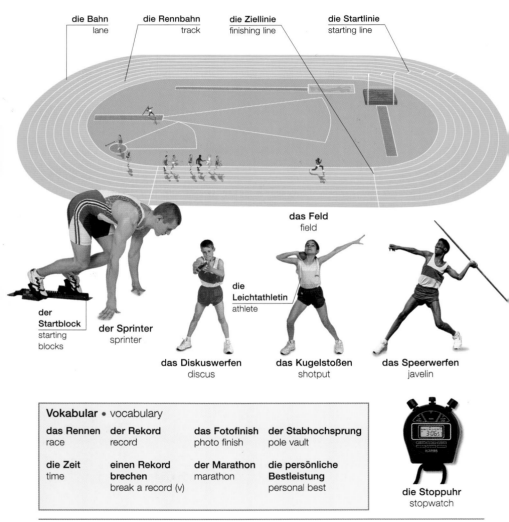

die Bahn
lane

die Rennbahn
track

die Ziellinie
finishing line

die Startlinie
starting line

das Feld
field

der Startblock
starting blocks

der Sprinter
sprinter

die Leichtathletin
athlete

das Diskuswerfen
discus

das Kugelstoßen
shotput

das Speerwerfen
javelin

**Vokabular** • vocabulary

| | | | |
|---|---|---|---|
| **das Rennen**<br>race | **der Rekord**<br>record | **das Fotofinish**<br>photo finish | **der Stabhochsprung**<br>pole vault |
| **die Zeit**<br>time | **einen Rekord brechen**<br>break a record (v) | **der Marathon**<br>marathon | **die persönliche Bestleistung**<br>personal best |

die Stoppuhr
stopwatch

der Stab
baton

die Latte
crossbar

**der Staffellauf**
relay race

**der Hochsprung**
high jump

**der Weitsprung**
long jump

**der Hürdenlauf**
hurdles

## das Turnen • gymnastics

das Sprungbrett
springboard

die Turnerin
gymnast

das Pferd
horse

**der Salto**
somersault

**der Schwebebalken**
beam

das Gymnastikband
ribbon

die Matte
mat

**der Sprung**
vault

**das Bodenturnen**
floor exercises

**die Bodenakrobatik**
tumble

**die rhythmische Gymnastik**
rhythmic gymnastics

**Vokabular** • vocabulary

| **das Reck** horizontal bar | **der Stufenbarren** asymmetric bars | **die Ringe** rings | **die Medaillen** medals | **das Silber** silver |
|---|---|---|---|---|
| **der Barren** parallel bars | **das Seitpferd** pommel horse | **das Siegerpodium** podium | **das Gold** gold | **die Bronze** bronze |

# der Kampfsport • combat sports

der Gegner
opponent

der Kopfschutz
guard

der Handschuh
glove

der Gürtel
belt

das Taekwondo
tae-kwon-do

das Karate
karate

das Judo
judo

die Maske
mask

der Säbel
sword

das Aikido
aikido

das Kendo
kendo

das Kung-Fu
kung fu

das Kickboxen
kickboxing

das Ringen
wrestling

das Boxen
boxing

# die Techniken • actions

**das Fallen**
fall

**der Griff**
hold

**der Wurf**
throw

**das Fesseln**
pin

**der Seitfußstoß**
kick

**der Stoß**
punch

**der Angriff**
strike

**der Sprung**
jump

**der Block**
block

**der Hieb**
chop

### Vokabular • vocabulary

| | | | | |
|---|---|---|---|---|
| **der Boxring**<br>boxing ring | **die Runde**<br>round | **die Faust**<br>fist | **der schwarze Gürtel**<br>black belt | **das Capoeira**<br>capoeira |
| **die Boxhandschuhe**<br>boxing gloves | **der Kampf**<br>bout | **der Knockout**<br>knock out | **die Selbstverteidigung**<br>self defence | **das Sumo**<br>sumo wrestling |
| **der Mundschutz**<br>mouth guard | **das Sparren**<br>sparring | **der Sandsack**<br>punch bag | **die Kampfsportarten**<br>martial arts | **das Tai Chi**<br>tai-chi |

# der Schwimmsport • swimming
## die Ausrüstung • equipment

**der Schwimmflügel**
armband

**die Schwimmbrille**
goggles

**die Nasenklemme**
nose clip

**das Schwimmfloß**
float

**der Badeanzug**
swimsuit

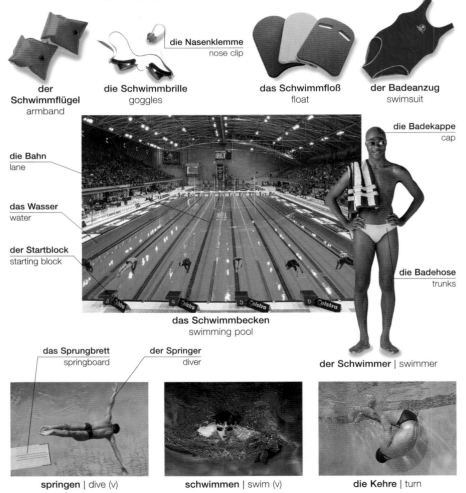

**die Badekappe**
cap

**die Bahn**
lane

**das Wasser**
water

**der Startblock**
starting block

**die Badehose**
trunks

**das Schwimmbecken**
swimming pool

**der Schwimmer** | swimmer

**das Sprungbrett**
springboard

**der Springer**
diver

**springen** | dive (v)

**schwimmen** | swim (v)

**die Kehre** | turn

# die Schwimmstile • styles

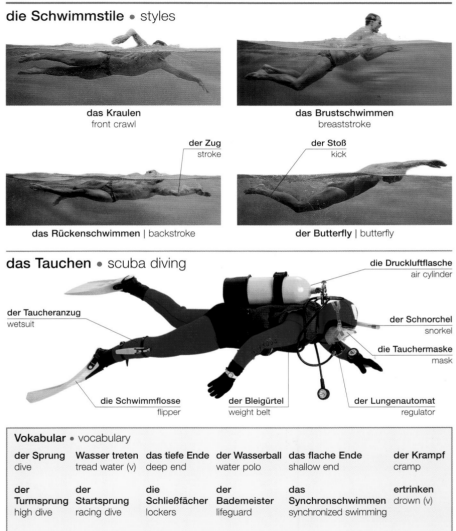

**das Kraulen**
front crawl

**das Brustschwimmen**
breaststroke

der Zug
stroke

der Stoß
kick

**das Rückenschwimmen** | backstroke

**der Butterfly** | butterfly

# das Tauchen • scuba diving

die Druckluftflasche
air cylinder

der Taucheranzug
wetsuit

der Schnorchel
snorkel

die Tauchermaske
mask

die Schwimmflosse
flipper

der Bleigürtel
weight belt

der Lungenautomat
regulator

## Vokabular • vocabulary

| der Sprung | Wasser treten | das tiefe Ende | der Wasserball | das flache Ende | der Krampf |
|---|---|---|---|---|---|
| dive | tread water (v) | deep end | water polo | shallow end | cramp |
| der Turmsprung | der Startsprung | die Schließfächer | der Bademeister | das Synchronschwimmen | ertrinken |
| high dive | racing dive | lockers | lifeguard | synchronized swimming | drown (v) |

# der Segelsport • sailing

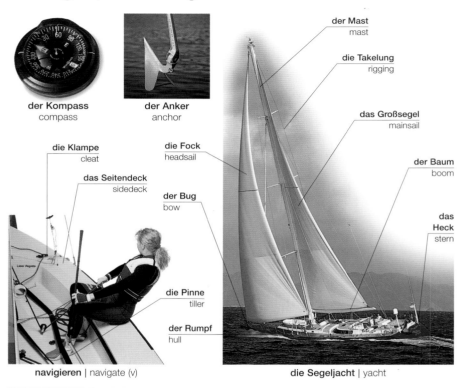

**der Kompass**
compass

**der Anker**
anchor

**der Mast**
mast

**die Takelung**
rigging

**das Großsegel**
mainsail

**die Klampe**
cleat

**die Fock**
headsail

**der Baum**
boom

**das Seitendeck**
sidedeck

**der Bug**
bow

**das Heck**
stern

**die Pinne**
tiller

**der Rumpf**
hull

**navigieren** | navigate (v)

**die Segeljacht** | yacht

# die Sicherheit • safety

**die Leuchtrakete**
flare

**der Rettungsring**
lifebuoy

**die Schwimmweste**
life jacket

**das Rettungsboot**
life raft

# der Wassersport • watersports

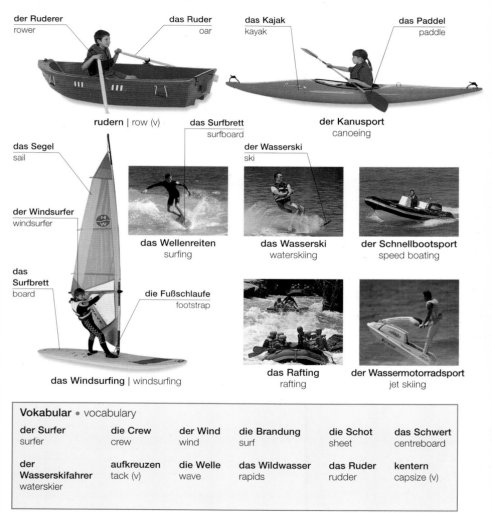

der Ruderer
rower

das Ruder
oar

das Kajak
kayak

das Paddel
paddle

**rudern** | row (v)

der Kanusport
canoeing

das Surfbrett
surfboard

das Segel
sail

der Wasserski
ski

der Windsurfer
windsurfer

das
Surfbrett
board

die Fußschlaufe
footstrap

**das Wellenreiten**
surfing

**das Wasserski**
waterskiing

**der Schnellbootsport**
speed boating

**das Windsurfing** | windsurfing

**das Rafting**
rafting

**der Wassermotorradsport**
jet skiing

---

**Vokabular** • vocabulary

| der Surfer<br>surfer | die Crew<br>crew | der Wind<br>wind | die Brandung<br>surf | die Schot<br>sheet | das Schwert<br>centreboard |
|---|---|---|---|---|---|
| der<br>Wasserskifahrer<br>waterskier | aufkreuzen<br>tack (v) | die Welle<br>wave | das Wildwasser<br>rapids | das Ruder<br>rudder | kentern<br>capsize (v) |

---

# der Reitsport • horse riding

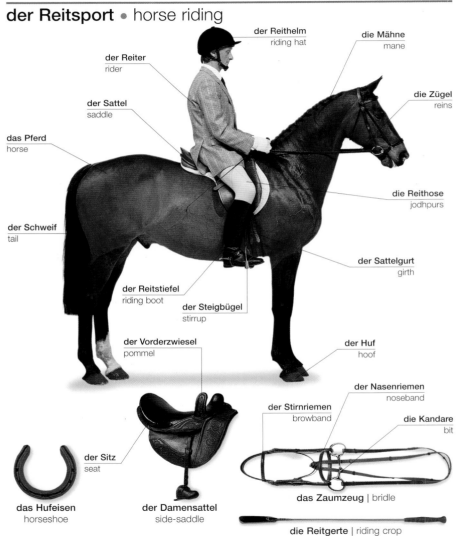

der Reithelm
riding hat

die Mähne
mane

der Reiter
rider

die Zügel
reins

der Sattel
saddle

das Pferd
horse

die Reithose
jodhpurs

der Schweif
tail

der Sattelgurt
girth

der Reitstiefel
riding boot

der Steigbügel
stirrup

der Huf
hoof

der Vorderzwiesel
pommel

der Nasenriemen
noseband

der Stirnriemen
browband

die Kandare
bit

der Sitz
seat

**das Zaumzeug** | bridle

**das Hufeisen**
horseshoe

**der Damensattel**
side-saddle

**die Reitgerte** | riding crop

# die Veranstaltungen • events

das Rennpferd
racehorse

das Hindernis
fence

**das Pferderennen**
horse race

**das Jagdrennen**
steeplechase

**das Trabrennen**
harness race

**das Rodeo**
rodeo

**das Springreiten**
showjumping

**das Zweispännerrennen**
carriage race

**das Trekking**
trekking

**das Dressurreiten**
dressage

**das Polo**
polo

## Vokabular • vocabulary

| | | | | | |
|---|---|---|---|---|---|
| **der Schritt**<br>walk | **der Kanter**<br>canter | **der Sprung**<br>jump | **das Halfter**<br>halter | **die Koppel**<br>paddock | **das Flachrennen**<br>flat race |
| **der Trab**<br>trot | **der Galopp**<br>gallop | **der Stallbursche**<br>groom | **der Pferdestall**<br>stable | **der Turnierplatz**<br>arena | **die Rennbahn**<br>racecourse |

# der Angelsport • fishing

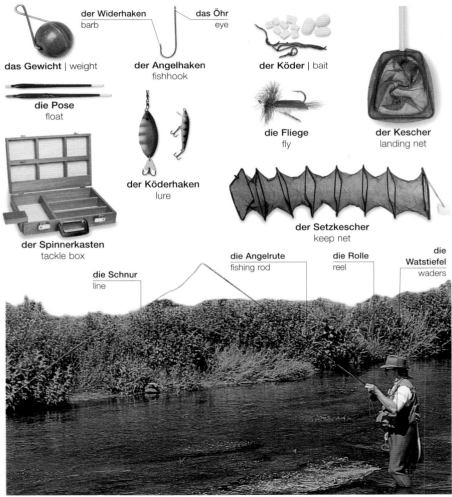

**der Widerhaken**
barb

**das Öhr**
eye

**das Gewicht** | weight

**der Angelhaken**
fishhook

**der Köder** | bait

**die Pose**
float

**die Fliege**
fly

**der Kescher**
landing net

**der Köderhaken**
lure

**der Spinnerkasten**
tackle box

**der Setzkescher**
keep net

**die Angelrute**
fishing rod

**die Rolle**
reel

**die Watstiefel**
waders

**die Schnur**
line

**der Angler** | angler

# die Fischfangarten • types of fishing

**das Süßwasserangeln**
freshwater fishing

**das Fliegenangeln**
fly fishing

**das Sportangeln**
sport fishing

**die Hochseefischerei**
deep sea fishing

**das Brandungsangeln**
surfcasting

# die Aktivitäten • activities

**auswerfen**
cast (v)

**fangen**
catch (v)

**einholen**
reel in (v)

**mit dem Netz fangen**
net (v)

**loslassen**
release (v)

---

**Vokabular** • vocabulary

| | | | | |
|---|---|---|---|---|
| **ködern**<br>bait (v) | **die Angelgeräte**<br>tackle | **die Regenhaut**<br>waterproofs | **der Angelschein**<br>fishing permit | **der Fischkorb**<br>creel |
| **anbeißen**<br>bite (v) | **die Rolle**<br>spool | **die Stake**<br>pole | **die Seefischerei**<br>marine fishing | **das Speerfischen**<br>spearfishing |

---

# **der Skisport**• skiing

**der Skihang**
ski slope

**der Sessellift**
chairlift

**der Kabinenlift**
cable car

**der Skianzug**
ski suit

**der Skistock**
ski pole

**der Handschuh**
glove

**die Skipiste**
ski run

**die Sicherheitssperre**
safety barrier

**der Skistiefel**
ski boot

**der Ski**
ski

**die Kante**
edge

**die Skiläuferin**
skier

**die Spitze**
tip

# die Disziplinen • events

**das Tor**
gate

**der Abfahrtslauf**
downhill skiing

**der Slalom**
slalom

**der Skisprung**
ski jump

**der Langlauf**
cross-country skiing

# der Wintersport • winter sports

**die Skibrille**
goggles

**der Schlittschuh**
skate

**das Eisklettern**
ice climbing

**das Eislaufen**
ice-skating

**der Eiskunstlauf**
figure skating

**das Snowboarding**
snowboarding

**der Bobsport**
bobsleigh

**das Rennrodeln**
luge

**das Schneemobil**
snowmobile

**das Schlittenfahren**
sledding

**Vokabular** • vocabulary

**die alpine Kombination**
alpine skiing

**der Riesenslalom**
giant slalom

**abseits der Piste**
off-piste

**das Curling**
curling

**das Hundeschlittenfahren**
dog sledding

**das Eisschnelllauf**
speed skating

**das Biathlon**
biathlon

**die Lawine**
avalanche

# die anderen Sportarten • other sports

**das Segelflugzeug**
glider

**der Drachen**
hang-glider

**das Segelfliegen**
gliding

**der Fallschirm**
parachute

**das Drachenfliegen**
hang-gliding

**das Seil**
rope

**das Klettern**
rock climbing

**das Fallschirmspringen**
parachuting

**das Gleitschirmfliegen**
paragliding

**das Fallschirmspringen**
skydiving

**das Abseilen**
abseiling

**das Bungeejumping**
bungee jumping

**das Rallyefahren**
rally driving

der
**Rennfahrer**
racing driver

**der Rennsport**
motor racing

**das Motocross**
motorcross

**das Motorradrennen**
motorbike racing

**das Skateboard**
skateboard

**der Rollschuh**
rollerskate

**der Lacrosseschläger**
stick

**das Florett**
foil

**die Maske**
mask

**das Skateboard-
fahren**
skateboarding

**das Rollschuhfahren**
roller skating

**das Lacrosse**
lacrosse

**das Fechten**
fencing

**der Kegel**
pin

**der Bogen**
bow

**die Zielscheibe**
target

**der Pfeil**
arrow

**der Köcher**
quiver

**das Bogenschießen**
archery

**das
Scheibenschießen**
target shooting

die
**Bowlingkugel**
bowling ball

**das Bowling**
bowling

**das Poolbillard**
pool

**das Snooker**
snooker

# die Fitness • fitness

**das Trainingsrad**
exercise bike

**das Fitnessgerät**
gym machine

**die Bank**
bench

**die Gewichte**
free weights

**die Stange**
bar

**das Fitnesscenter**
gym

**die Rudermaschine**
rowing machine

**das Laufband**
treadmill

**die Langlaufmaschine**
cross trainer

**die private Fitness-
trainerin**
personal trainer

**die Tretmaschine**
step machine

**das Schwimmbecken**
swimming pool

**die Sauna**
sauna

# die Übungen • exercises

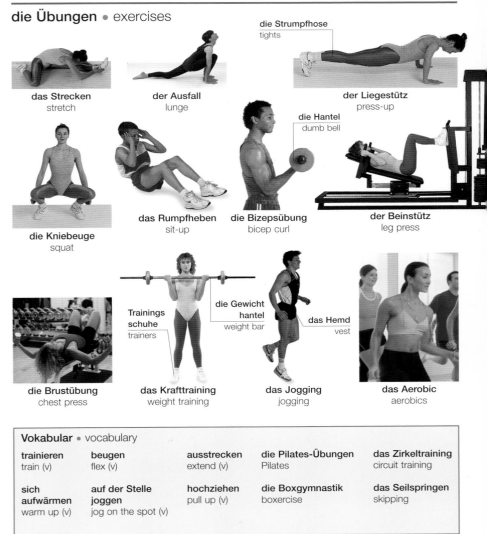

**das Strecken**
stretch

**der Ausfall**
lunge

**die Strumpfhose**
tights

**der Liegestütz**
press-up

**die Kniebeuge**
squat

**das Rumpfheben**
sit-up

**die Hantel**
dumb bell

**die Bizepsübung**
bicep curl

**der Beinstütz**
leg press

**die Brustübung**
chest press

**Trainings schuhe**
trainers

**das Krafttraining**
weight training

**die Gewicht hantel**
weight bar

**das Jogging**
jogging

**das Hemd**
vest

**das Aerobic**
aerobics

---

**Vokabular** • vocabulary

| | | | | |
|---|---|---|---|---|
| **trainieren**<br>train (v) | **beugen**<br>flex (v) | **ausstrecken**<br>extend (v) | **die Pilates-Übungen**<br>Pilates | **das Zirkeltraining**<br>circuit training |
| **sich aufwärmen**<br>warm up (v) | **auf der Stelle joggen**<br>jog on the spot (v) | **hochziehen**<br>pull up (v) | **die Boxgymnastik**<br>boxercise | **das Seilspringen**<br>skipping |

---

**die Freizeit**
leisure

# das Theater • theatre

der Vorhang
curtain

die Kulisse
wings

das Bühnenbild
set

das Publikum
audience

das Orchester
orchestra

die Bühne | stage

der Sitzplatz
seat

der zweite Rang
upper circle

die Reihe
row

die Loge
box

der erste Rang
circle

der Balkon
balcony

der Gang
aisle

das Parkett
stalls

die Bestuhlung | seating

## Vokabular • vocabulary

| | | |
|---|---|---|
| **das Theaterstück** play | **der Regisseur** director | **die Premiere** first night |
| **die Besetzung** cast | **der Prospekt** backdrop | **die Pause** interval |
| **der Schauspieler** actor | **das Rollenheft** script | **das Programm** programme |
| **die Schauspielerin** actress | **der Regisseur** producer | **der Orchestergraben** orchestra pit |

**das Konzert**
concert

**das Musical**
musical

das
**Theaterkostüm**
costume

**das Ballett**
ballet

### Vokabular • vocabulary

**der Platzanweiser**
usher

**die klassische Musik**
classical music

**die Noten**
musical score

**die Tonspur**
soundtrack

**applaudieren**
applaud (v)

**die Zugabe**
encore

**Ich möchte zwei Karten für die Aufführung heute Abend.**
I'd like two tickets for tonight's performance.

**Um wieviel Uhr beginnt die Aufführung?**
What time does it start?

**die Oper**
opera

## das Kino • cinema

das
**Popcorn**
popcorn

das
**Plakat**
poster

das **Foyer**
lobby

**die Kasse**
box office

**der Kinosaal**
cinema hall

**die Leinwand**
screen

### Vokabular • vocabulary

**die Komödie**
comedy

**der Thriller**
thriller

**der Horrorfilm**
horror film

**der Western**
western

**der Liebesfilm**
romance

**der Science-Fiction-Film**
science fiction film

**der Abenteuerfilm**
adventure

**der Zeichentrickfilm**
animated film

# das Orchester • orchestra

## die Saiteninstrumente • strings

die Harfe
harp

der Dirigent
conductor

der Kontrabass
double bass

die Geige
violin

das Podium
podium

die Bratsche
viola

das Cello
cello

die Noten
score

der
Violinschlüssel
treble clef

die Note
note

das
Liniensystem
staff

der
Bassschlüssel
bass clef

das Klavier | piano

die Notation | notation

---

**Vokabular • vocabulary**

| | | | | | |
|---|---|---|---|---|---|
| die Ouvertüre<br>overture | die Sonate<br>sonata | die Tonhöhe<br>pitch | das Kreuz<br>sharp | der Taktstrich<br>bar | die Tonleiter<br>scale |
| die<br>Symphonie<br>symphony | die Musikins<br>trumente<br>instruments | das Pausen-<br>zeichen<br>rest | das B<br>flat | das Auflösungs<br>zeichen<br>natural | der<br>Taktstock<br>baton |

---

# die Holzblasinstrumente • woodwind

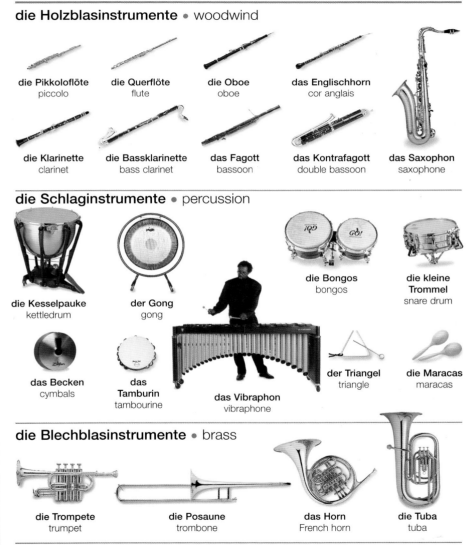

**die Pikkoloflöte**
piccolo

**die Querflöte**
flute

**die Oboe**
oboe

**das Englischhorn**
cor anglais

**die Klarinette**
clarinet

**die Bassklarinette**
bass clarinet

**das Fagott**
bassoon

**das Kontrafagott**
double bassoon

**das Saxophon**
saxophone

# die Schlaginstrumente • percussion

**die Bongos**
bongos

**die kleine Trommel**
snare drum

**die Kesselpauke**
kettledrum

**der Gong**
gong

**das Becken**
cymbals

**das Tamburin**
tambourine

**das Vibraphon**
vibraphone

**der Triangel**
triangle

**die Maracas**
maracas

# die Blechblasinstrumente • brass

**die Trompete**
trumpet

**die Posaune**
trombone

**das Horn**
French horn

**die Tuba**
tuba

# das Konzert • concert

der **Leadsänger** lead singer

das **Mikrophon** microphone

der **Schlag-zeuger** drummer

der **Gitarrist** guitarist

die **Fans** fans

der **Bassgitarrist** bass guitarist

der **Lautsprecher** speaker

**das Rockkonzert** | rock concert

# die Instrumente • instruments

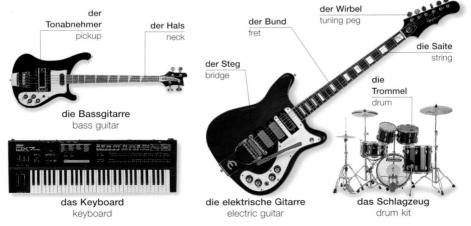

der **Tonabnehmer** pickup

der **Hals** neck

der **Bund** fret

der **Wirbel** tuning peg

die **Saite** string

der **Steg** bridge

die **Trommel** drum

**die Bassgitarre** bass guitar

**das Keyboard** keyboard

**die elektrische Gitarre** electric guitar

**das Schlagzeug** drum kit

# die Musikstile • musical styles

**der Jazz**
jazz

**der Blues**
blues

**die Punkmusik**
punk

**der Folk**
folk music

**der Pop**
pop

**die Tanzmusik**
dance

**der Rap**
rap

**das Heavymetal**
heavy metal

**die klassische Musik**
classical music

---

**Vokabular** • vocabulary

| **das Lied** | **der Text** | **die Melodie** | **der Beat** | **der Reggae** | **die Countrymusic** |
|---|---|---|---|---|---|
| song | lyrics | melody | beat | reggae | country |

---

# die Besichtigungstour • sightseeing

**der Tourist**
tourist

**die Route**
itinerary

**mit offenem Oberdeck**
open-top

**der Stadtrundfahrtbus** | tour bus

**die Touristenattraktion** | tourist attraction

**die Fremdenführerin**
tour guide

**die Führung**
guided tour

**die Figur**
statuette

**die Andenken**
souvenirs

---

**Vokabular** • vocabulary

| | | | | |
|---|---|---|---|---|
| **geöffnet**<br>open | **der Film**<br>film | **der Camcorder**<br>camcorder | **links**<br>left | **Wo ist...?**<br>Where is…? |
| **geschlossen**<br>closed | **die Batterien**<br>batteries | **die Kamera**<br>camera | **rechts**<br>right | **Ich habe mich verlaufen.**<br>I'm lost. |
| **das Eintrittsgeld**<br>entrance fee | **der Reiseführer**<br>guide book | **die Richtungs-angaben**<br>directions | **geradeaus**<br>straight on | **Können Sie mir sagen, wie ich nach... komme?**<br>Can you tell me the way to….? |

---

# die Sehenswürdigkeiten • attractions

**das Gemälde**
painting

**das Aussellungs stück**
exhibit

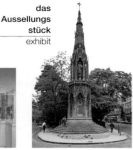

**die Ausstellung**
exhibition

**die berühmte Ruine**
famous ruin

**die Kunstgalerie**
art gallery

**das Monument**
monument

**das Museum**
museum

**das historische Gebäude**
historic building

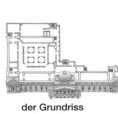

**das Kasino**
casino

**der Park**
gardens

**der Nationalpark**
national park

# die Information • information

**die Zeiten**
times

**der Grundriss**
floor plan

**der Stadtplan**
map

**der Fahrplan**
timetable

**die Touristeninformation**
tourist information

# die Aktivitäten im Freien • outdoor activities

**der Fußweg**
footpath

**die Sonnenuhr**
sundial

**das Café**
café

**der Park** | park

**das Gras**
grass

**die Bank**
bench

**die Gartenanlagen**
formal gardens

**die Berg-und-Talbahn**
roller coaster

**der Jahrmarkt**
fairground

**der Vergnügungspark**
theme park

**der Safaripark**
safari park

**der Zoo**
zoo

## die Aktivitäten • activites

**das Radfahren**
cycling

**das Jogging**
jogging

**das Skateboardfahren**
skateboarding

**das Inlinerfahren**
rollerblading

der Reitweg
bridle path

**das Vogelbeobachten**
bird watching

**das Reiten**
horse riding

**das Wandern**
hiking

der Pick-
nickkorb
hamper

**das Picknick**
picnic

## der Spielplatz • playground

**der Sandkasten**
sandpit

**das Planschbecken**
paddling pool

**die Schaukel**
swings

**die Wippe** | seesaw

**die Rutsche**
slide

**das Klettergerüst**
climbing frame

# der Strand • beach

das **Hotel**
hotel

der **Sonnenschirm**
beach umbrella

das **Strandhäuschen**
beach hut

der **Sand**
sand

die **Welle**
wave

das **Meer**
sea

die **Strandtasche**
beach bag

der **Bikini**
bikini

**sonnenbaden** | sunbathe (v)

der
**Rettungsschwimmer**
lifeguard

**der Rettungsturm**
lifeguard tower

**der Windschutz**
windbreak

**die Promenade**
promenade

**der Liegestuhl**
deck chair

**die Sonnenbrille**
sunglasses

**der Sonnenhut**
sunhat

**die Sonnenmilch**
suntan lotion

**der Sonnenblock**
sunblock

**der Wasserball**
beach ball

**der Schwimmreifen**
rubber ring

**das Strandtuch**
beach towel

**der Badeanzug**
swimsuit

**die Schaufel**
spade

**der Eimer**
bucket

**die Sandburg**
sandcastle

**die Muschel**
shell

# das Camping • camping

**die Toiletten**
toilets

**die Mülleimer**
waste disposal

**die Duschen**
shower block

**der Stromanschluss**
electric hook-up

**das Überdach**
flysheet

**der Hering**
tent peg

**der Campingplatz**
campsite

**die Zeltspannleine**
guy rope

**der Wohnwagen**
caravan

---

**Vokabular** • vocabulary

**zelten**
camp (v)

**Zeltplätze frei**
pitches available

**voll**
full

**die Campingplatzverwaltung**
site manager's office

**der Zeltplatz**
pitch

**die Zeltstange**
tent pole

**das Faltbett**
camp bed

**ein Zelt aufschlagen**
pitch a tent (v)

**die Picknickbank**
picnic bench

**die Hängematte**
hammock

**das Wohnmobil**
camper van

**der Anhänger**
trailer

**die Holzkohle**
charcoal

**der Feueranzünder**
firelighter

**ein Feuer machen**
light a fire (v)

**das Lagerfeuer**
campfire

---

das
**Gestänge**
frame

**der Zeltboden**
ground sheet

**die Thermos
flasche**
vacuum flask

**der Rucksack**
backpack

**die Wasserflasche**
water bottle

**das Zelt**
tent

**der Insektenspray**
insect repellent

**die Taschenlampe**
torch

**das Moskitonetz**
mosquito net

**die Thermowäsche**
thermals

**die Wanderschuhe**
walking boots

**die Regenhaut**
waterproofs

**der Schlafsack**
sleeping bag

**die Schlafmatte**
sleeping mat

**der Gasbrenner**
camping stove

**der Grill**
barbecue

**die Luftmatratze** | air mattress

# die Privatunterhaltung • home entertainment

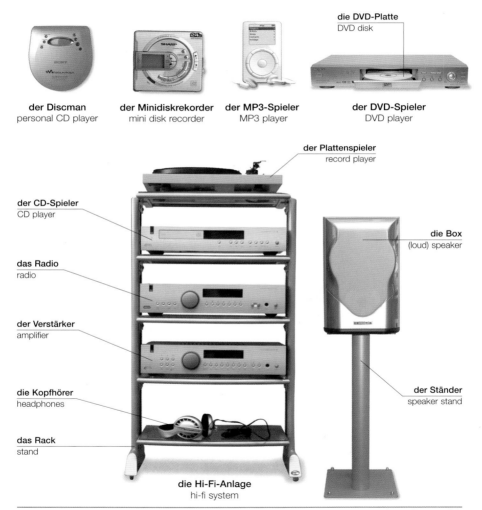

**der Discman**
personal CD player

**der Minidiskrekorder**
mini disk recorder

**der MP3-Spieler**
MP3 player

**die DVD-Platte**
DVD disk

**der DVD-Spieler**
DVD player

**der Plattenspieler**
record player

**der CD-Spieler**
CD player

**das Radio**
radio

**der Verstärker**
amplifier

**die Kopfhörer**
headphones

**das Rack**
stand

**die Hi-Fi-Anlage**
hi-fi system

**die Box**
(loud) speaker

**der Ständer**
speaker stand

die Videokassette
video tape

der Bildschirm
screen

die Okularmuschel
eyecup

der Videorekorder
video recorder

der Camcorder
camcorder

die Satellitenschüssel
satellite dish

der Breitbildfernseher
widescreen television

das Pult
console

der Vorlauf
fast forward

die Pause
pause

die Aufnahme
record

die Lautstärke
volume

der Steuerhebel
controller

der Rücklauf
rewind

das Abspielen
play

der Stop
stop

das Videospiel | video game

die Fernbedienung
remote control

**Vokabular** • vocabulary

| | | | | |
|---|---|---|---|---|
| die CD-Platte<br>compact disc | der Spielfilm<br>feature film | das Kabelfernsehen<br>cable television | digital<br>digital | stereo<br>stereo |
| die Kassette<br>cassette tape | die Werbung<br>advertisement | das Programm<br>programme | fernsehen<br>watch television (v) | das Radio<br>einstellen<br>tune the radio (v) |
| der<br>Kassettenrekorder<br>cassette player | der Pay-Kanal<br>pay per view<br>channel | den Kanal<br>wechseln<br>change channel (v) | den Fernseher<br>einschalten<br>turn the television<br>on (v) | den Fernseher<br>abschalten<br>turn the television<br>off (v) |

# die Fotografie • photography

**der Zähler**
frame counter

**der Blitz**
flash

**der Blendenregler**
aperture dial

**der Filter**
filter

**der Auslöser**
shutter release

**die Schutzkappe**
lens caps

**die Zeiteinstellscheibe**
shutter-speed dial

**die Linse**
lens

**die Spiegelreflexkamera** | SLR camera

**der Elektronenblitz**
flash gun

**der Belichtungsmesser**
lightmeter

**das Zoom**
zoom lens

**das Stativ**
tripod

# die Fotoapparattypen • types of camera

**die Digitalkamera**
digital camera

**die Kamera für APS-Film**
APS camera

**die Sofortbildkamera**
instant camera

**die Einwegkamera**
disposable camera

# fotografieren • photograph (v)

die
**Filmspule**
film spool

**der Film**
film

**einstellen**
focus (v)

**entwickeln**
develop (v)

**das Negativ**
negative

**quer**
landscape

**hoch**
portrait

**das Foto** | photograph

**das Fotoalbum**
photo album

**der Fotorahmen**
photo frame

# die Probleme • problems

**unterbelichtet**
underexposed

**überbelichtet**
overexposed

**unscharf**
out of focus

**die Rotfärbung der Augen**
red eye

**Vokabular** • vocabulary

| | |
|---|---|
| **der Bildsucher**<br>viewfinder | **der Abzug**<br>print |
| **die Kameratasche**<br>camera case | **matt**<br>mat |
| **die Belichtung**<br>exposure | **hochglanz**<br>gloss |
| **die Dunkelkammer**<br>darkroom | **die Vergrößerung**<br>enlargement |

**Könnten Sie diesen Film entwickeln lassen?**
I'd like this film processed

# die Spiele • games

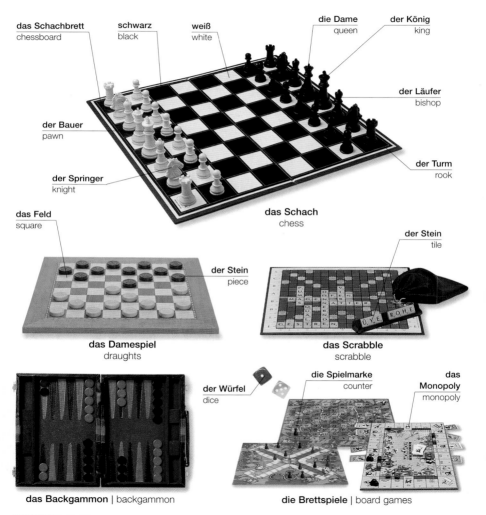

**das Schachbrett**
chessboard

**schwarz**
black

**weiß**
white

**die Dame**
queen

**der König**
king

**der Läufer**
bishop

**der Bauer**
pawn

**der Turm**
rook

**der Springer**
knight

**das Schach**
chess

**das Feld**
square

**der Stein**
piece

**der Stein**
tile

**das Damespiel**
draughts

**das Scrabble**
scrabble

**der Würfel**
dice

**die Spielmarke**
counter

**das Monopoly**
monopoly

**das Backgammon** | backgammon

**die Brettspiele** | board games

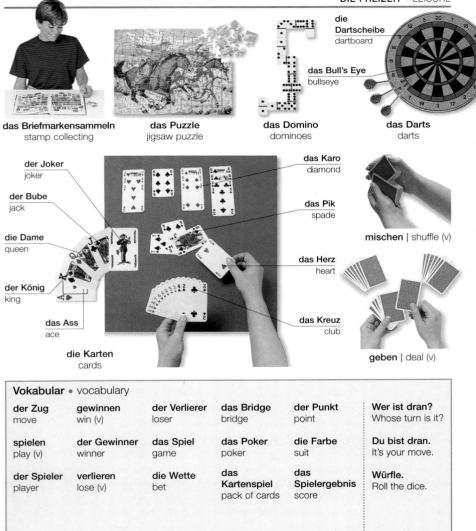

**das Briefmarkensammeln**
stamp collecting

**das Puzzle**
jigsaw puzzle

**das Domino**
dominoes

**die Dartscheibe**
dartboard

**das Bull's Eye**
bullseye

**das Darts**
darts

**der Joker**
joker

**der Bube**
jack

**die Dame**
queen

**der König**
king

**das Ass**
ace

**das Karo**
diamond

**das Pik**
spade

**das Herz**
heart

**das Kreuz**
club

**die Karten**
cards

**mischen** | shuffle (v)

**geben** | deal (v)

| **Vokabular** • vocabulary | | | | | |
|---|---|---|---|---|---|
| **der Zug**<br>move | **gewinnen**<br>win (v) | **der Verlierer**<br>loser | **das Bridge**<br>bridge | **der Punkt**<br>point | **Wer ist dran?**<br>Whose turn is it? |
| **spielen**<br>play (v) | **der Gewinner**<br>winner | **das Spiel**<br>game | **das Poker**<br>poker | **die Farbe**<br>suit | **Du bist dran.**<br>It's your move. |
| **der Spieler**<br>player | **verlieren**<br>lose (v) | **die Wette**<br>bet | **das Kartenspiel**<br>pack of cards | **das Spielergebnis**<br>score | **Würfle.**<br>Roll the dice. |

# das Kunsthandwerk 1 • arts and crafts 1

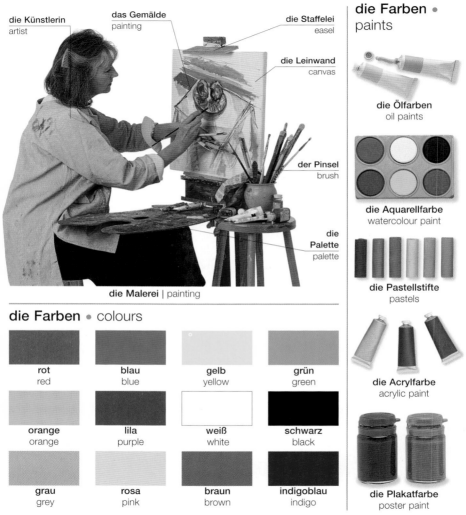

die Künstlerin
artist

das Gemälde
painting

die Staffelei
easel

die Leinwand
canvas

der Pinsel
brush

die Palette
palette

die Malerei | painting

## die Farben • paints

die Ölfarben
oil paints

die Aquarellfarbe
watercolour paint

die Pastellstifte
pastels

die Acrylfarbe
acrylic paint

die Plakatfarbe
poster paint

## die Farben • colours

| rot red | blau blue | gelb yellow | grün green |
| orange orange | lila purple | weiß white | schwarz black |
| grau grey | rosa pink | braun brown | indigoblau indigo |

# andere Kunstfertigkeiten • other crafts

**der Skizzenblock**
sketch pad

**die Skizze**
sketch

**die Druck farbe**
ink

**der Bleistift**
pencil

der Kohlestift
charcoal

**das Zeichnen** | drawing

**das Drucken**
printing

**das Gravieren**
engraving

**der Stein**
stone

**der Schlegel**
mallet

**der Meißel**
chisel

**das Holz**
wood

**das Modellierholz**
modelling tool

**die Drehscheibe**
potter's wheel

**die Bildhauerei**
sculpting

**die Holzarbeit**
woodworking

**der Ton**
clay

**der Klebstoff**
glue

**die Pappe**
cardboard

**die Collage** | collage

**die Töpferei**
pottery

**die Juwelierarbeit**
jewellery making

**das Papiermaché**
papier-mâché

**das Origami**
origami

**der Modellbau**
model making

# das Kunsthandwerk 2 • arts and crafts 2

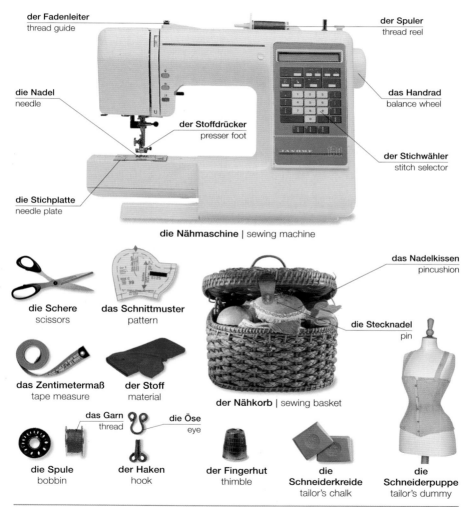

**der Fadenleiter**
thread guide

**der Spuler**
thread reel

**die Nadel**
needle

**das Handrad**
balance wheel

**der Stoffdrücker**
presser foot

**die Stichplatte**
needle plate

**der Stichwähler**
stitch selector

**die Nähmaschine** | sewing machine

**die Schere**
scissors

**das Schnittmuster**
pattern

**das Nadelkissen**
pincushion

**die Stecknadel**
pin

**das Zentimetermaß**
tape measure

**der Stoff**
material

**der Nähkorb** | sewing basket

**das Garn**
thread

**die Öse**
eye

**die Spule**
bobbin

**der Haken**
hook

**der Fingerhut**
thimble

**die Schneiderkreide**
tailor's chalk

**die Schneiderpuppe**
tailor's dummy

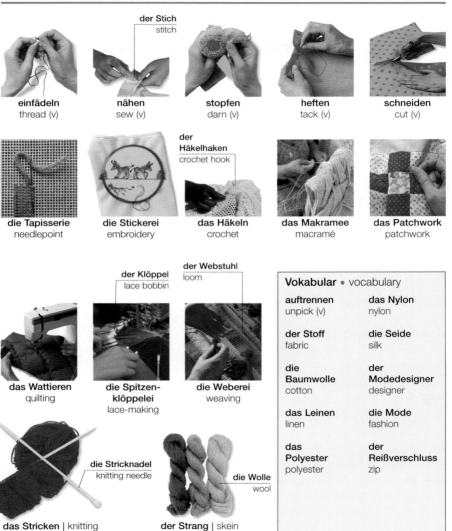

**der Stich**
stitch

**einfädeln**
thread (v)

**nähen**
sew (v)

**stopfen**
darn (v)

**heften**
tack (v)

**schneiden**
cut (v)

**die Tapisserie**
needlepoint

**die Stickerei**
embroidery

**der Häkelhaken**
crochet hook

**das Häkeln**
crochet

**das Makramee**
macramé

**das Patchwork**
patchwork

**der Klöppel**
lace bobbin

**der Webstuhl**
loom

**das Wattieren**
quilting

**die Spitzen-klöppelei**
lace-making

**die Weberei**
weaving

**die Stricknadel**
knitting needle

**die Wolle**
wool

**das Stricken** | knitting

**der Strang** | skein

**Vokabular** • vocabulary

| | |
|---|---|
| **auftrennen** unpick (v) | **das Nylon** nylon |
| **der Stoff** fabric | **die Seide** silk |
| **die Baumwolle** cotton | **der Modedesigner** designer |
| **das Leinen** linen | **die Mode** fashion |
| **das Polyester** polyester | **der Reißverschluss** zip |

**die Umwelt**
environment

# der Weltraum • space

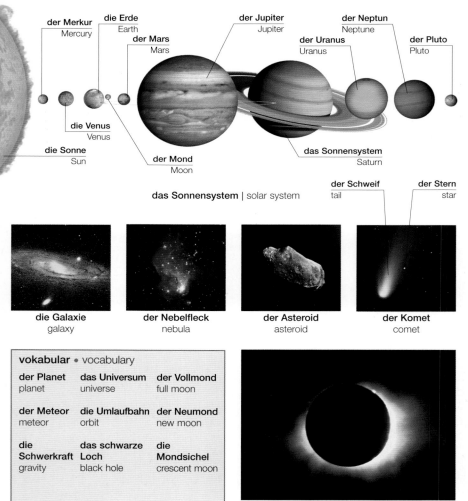

der Merkur
Mercury

die Erde
Earth

der Mars
Mars

der Jupiter
Jupiter

der Neptun
Neptune

der Uranus
Uranus

der Pluto
Pluto

die Venus
Venus

die Sonne
Sun

der Mond
Moon

das Sonnensystem
Saturn

**das Sonnensystem** | solar system

der Schweif
tail

der Stern
star

die Galaxie
galaxy

der Nebelfleck
nebula

der Asteroid
asteroid

der Komet
comet

**vokabular** • vocabulary

| | | |
|---|---|---|
| **der Planet**<br>planet | **das Universum**<br>universe | **der Vollmond**<br>full moon |
| **der Meteor**<br>meteor | **die Umlaufbahn**<br>orbit | **der Neumond**<br>new moon |
| **die Schwerkraft**<br>gravity | **das schwarze Loch**<br>black hole | **die Mondsichel**<br>crescent moon |

**die Finsternis** | eclipse

# die Raumforschung • space exploration

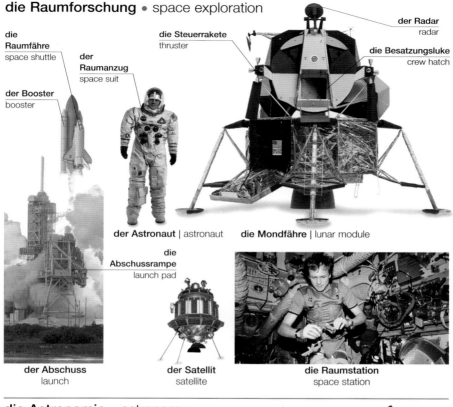

**der Radar**
radar

**die Steuerrakete**
thruster

**die Besatzungsluke**
crew hatch

**die Raumfähre**
space shuttle

**der Raumanzug**
space suit

**der Booster**
booster

**der Astronaut** | astronaut

**die Mondfähre** | lunar module

**die Abschussrampe**
launch pad

**der Abschuss**
launch

**der Satellit**
satellite

**die Raumstation**
space station

# die Astronomie • astronomy

**das Sternbild**
constellation

**das Fernglas**
binoculars

**das Teleskop**
telescope

**das Stativ**
tripod

# **die Erde** • Earth

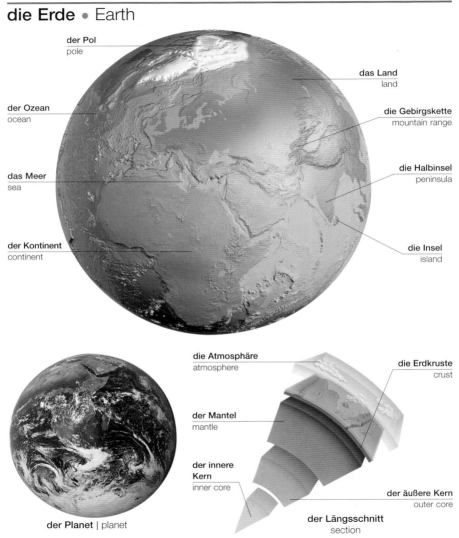

**der Pol**
pole

**das Land**
land

**der Ozean**
ocean

**die Gebirgskette**
mountain range

**das Meer**
sea

**die Halbinsel**
peninsula

**der Kontinent**
continent

**die Insel**
island

**die Atmosphäre**
atmosphere

**die Erdkruste**
crust

**der Mantel**
mantle

**der innere Kern**
inner core

**der äußere Kern**
outer core

**der Planet** | planet

**der Längsschnitt**
section

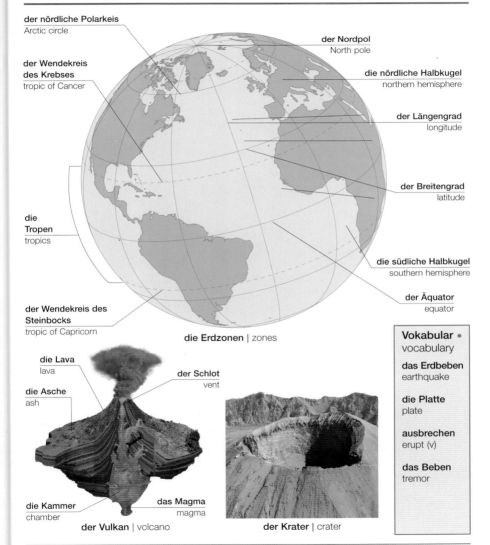

**der nördliche Polarkeis**
Arctic circle

**der Wendekreis des Krebses**
tropic of Cancer

**der Nordpol**
North pole

**die nördliche Halbkugel**
northern hemisphere

**der Längengrad**
longitude

**der Breitengrad**
latitude

**die Tropen**
tropics

**die südliche Halbkugel**
southern hemisphere

**der Äquator**
equator

**der Wendekreis des Steinbocks**
tropic of Capricorn

**die Erdzonen** | zones

**die Lava**
lava

**der Schlot**
vent

**die Asche**
ash

**die Kammer**
chamber

**das Magma**
magma

**der Vulkan** | volcano

**der Krater** | crater

**Vokabular** •
vocabulary

**das Erdbeben**
earthquake

**die Platte**
plate

**ausbrechen**
erupt (v)

**das Beben**
tremor

# die Landschaft • landscape

**der Berg**
mountain

**der Hang**
slope

**das Ufer**
bank

**der Fluss**
river

**die Strom schnellen**
rapids

**die Felsen**
rocks

**der Gletscher**
glacier

**das Tal** | valley

**der Hügel**
hill

**das Plateau**
plateau

**die Schlucht**
gorge

**die Höhle**
cave

**die Ebene** | plain

**die Wüste** | desert

**der Wald** | forest

**der Wald** | wood

**der Regenwald**
rainforest

**der Sumpf**
swamp

**die Wiese label**
meadow

**das Grasland**
grassland

**der Wasserfall**
waterfall

**der Bach**
stream

**der See**
lake

**der Geysir**
geyser

**die Küste**
coast

**die Klippe**
cliff

**das Korallenriff**
coral reef

**die Flussmündung**
estuary

# das Wetter • weather

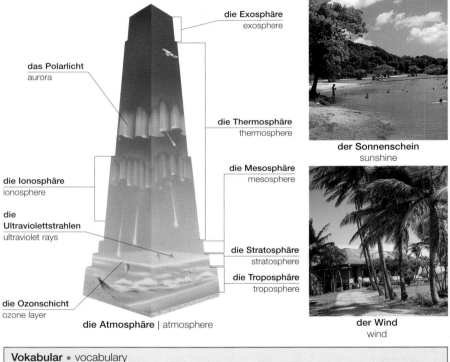

die Exosphäre
exosphere

das Polarlicht
aurora

die Thermosphäre
thermosphere

die Mesosphäre
mesosphere

die Ionosphäre
ionosphere

die Ultraviolettstrahlen
ultraviolet rays

die Stratosphäre
stratosphere

die Troposphäre
troposphere

die Ozonschicht
ozone layer

**die Atmosphäre** | atmosphere

**der Sonnenschein**
sunshine

**der Wind**
wind

---

## Vokabular • vocabulary

| | | | | | |
|---|---|---|---|---|---|
| **der Schneeregen** sleet | **der Schauer** shower | **heiß** hot | **trocken** dry | **windig** windy | **Mir ist heiß/kalt.** I'm hot/cold. |
| **der Hagel** hail | **sonnig** sunny | **kalt** cold | **nass** wet | **der Sturm** gale | **Es regnet.** It's raining. |
| **der Donner** thunder | **bewölkt** cloudy | **warm** warm | **feucht** humid | **die Temperatur** temperature | **Es sind … Grad.** It's … degrees. |

**die Wolke**
cloud

**der Regen**
rain

**der Blitz**
lightning

**das Gewitter**
storm

**der feine Nebel**
mist

**der dichte Nebel**
fog

**der Regenbogen**
rainbow

**der Schnee**
snow

**der Raureif**
frost

**der Eiszapfen**
icicle

**das Eis**
ice

**der Frost**
freeze

**der Hurrikan**
hurricane

**der Tornado**
tornado

**der Monsun**
monsoon

**die Überschwemmung**
flood

# das Gestein • rocks

## eruptiv • igneous

**der Granit**
granite

**der Obsidian**
obsidian

**der Basalt**
basalt

**der Bimsstein**
pumice

## sedimentär • sedimentary

**der Sandstein**
sandstone

**der Kalkstein**
limestone

**die Kreide**
chalk

**der Feuerstein**
flint

**das Konglomerat**
conglomerate

**die Kohle**
coal

## metamorph • metamorphic

**der Schiefer**
slate

**der Glimmers**
schist

**der Gneis**
gneiss

**der Marmor**
marble

## die Schmucksteine • gems

**der Rubin**
ruby

**der Aquamarin**
aquamarine

**der Amethyst**
amethyst

**der Diamant**
diamond

**der Jade**
jade

**der Jett**
jet

**der Smaragd**
emerald

**der Opal**
opal

**der Saphir**
sapphire

**der Mondstein**
moonstone

**der Turmalin**
tourmaline

**der Granat**
garnet

**der Topas**
topaz

# die Mineralien • minerals

**der Quarz**
quartz

**der Glimmer**
mica

**der Schwefel**
sulphur

**der Hämatit**
hematite

**der Kalzit**
calcite

**der Malachit**
malachite

**der Türkis**
turquoise

**der Onyx**
onyx

**der Achat**
agate

**der Graphit**
graphite

# die Metalle • metals

**das Gold**
gold

**das Silber**
silver

**das Platin**
platinum

**das Nickel**
nickel

**das Eisen**
iron

**das Kupfer**
copper

**das Zinn**
tin

**das Aluminium**
aluminium

**das Quecksilber**
mercury

**das Zink**
zinc

# die Tiere 1 • animals 1
## die Säugetiere • mammals

die Schnurrhaare
whiskers

der Schwanz
tail

das Kaninchen
rabbit

der Hamster
hamster

die Maus
mouse

die Ratte
rat

der Igel
hedgehog

das Eichhörnchen
squirrel

die Fledermaus
bat

der Waschbär
raccoon

der Fuchs
fox

der Wolf
wolf

der Welpe
puppy

das Kätzchen
kitten

das Junge
pup

der Hund
dog

die Katze
cat

der Otter
otter

die Robbe
seal

die Flosse
flipper

das Atemloch
blowhole

der Seelöwe
sea lion

das Walross
walrus

der Wal
whale

der Delphin
dolphin

das Geweih
antler

die Mähne
mane

der Huf
hoof

der Höcker
hump

**der Hirsch**
deer

**das Zebra**
zebra

**die Giraffe**
giraffe

**das Kamel**
camel

der Rüssel
trunk

der Stoßzahn
tusk

das Horn
horn

**das Nilpferd**
hippopotamus

**der Elefant**
elephant

**das Nashorn**
rhinoceros

**der Tiger**
tiger

die Mähne
mane

**der Löwe**
lion

**der Affe**
monkey

**der Gorilla**
gorilla

**der Koalabär**
koala

der Beutel
pouch

**der Pandabär**
panda

die Klaue
claw

**das Känguru**
kangaroo

**der Bär**
bear

**der Eisbär**
polar bear

# die Tiere 2 • animals 2
## die Vögel • birds

der Schwanz
tail

**der Kanarienvogel**
canary

**der Spatz**
sparrow

**der Kolibri**
hummingbird

**die Schwalbe**
swallow

**die Krähe**
crow

**die Taube**
pigeon

**der Specht**
woodpecker

**der Falke**
falcon

**die Eule**
owl

**die Möwe**
gull

**der Adler**
eagle

**der Pelikan**
pelican

**der Flamingo**
flamingo

**der Storch**
stork

**der Kranich**
crane

**der Pinguin**
penguin

**der Strauß**
ostrich

## die Reptilien • reptiles

**die Gans** | goose

**der Schwan**
swan

**der Pfau**
peacock

**der Fasan**
pheasant

**der Truthahn**
turkey

**der Kakadu**
cockatoo

**der Schnabel**
bill

**die Feder**
feather

**der Flügel**
wing

**die Kralle**
claw

**der Papagei**
parrot

**die Schuppen**
scales

**der Alligator**
alligator

**die Eidechse**
lizard

**der Leguan**
iguana

**der Panzer**
shell

**die Wasserschildkröte**
turtle

**die Schildkröte**
tortoise

**die Schlange**
snake

**die Schnauze**
snout

**das Krokodil**
crocodile

# die Tiere 3 • animals 3
## die Amphibien • amphibians

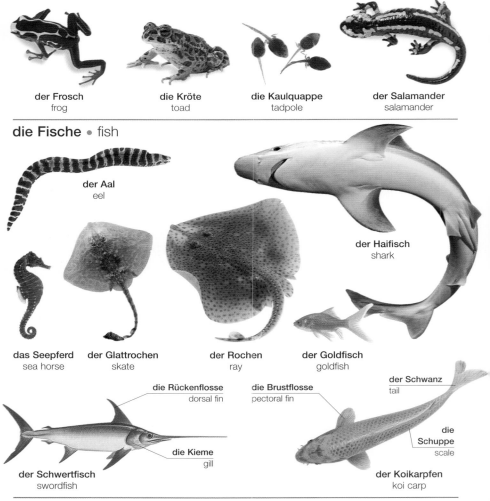

**der Frosch**
frog

**die Kröte**
toad

**die Kaulquappe**
tadpole

**der Salamander**
salamander

# die Fische • fish

**der Aal**
eel

**der Haifisch**
shark

**das Seepferd**
sea horse

**der Glattrochen**
skate

**der Rochen**
ray

**der Goldfisch**
goldfish

**die Rückenflosse**
dorsal fin

**die Brustflosse**
pectoral fin

**der Schwanz**
tail

**die Schuppe**
scale

**die Kieme**
gill

**der Schwertfisch**
swordfish

**der Koikarpfen**
koi carp

# die Wirbellosen • invertebrates

**die Ameise**
ant

**die Termite**
termite

**die Biene**
bee

**die Wespe**
wasp

**der Käfer**
beetle

**der Kakerlak**
cockroach

**die Motte**
moth

der Fühler
antenna

**der Schmetterling**
butterfly

**der Kokon**
cocoon

**die Raupe**
caterpillar

**die Grille**
cricket

**die Heuschrecke**
grasshopper

**die Gottesanbeterin**
praying mantis

der
**Stachel**
sting

**der Skorpion**
scorpion

**der
Tausendfüßer**
centipede

**die Libelle**
dragonfly

**die Fliege**
fly

**die Stechmücke**
mosquito

**der Marienkäfer**
ladybird

**die Spinne**
spider

**die
Wegschnecke**
slug

**die Schnecke**
snail

**der Wurm**
worm

**der Seestern**
starfish

**die Muschel**
mussel

**der Krebs**
crab

**der Hummer**
lobster

**der Krake**
octopus

**der Tintenfisch**
squid

**die Qualle**
jellyfish

# die Pflanzen • plants

## der Baum • tree

**das Blatt**
leaf

**der Zweig**
twig

**der Ast**
branch

**die Rinde**
bark

**die Wurzel**
root

**der Stamm**
trunk

**die Eiche**
oak

**die Weide**
willow

**die Pappel**
poplar

**der Eukalyptus**
eucalyptus

**die Lärche**
larch

**die Buche**
beech

**die Birke**
birch

**die Kiefer**
pine

**die Zeder**
cedar

**der Ahorn**
maple

**die Ulme**
elm

**die Linde**
lime

**die Stechpalme**
holly

**die Beere**
berry

**die Palme**
palm

# die blühende Pflanze • flowering plant

die Blüte
flower

das
Staubgefäß
stamen

das
Blütenblatt
petal

der Kelch
calyx

der Stängel
stalk

der Stiel
stem

die Knospe
bud

**der Hahnenfuß**
buttercup

**das
Gänseblümchen**
daisy

**die Distel**
thistle

**der Löwenzahn**
dandelion

**das Heidekraut**
heather

**der
Klatschmohn**
poppy

**der Fingerhut**
foxglove

**das Geißblatt**
honeysuckle

**die
Sonnenblume**
sunflower

**der Klee**
clover

**die
Sternhyazinthen**
bluebells

**die
Schlüsselblume**
primrose

**die Lupinen**
lupins

**die Nessel**
nettle

# die Stadt • town

die Straße
street

die Bordkante
kerb

die Straßenecke
street corner

der Laden
shop

die Kreuzung
intersection

die Einbahn
straße
one-way
system

der
Bürgersteig
pavement

das
Bürogebäude
office block

der
Wohnblock
apartment
block

die Gasse
alley

der Parkplatz
car park

das Straßenschild
street sign

der Poller
bollard

die Straßenlaterne
street light

# die Gebäude • buildings

**das Rathaus**
town hall

**die Bibliothek**
library

**das Kino**
cinema

**das Theater**
theatre

**die Universität**
university

**der Wolkenkratzer**
skyscraper

## die Wohngegend • areas

**das Industriegebiet**
industrial estate

**die Stadt**
city

**die Schule**
school

**der Vorort**
suburb

**das Dorf**
village

---

## Vokabular • vocabulary

| | | | | |
|---|---|---|---|---|
| **die Fußgängerzone**<br>pedestrian zone | **die Seitenstraße**<br>side street | **der Kanalschacht**<br>manhole | **der Rinnstein**<br>gutter | **die Kirche**<br>church |
| **die Allee**<br>avenue | **der Platz**<br>square | **die Bushaltestelle**<br>bus stop | **die Fabrik**<br>factory | **der Kanal**<br>drain |

---

# die Architektur • architecture

## die Gebäude und Strukturen • buildings and structures

**der Wolkenkratzer**
skyscraper

**die Burg**
castle

**die Kirche**
church

**die Moschee**
mosque

**der Tempel**
temple

**die Synagoge**
synagogue

**der Staudamm**
dam

**die Brücke**
bridge

die
**Kreuzblume**
finial

die
**Turmspitze**
spire

**der Mauerturm**
turret

**der Burggraben**
moat

**der Giebel**
gable

**die Kuppel**
dome

**der Turm**
tower

**das Gewölbe**
vault

**das Gesims**
cornice

**die Säule**
pillar

**die Kathedrale** | cathedral

# die Baustile • styles

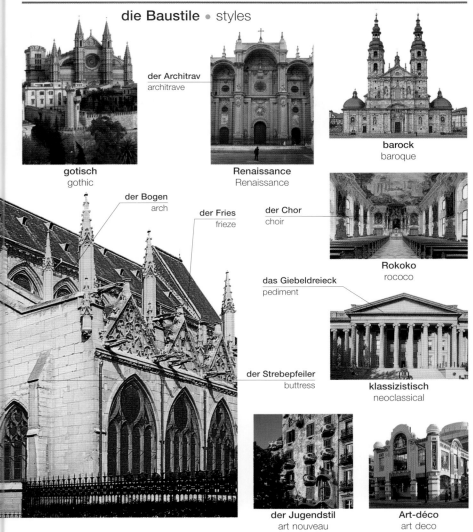

**gotisch**
gothic

**der Architrav**
architrave

**Renaissance**
Renaissance

**barock**
baroque

**der Bogen**
arch

**der Fries**
frieze

**der Chor**
choir

**Rokoko**
rococo

**das Giebeldreieck**
pediment

**der Strebepfeiler**
buttress

**klassizistisch**
neoclassical

**der Jugendstil**
art nouveau

**Art-déco**
art deco

**die Information**
reference

# die Uhrzeit • time

**der Minutenzeiger**
minute hand

**der Stundenzeiger**
hour hand

**die Uhr**
clock

## Vokabular • vocabulary

| | | |
|---|---|---|
| **die Stunde** hour | **jetzt** now | **zwanzig Minuten** twenty minutes |
| **die Minute** minute | **später** later | **vierzig Minuten** forty minutes |
| **die Sekunde** second | **eine halbe stunde** half an hour | **eine Viertelstunde** a quarter of an hour |

**Wie spät ist es?**
What time is it?

**Es ist drei Uhr.**
It's three o'clock.

**fünf nach eins**
five past one

**zehn nach eins**
ten past one

**Viertel nach eins**
quarter past one

**zwanzig nach eins**
twenty past one

**fünf vor halb zwei**
twenty five past one

**der Sekundenzeiger**
second hand

**ein Uhr dreißig**
one thirty

**fünf nach halb zwei**
twenty five to two

**zwanzig vor zwei**
twenty to two

**Viertel vor zwei**
quarter to two

**zehn vor zwei**
ten to two

**fünf vor zwei**
five to two

**zwei Uhr**
two o'clock

# die Nacht und der Tag • night and day

**die Mitternacht**
midnight

**der Sonnenaufgang**
sunrise

**die Morgendämmerung**
dawn

**der Morgen**
morning

**der Sonnenuntergang**
sunset

**der Mittag**
midday

**die Abenddämmerung**
dusk

**der Abend**
evening

**der Nachmittag**
afternoon

## Vokabular • vocabulary

| | | | |
|---|---|---|---|
| **früh**<br>early | **Du bist früh.**<br>You're early. | **Sei bitte pünktlich.**<br>Please be on time. | **Wann ist es zu Ende?**<br>What time does it finish? |
| **pünktlich**<br>on time | **Du hast dich verspätet.**<br>You're late. | **Bis später.**<br>I'll see you later. | **Wie lange dauert es?**<br>How long will it last? |
| **spät**<br>late | **Ich werde bald dort sein.**<br>I'll be there soon. | **Wann fängt es an?**<br>What time does it start? | **Es ist schon spät.**<br>It's getting late. |

# der Kalender • calendar

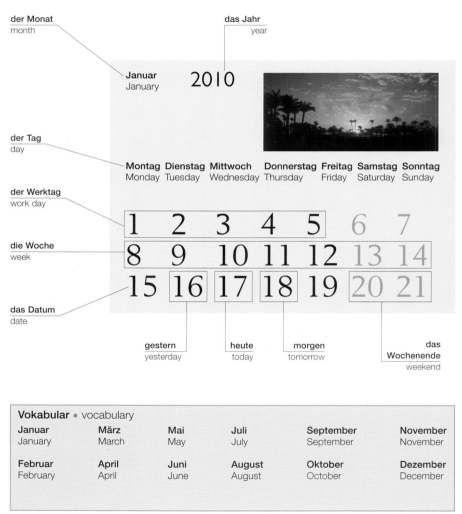

**der Monat**
month

**das Jahr**
year

**Januar**
January

**2010**

**der Tag**
day

| Montag | Dienstag | Mittwoch | Donnerstag | Freitag | Samstag | Sonntag |
|--------|----------|----------|------------|---------|---------|---------|
| Monday | Tuesday | Wednesday | Thursday | Friday | Saturday | Sunday |

**der Werktag**
work day

| 1 | 2 | 3 | 4 | 5 | 6 | 7 |

**die Woche**
week

| 8 | 9 | 10 | 11 | 12 | 13 | 14 |

| 15 | 16 | 17 | 18 | 19 | 20 | 21 |

**das Datum**
date

**gestern**
yesterday

**heute**
today

**morgen**
tomorrow

**das Wochenende**
weekend

---

**Vokabular** • vocabulary

| **Januar** January | **März** March | **Mai** May | **Juli** July | **September** September | **November** November |
|---|---|---|---|---|---|
| **Februar** February | **April** April | **Juni** June | **August** August | **Oktober** October | **Dezember** December |

---

306     **deutsch** • english

# die Jahre • years

1900    **neunzehnhundert** • nineteen hundred

1901    **neunzehnhunderteins** • nineteen hundred and one

1910    **neunzehnhundertzehn** • nineteen ten

2000    **zweitausend** • two thousand

2001    **zweitausendeins** • two thousand and one

## die Jahreszeiten • seasons

**der Frühling**
spring

**der Sommer**
summer

**der Herbst**
autumn

**der Winter**
winter

### Vokabular • vocabulary

**das Jahrhundert**
century

**das Jahrzehnt**
decade

**das Jahrtausend**
millennium

**vierzehn Tage**
fortnight

**diese Woche**
this week

**letzte Woche**
last week

**nächste Woche**
next week

**vorgestern**
the day before yesterday

**übermorgen**
the day after tomorrow

**wöchentlich**
weekly

**monatlich**
monthly

**jährlich**
annual

**Welches Datum haben wir heute?**
What's the date today?

**Heute ist der siebte Februar zweitausendzwei.**
It's February seventh, two thousand and two.

# die Zahlen • numbers

| | | | |
|---|---|---|---|
| 0 | **null** • zero | 20 | **zwanzig** • twenty |
| 1 | **eins** • one | 21 | **einundzwanzig** • twenty-one |
| 2 | **zwei** • two | 22 | **zweiundzwanzig** • twenty-two |
| 3 | **drei** • three | 30 | **dreißig** • thirty |
| 4 | **vier** • four | 40 | **vierzig** • forty |
| 5 | **fünf** • five | 50 | **fünfzig** • fifty |
| 6 | **sechs** • six | 60 | **sechzig** • sixty |
| 7 | **sieben** • seven | 70 | **siebzig** • seventy |
| 8 | **acht** • eight | 80 | **achtzig** • eighty |
| 9 | **neun** • nine | 90 | **neunzig** • ninety |
| 10 | **zehn** • ten | 100 | **hundert** • one hundred |
| 11 | **elf** • eleven | 110 | **hundertzehn** • one hundred and ten |
| 12 | **zwölf** • twelve | 200 | **zweihundert** • two hundred |
| 13 | **dreizehn** • thirteen | 300 | **dreihundert** • three hundred |
| 14 | **vierzehn** • fourteen | 400 | **vierhundert** • four hundred |
| 15 | **fünfzehn** • fifteen | 500 | **fünfhundert** • five hundred |
| 16 | **sechzehn** • sixteen | 600 | **sechshundert** • six hundred |
| 17 | **siebzehn** • seventeen | 700 | **siebenhundert** • seven hundred |
| 18 | **achtzehn** • eighteen | 800 | **achthundert** • eight hundred |
| 19 | **neunzehn** • nineteen | 900 | **neunhundert** • nine hundred |

| | | |
|---|---|---|
| 1,000 | **tausend** • one thousand | |
| 10,000 | **zehntausend** • ten thousand | |
| 20,000 | **zwanzigtausend** • twenty thousand | |
| 50,000 | **fünfzigtausend** • fifty thousand | |
| 55,500 | **fünfundfünfzigtausend-fünfhundert** • fifty-five thousand five hundred | |
| 100,000 | **hunderttausend** • one hundred thousand | |
| 1,000,000 | **eine Million** • one million | |
| 1,000,000,000 | **eine Milliarde** • one billion | |

**erster** / first    **zweiter** / second    **dritter** / third

**vierter** • fourth

**fünfter** • fifth

**sechster** • sixth

**siebter** • seventh

**achter** • eighth

**neunter** • ninth

**zehnter** • tenth

**elfter** • eleventh

**zwölfter** • twelfth

**dreizehnter** • thirteenth

**vierzehnter** • fourteenth

**fünfzehnter** • fifteenth

**sechzehnter**
• sixteenth

**siebzehnter**
• seventeenth

**achtzehnter**
• eighteenth

**neunzehnter**
• nineteenth

**zwanzigster**
• twentieth

**einundzwanzigster**
• twenty-first

**zweiundzwanzigster**
• twenty-second

**dreiundzwanzigster**
• twenty-third

**dreißigster**
• thirtieth

**vierzigster**
• fortieth

**fünfzigster**
• fiftieth

**sechzigster**
• sixtieth

**siebzigster**
• seventieth

**achtzigster**
• eightieth

**neunzigster**
• ninetieth

**hundertster**
• hundredth

# die Maße und Gewichte • weights and measures

## die Fläche • area

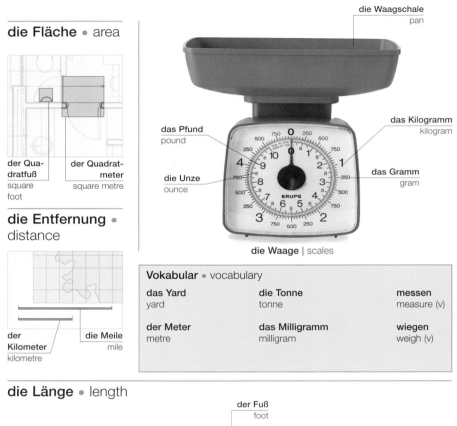

der Qua-
dratfuß
square
foot

der Quadrat-
meter
square metre

## die Entfernung •
distance

der
Kilometer
kilometre

die Meile
mile

die Waagschale
pan

das Pfund
pound

das Kilogramm
kilogram

die Unze
ounce

das Gramm
gram

KRUPS

die Waage | scales

### Vokabular • vocabulary

| das Yard | die Tonne | messen |
|---|---|---|
| yard | tonne | measure (v) |
| der Meter | das Milligramm | wiegen |
| metre | milligram | weigh (v) |

## die Länge • length

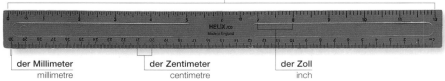

der Fuß
foot

HELIX JCB
Made in England

der Millimeter
millimetre

der Zentimeter
centimetre

der Zoll
inch

# das Fassungsvermögen • capacity

der halbe Liter
half-litre

das Pint
pint

das Volumen
volume

**Vokabular •**
vocabulary

**die Gallone**
gallon

**das Quart**
quart

**der Liter**
litre

der Milliliter
millilitre

**der Messbecher**
measuring jug

**das Flüssigkeitsmaß**
liquid measure

# der Behälter • container

**die Tüte**
carton

**das Päckchen**
packet

**die Flasche**
bottle

**der Beutel**
bag

**die Dose** | tub

**das Glas** | jar

die Dose
can

**die Dose** | tin

**die Spritze**
liquid dispenser

das Stück
bar

**die Tube**
tube

**die Rolle**
roll

**das Päckchen**
pack

**die Sprühdose**
spray can

# die Weltkarte • world map

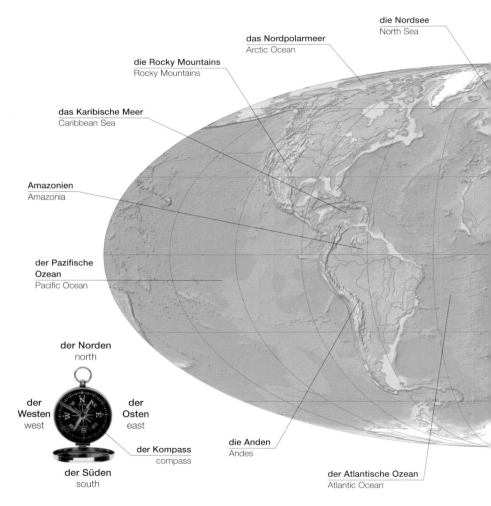

die Nordsee
North Sea

das Nordpolarmeer
Arctic Ocean

die Rocky Mountains
Rocky Mountains

das Karibische Meer
Caribbean Sea

Amazonien
Amazonia

der Pazifische
Ozean
Pacific Ocean

der Norden
north

der
Westen
west

der
Osten
east

der Kompass
compass

die Anden
Andes

der Süden
south

der Atlantische Ozean
Atlantic Ocean

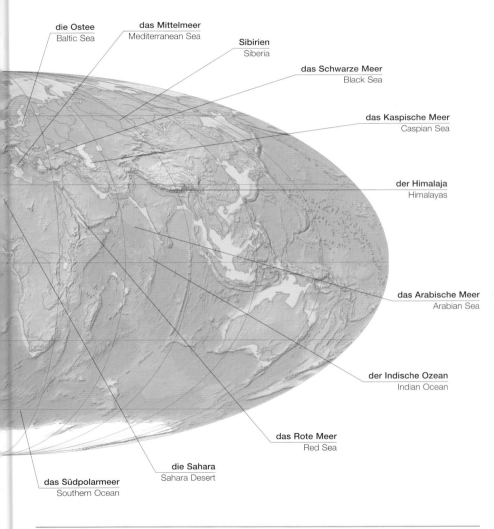

die Ostee
Baltic Sea

das Mittelmeer
Mediterranean Sea

Sibirien
Siberia

das Schwarze Meer
Black Sea

das Kaspische Meer
Caspian Sea

der Himalaja
Himalayas

das Arabische Meer
Arabian Sea

der Indische Ozean
Indian Ocean

das Rote Meer
Red Sea

die Sahara
Sahara Desert

das Südpolarmeer
Southern Ocean

# Nord- und Mittelamerika • North and Central America

**Hawaii**
Hawaii

1 **Alaska** • Alaska
2 **Kanada** • Canada
3 **Grönland** • Greenland
4 **die Vereinigten Staten**
  • United States of America
5 **Mexiko** • Mexico
6 **Guatemala** • Guatemala
7 **Belize** • Belize
8 **El Salvador** • El Salvador
9 **Honduras** • Honduras
10 **Nicaragua** • Nicaragua
11 **Costa Rica** • Costa Rica
12 **Panama** • Panama
13 **Kuba** • Cuba
14 **die Bahamas** • Bahamas
15 **Jamaika** • Jamaica
16 **Haiti** • Haiti
17 **die Dominikanische Republik**
  • Dominican Republic
18 **Puerto Rico** • Puerto Rico
19 **Barbados** • Barbados
20 **Trinidad und Tobago** • Trinidad and Tobago
21 **Saint Kitts und Nevis** • St. Kitts and Nevis

22 **Antigua und Barbuda** • Antigua and Barbuda
23 **Dominica** • Dominica
24 **Saint Lucia** • St Lucia
25 **Saint Vinzent und die Grenadinen**
  • St Vincent and The Grenadines
26 **Grenada** • Grenada

# Südamerika • South America

1 **Venezuela** • Venezuela

2 **Kolumbien** • Colombia

3 **Ecuador** • Ecuador

4 **Peru** • Peru

5 **die Galapagosinseln**
 • Galapagos Islands

6 **Guyana** • Guyana

7 **Suriname** • Suriname

8 **Französisch-Guayana**
 • French Guiana

9 **Brasilien** • Brazil

10 **Bolivien** • Bolivia

11 **Chile** • Chile

12 **Argentinien** • Argentina

13 **Paraguay** • Paraguay

14 **Uruguay** • Uruguay

15 **die Falklandinseln**
 • Falkland Islands

| **Vokabular** • vocabulary | | |
|---|---|---|
| **der Staat** state | **die Kolonie** colony | **die Zone** zone |
| **das Land** country | **die Provinz** province | **die Region** region |
| **die Nation** nation | **das Territorium** territory | **der Bezirk** district |
| **der Kontinent** continent | **das Fürstentum** principality | **die Hauptstadt** capital |

# Europa • Europe

1 **Irland** • Ireland
2 **das Vereinigte Königreich**
   • United Kingdom
3 **Portugal** • Portugal
4 **Spanien** • Spain
5 **die Balearen**
   • Balearic Islands
6 **Andorra** • Andorra
7 **Frankreich** • France
8 **Belgien** • Belgium
9 **die Niederlande**
   • Netherlands
10 **Luxemburg** • Luxembourg
11 **Deutschland** • Germany
12 **Dänemark** • Denmark
13 **Norwegen** • Norway
14 **Schweden** • Sweden
15 **Finnland** • Finland
16 **Estland** • Estonia
17 **Lettland** • Latvia
18 **Litauen** • Lithuania
19 **Kaliningrad**
   • Kaliningrad
20 **Polen** • Poland
21 **die Tschechische**
   **Republik**
   • Czech Republic
22 **Österreich** • Austria
23 **Liechtenstein**
   • Liechtenstein
24 **die Schweiz**
   • Switzerland
25 **Italien** • Italy
26 **Monaco**
   • Monaco
27 **Korsika** • Corsica
28 **Sardinien** • Sardinia

29 **San Marino** • San Marino
30 **die Vatikanstadt**
   • Vatican City
31 **Sizilien** • Sicily
32 **Malta** • Malta
33 **Slowenien** • Slovenia
34 **Kroatien** • Croatia
35 **Ungarn** • Hungary
36 **die Slowakei** • Slovakia
37 **die Ukraine** • Ukraine
38 **Weißrussland** • Belarus

39 **Moldawien** • Moldova
40 **Rumänien** • Romania
41 **Serbien** • Serbia
42 **Bosnien und Herzegowina**
   • Bosnia and Herzogovina
43 **Albanien** • Albania
44 **Mazedonien** • Macedonia
45 **Bulgarien** • Bulgaria
46 **Griechenland** • Greece
47 **Kosovo** • Kosovo (disputed)
48 **Montenegro** • Montenegro

# Afrika • Africa

1 **Marokko** • Morocco
2 **Westsahara** • Western Sahara
3 **Mauretanien** • Mauritania
4 **Senegal** • Senegal
5 **Gambia** • Gambia
6 **Guinea-Bissau** • Guinea-Bissau
7 **Guinea** • Guinea
8 **Sierra Leone** • Sierra Leone
9 **Liberia** • Liberia
10 **Elfenbeinküste** • Ivory Coast
11 **Burkina Faso** • Burkina Faso
12 **Mali** • Mali
13 **Algerien** • Algeria
14 **Tunesien** • Tunisia
15 **Libyen** • Libya
16 **Niger** • Niger
17 **Ghana** • Ghana
18 **Togo** • Togo
19 **Benin** • Benin
20 **Nigeria** • Nigeria

21 **São Tomé und Príncipe** • São Tomé and Principe
22 **Äquatorialguinea** • Equatorial Guinea
23 **Kamerun** • Cameroon
24 **Tschad** • Chad
25 **Ägypten** • Egypt
26 **der Sudan** • Sudan
27 **Eritrea** • Eritrea
28 **Dschibuti** • Djibouti
29 **Äthiopien** • Ethiopia
30 **Somalia** • Somalia
31 **Kenia** • Kenya

32 **Uganda** • Uganda
33 **die Zentralafrikanische Republik** • Central African Republic
34 **Gabun** • Gabon
35 **Kongo** • Congo
36 **Kabinda (Angola)** • Cabinda (Angola)
37 **die Demokratische Republik Kongo** • Democratic Republic of the Congo
38 **Ruanda** • Rwanda
39 **Burundi** • Burundi
40 **Tansania** • Tanzania
41 **Mosambik** • Mozambique
42 **Malawi** • Malawi
43 **Sambia** • Zambia
44 **Angola** • Angola
45 **Namibia** • Namibia
46 **Botsuana** • Botswana
47 **Simbabwe** • Zimbabwe
48 **Südafrika** • South Africa
49 **Lesotho** • Lesotho
50 **Swasiland** • Swaziland
51 **die Komoren** • Comoros
52 **Madagaskar** • Madagascar
53 **Mauritius** • Mauritius

# Asien • Asia

1 **die Türkei** • Turkey

2 **Zypern** • Cyprus

3 **die Russische Föderation**
 • Russian Federation

4 **Georgien** • Georgia

5 **Armenien** • Armenia

6 **Aserbaidschan** • Azerbaijan

7 **der Iran** • Iran

8 **der Irak** • Iraq

9 **Syrien** • Syria

10 **der Libanon** • Lebanon

11 **Israel** • Israel

12 **Jordanien** • Jordan

13 **Saudi-Arabien**
 • Saudi Arabia

14 **Kuwait** • Kuwait

15 **Bahrain** • Bahrain

16 **Katar** • Qatar

17 **Vereinigte Arabische Emirate**
 • United Arab Emirates

18 **Oman** • Oman

19 **der Jemen** • Yemen

20 **Kasachstan** • Kazakhstan

21 **Usbekistan** • Uzbekistan

22 **Turkmenistan** • Turkmenistan

23 **Afghanistan** • Afghanistan

24 **Tadschikistan** • Tajikistan

25 **Kirgisistan** • Kyrgyzstan

26 **Pakistan** • Pakistan

27 **Indien** • India

28 **die Malediven** • Maldives

29 **Sri Lanka** • Sri Lanka

30 **China** • China

31 **die Mongolei** • Mongolia

32 **Nordkorea** • North Korea

33 **Südkorea** • South Korea

34 **Japan** • Japan

35 **Nepal** • Nepal

36 **Bhutan** • Bhutan

37 **Bangladesch** • Bangladesh

38 **Birmania (Myanmar)**
 • Burma (Myanmar)

39 **Thailand** • Thailand

40 **Laos** • Laos

41 **Vietnam** • Vietnam

42 **Kambodscha** • Cambodia

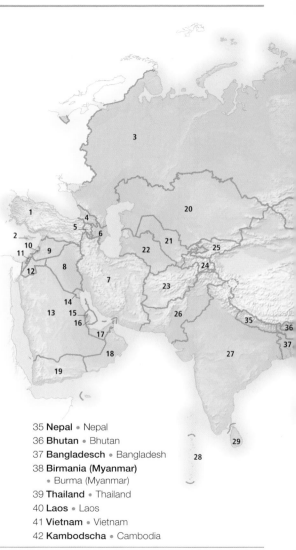

**deutsch** • english

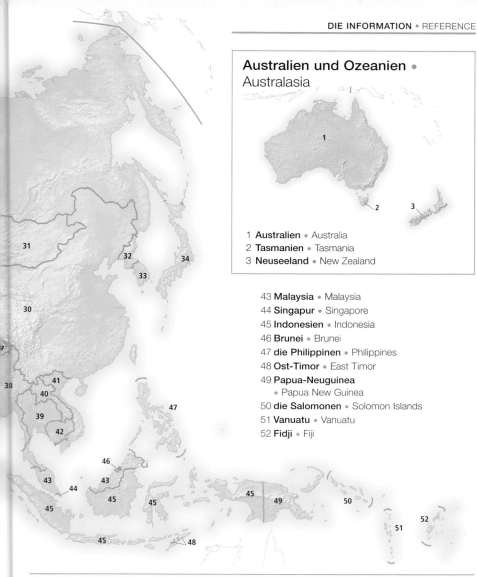

## Australien und Ozeanien •
Australasia

1 **Australien** • Australia
2 **Tasmanien** • Tasmania
3 **Neuseeland** • New Zealand

43 **Malaysia** • Malaysia
44 **Singapur** • Singapore
45 **Indonesien** • Indonesia
46 **Brunei** • Brunei
47 **die Philippinen** • Philippines
48 **Ost-Timor** • East Timor
49 **Papua-Neuguinea**
   • Papua New Guinea
50 **die Salomonen** • Solomon Islands
51 **Vanuatu** • Vanuatu
52 **Fidji** • Fiji

# Partikeln und Antonyme • particles and antonyms

| | | | |
|---|---|---|---|
| **zu, nach**<br>to | **von, aus**<br>from | **für**<br>for | **zu**<br>towards |
| **über**<br>over | **unter**<br>under | **entlang**<br>along | **über**<br>across |
| **vor**<br>in front of | **hinter**<br>behind | **mit**<br>with | **ohne**<br>without |
| **auf**<br>onto | **in**<br>into | **vor**<br>before | **nach**<br>after |
| **in**<br>in | **aus**<br>out | **bis**<br>by | **bis**<br>until |
| **über**<br>above | **unter**<br>below | **früh**<br>early | **spät**<br>late |
| **innerhalb**<br>inside | **außerhalb**<br>outside | **jetzt**<br>now | **später**<br>later |
| **hinauf**<br>up | **hinunter**<br>down | **immer**<br>always | **nie**<br>never |
| **an, bei**<br>at | **jenseits**<br>beyond | **oft**<br>often | **selten**<br>rarely |
| **durch**<br>through | **um**<br>around | **gestern**<br>yesterday | **morgen**<br>tomorrow |
| **auf**<br>on top of | **neben**<br>beside | **erste**<br>first | **letzte**<br>last |
| **zwischen**<br>between | **gegenüber**<br>opposite | **jede**<br>every | **etwas**<br>some |
| **nahe**<br>near | **weit**<br>far | **gegen**<br>about | **genau**<br>exactly |
| **hier**<br>here | **dort**<br>there | **ein wenig**<br>a little | **viel**<br>a lot |

| | | | |
|---|---|---|---|
| **groß** large | **klein** small | **heiß** hot | **kalt** cold |
| **breit** wide | **schmal** narrow | **offen** open | **geschlossen** closed |
| **groß** tall | **kurz** short | **voll** full | **leer** empty |
| **hoch** high | **niedrig** low | **neu** new | **alt** old |
| **dick** thick | **dünn** thin | **hell** light | **dunkel** dark |
| **leicht** light | **schwer** heavy | **leicht** easy | **schwer** difficult |
| **hart** hard | **weich** soft | **frei** free | **besetzt** occupied |
| **nass** wet | **trocken** dry | **stark** strong | **schwach** weak |
| **gut** good | **schlecht** bad | **dick** fat | **dünn** thin |
| **schnell** fast | **langsam** slow | **jung** young | **alt** old |
| **richtig** correct | **falsch** wrong | **besser** better | **schlechter** worse |
| **sauber** clean | **schmutzig** dirty | **schwarz** black | **weiß** white |
| **schön** beautiful | **hässlich** ugly | **interessant** interesting | **langweilig** boring |
| **teuer** expensive | **billig** cheap | **krank** sick | **wohl** well |
| **leise** quiet | **laut** noisy | **der Anfang** beginning | **das Ende** end |

# praktische Redewendungen • useful phrases

## wesentliche Redewendungen
• essential phrases

**Ja**
Yes

**Nein**
No

**Vielleicht**
Maybe

**Bitte**
Please

**Danke**
Thank you

**Bitte sehr**
You're welcome

**Entschuldigung**
Excuse me

**Es tut mir Leid**
I'm sorry

**Nicht**
Don't

**Okay**
OK

**In Ordnung**
That's fine

**Das ist richtig**
That's correct

**Das ist falsch**
That's wrong

## Begrüßungen
• greetings

**Guten Tag**
Hello

**Auf Wiedersehen**
Goodbye

**Guten Morgen**
Good morning

**Guten Tag**
Good afternoon

**Guten Abend**
Good evening

**Gute Nacht**
Good night

**Wie geht es Ihnen?**
How are you?

**Ich heiße…**
My name is…

**Wie heißen Sie?**
What is your name?

**Wie heißt er/sie?**
What is his/her name?

**Darf ich… vorstellen**
May I introduce…

**Das ist…**
This is…

**Angenehm**
Pleased to meet you

**Bis später**
See you later

## Schilder • signs

**Touristen-Information**
Tourist information

**Eingang**
Entrance

**Ausgang**
Exit

**Notausgang**
Emergency exit

**Drücken**
Push

**Lebensgefahr**
Danger

**Rauchen verboten**
No smoking

**Außer Betrieb**
Out of order

**Öffnungszeiten**
Opening times

**Eintritt frei**
Free admission

**Sonderangebot**
Special offer

**Reduziert**
Reduced

**Ausverkauf**
Sale

**Bitte anklopfen**
Knock before entering

**Betreten des Rasens verboten**
Keep off the grass

## Hilfe • help

**Können Sie mir helfen?**
Can you help me?

**Ich verstehe nicht**
I don't understand

**Ich weiß nicht**
I don't know

**Sprechen Sie Englisch, Französisch…?**
Do you speak English, French…?

**Ich spreche Englisch, Spanisch…**
I speak English, Spanish…

**Sprechen Sie bitte langsamer**
Please speak more slowly

**Schreiben Sie es bitte für mich auf**
Please write it down for me

**Ich habe… verloren**
I have lost…

**Richtungsangaben**
• directions

**Ich habe mich verlaufen**
I am lost

**Wo ist der/die/das…?**
Where is the…?

**Wo ist der/die/das nächste…?**
Where is the nearest…?

**Wo sind die Toiletten?**
Where are the toilets?

**Wie komme ich nach…?**
How do I get to…?

**Nach rechts**
To the right

**Nach links**
To the left

**Geradeaus**
Straight ahead

**Wie weit ist…?**
How far is…?

**die Verkehrsschilder**
• road signs

**Langsam fahren**
Slow down

**Achtung**
Caution

**Keine Zufahrt**
No entry

**Umleitung**
Diversion

**Rechts fahren**
Keep to the right

**Autobahn**
Motorway

**Parkverbot**
No parking

**Sackgasse**
No through road

**Einbahnstraße**
One-way street

**Vorfahrt gewähren**
Give way

**Anlieger frei**
Residents only

**Baustelle**
Roadworks

**gefährliche Kurve**
Dangerous bend

**Unterkunft**
• accommodation

**Haben Sie Zimmer frei?**
Do you have any vacancies?

**Ich habe ein Zimmer reserviert**
I have a reservation

**Wo ist der Speisesaal?**
Where's the dining room?

**Wann gibt es Frühstück?**
What time is breakfast?

**Ich bin um … Uhr wieder da**
I'll be back at … o'clock

**Ich reise morgen ab**
I'm leaving tomorrow

**Essen und Trinken**
• eating and drinking

**Zum Wohl!**
Cheers!

**Es ist köstlich/ scheußlich**
It's delicious/awful

**Ich trinke/rauche nicht**
I don't drink/smoke

**Ich esse kein Fleisch**
I don't eat meat

**Nichts mehr, danke**
No more for me, thank you

**Könnte ich noch etwas mehr haben?**
May I have some more?

**Wir möchten bitte zahlen**
May we have the bill?

**Ich hätte gerne eine Quittung**
Can I have a receipt?

**Nichtraucherbereich**
No-smoking area

**die Gusundheit**
• health

**Ich fühle mich nicht wohl**
I don't feel well

**Mir ist schlecht**
I feel sick

**Können Sie einen Arzt holen?**
Can you get me a doctor?

**Wird er/sie sich wieder erholen?**
Will he/she be all right?

**Es tut hier weh**
It hurts here

**Ich habe Fieber**
I have a temperature

**Ich bin im … Monat schwanger**
I'm … months pregnant

**Ich brauche ein Rezept für …**
I need a prescription for …

**Ich nehme normalerweise …**
I normally take …

**Ich bin allergisch gegen …**
I'm allergic to …

# deutsches register • German index

deutsch

deutsch

deutsch

deutsch

Majonäse f 135
Majoran m 133
Make-up n 40
Makramee n 277
Makrele f 120
Mal n 229
mal 165
Malachit m 288
Malawi 317
Malaysia 318
Malediven 318
Malerei f 274
Malerin f 191
Mali 317
Malspieler m 228
Malta 316
Malzessig m 135
Malzgetränk n 144
Manager m 174
Manchego m 142
Mandarine f 126
Mandel f 129
Mandeln f 151
Mandelöl n 134
Mango f 128
Mangold m 123
Mangostane f 128
Maniküre f 41
Maniok m 124
Mann m 12, 23
männlich 21
Mannschaft f 220
Mansarde f 58
Mansardenfenster n 58
Manschette f 32
Manschettenknopf m 36
Mantel m 32, 282
Maracas f 257
Marathon m 234
Margarine f 137
Margerite f 110, 297
Marienkäfer m 295
Marina f 217
mariniert 143, 159
Marketingabteilung f 175
Markise f 148
Markt m 115
Marmor m 288
Marokko 317
Mars m 280
Marshmallow m 113
Martini m 151
März m 306
Marzipan n 141
Maschinen f 187
Maschinenbau m 169
Maschinengewehr n 189
Maschinenraum m 214
Masern f 44
Maske f 189, 236, 249
Maß n 150, 151
Massage f 54
Maße n 165
Mast m 240
Mastdarm m 21
Match n 230
Material n 187

Materialien n 79
Mathematik f 162, 164
Matratze f 70, 74
matt 83, 271
Matte f 54, 235
Mauer f 58, 186, 222
Mauerturm m 300
Mauerwerkbohrer m 80
Mauretanien 317
Mauritius 317
Maus f 176, 290
Mautstelle f 194
Mazedonien 316
MDF-Platte f 79
Mechanik f 202
Mechaniker m 188, 203
Medaillen f 235
Medien f 178
Medikament n 109
Meditation f 54
Medizin f 169
Meer n 264, 282
Meeresfrüchte f 121
Meerrettich m 125
Mehl n 138
Mehl mit Backpulver n 139
Mehl ohne Backpulver n 139
mehrjährig 86
Mehrkornbrot n 139
Meile f 310
Meißel m 81, 275
Meisterschaft f 230
melken 183
Melodie f 259
Melone f 127
Mensa f 168
Menschen m 12, 16, 39
Menstruation f 20
Menübalken m 177
Merkur m 280
Mesosphäre f 286
Messbecher m 69, 150, 311
messen 310
Messer n 65, 66
Messerschärfer m 68, 118
Messlöffel m 109
Metall n 79
Metallbohrer m 80
Metalle n 289
Metallsäge f 81
metamorph 288
Meteor m 280
Meter m 310
Metermaß n 80
Metzger m 118, 188
Metzgerei f 114
Mexiko 314
Mieder n 35
Miesmuschel f 121
Miete f 58
mieten 58
Mieter m 58
Migräne f 44
Mikrophon n 179, 258

Mikrophongalgen m 179
Mikroskop n 167
Mikrowelle f 66
Milch f 136, 156
Milchprodukte n 107, 136
Milchpulver n 137
Milchreis m 130, 140
Milchschokolade f 113
Milchshake m 137
Milchtüte f 136
Milliarde 309
Milligramm n 310
Milliliter m 311
Millimeter m 310
Million 309
Milz f 18
Mineralien n 289
Mineralwasser n 144
Minibar f 101
Minidiskrekorder m 268
minirock m 34
minus 165
Minute f
Minutenzeiger m
Minze f 133
mischen 273
Mischpult n 179
mit 320
mit Automatik 200
mit Formbügeln 35
mit Handschaltung 200
mit Kohlensäure 144
mit Kopfdünger düngen 90
mit offenem Oberdeck 260
mit Rasen bedecken 90
mit Schokolade überzogen 140
mit Schokoladenstückche n 141
mit Zahnseide reinigen 50
Mittag m 305
Mittagessen n 64
Mittagsmenü n 152
Mittelfeld n 228
Mittelfinger m 15
Mittelfußknochen m 17
Mittelhandknochen m 17
mittelharte Käse m 136
Mittelkreis m 222, 224, 226
Mittellinie f 226
Mittelmeer n 313
Mittelpunkt m 164
Mittelstreifen m 194
Mittelstürmer m 222
Mittelwelle f 179
Mitternacht f 305
mittlere Spur f 194
Mittwoch m 306
Mixer m 66
Mixerschüssel f 66
Möbel n 105
Möbelgeschäft n 115

Mobile n 74
Mode f 277
Modedesigner m 277
Modell n 169, 190
Modellbau m 275
Modellierholz n 275
Modem n 176
Moderator m 178
Mohn m 138
Moldawien 316
Monaco 316
Monat m 306
monatlich 307
Monatshygiene f 108
Mond m 280
Mondbohnen f 131
Mondfähre f 281
Mondsichel f 280
Mondstein m 288
Mongolei 318
Monitor m 53, 176
Monopoly n 272
Monsun m 287
Montag m 306
Monument n 261
Mopp m 77
Morgen m 305
morgen 306
Morgendämmerung f 305
Morgenrock m 31
Mörser m 68, 167
Mörtel m 187
Mosambik 317
Moschee f 300
Moskitonetz n 267
Motocross m 249
Motor m 88, 202, 204
Motorhaube f 198
Motorrad n 204
Motorradrennen n 249
Motorradständer m 205
Motte f 295
Mountainbike n 206
Mousse f 141
Möwe f 292
Mozzarella m 142
MP3-Spieler m 268
Muffin m 140
mulchen 91
Mülleimer m 67, 266
Müllschaufel f 77
Müllschlucker m 61
multiplizieren 165
Multivitaminmittel n 109
Mumps m 44
Mund m 14
Mundschutz m 237
Mundwasser n 72
Mungbohnen f 131
Münze f 97
Münzfernsprecher m 99
Münzrückgabe f 99
Muschel f 265
Museum n 261
Musical n 255
Musik f 162
Musiker m 191

Musikhochschule f 169
Musikinstrumente n 256
Musikstile f 259
Muskatblüte f 132
Muskatnuss f 132
Muskeln m 16
Mutter f 22, 80
Muttermal n 14
Mütze f 36
Myanmar n 318

**N**

Naan m 139
Nabe f 206
Nabel m 12
Nabelschnur f 52
nach 320
Nachbar m 24
Nachmittag m 305
Nachrichten f 100, 178
Nachrichtensprecher m 191
Nachrichtensprecherin f 179
nachschneiden 39
Nachspeisen f 140
nächste Woche 307
Nacht f 305
Nachthemd n 31, 35
Nachtisch m 70, 153
Nachttischlampe f 70
Nachtwäsche f 31
Nacken m 13
Nadel f 109, 276
Nadelbaum m 86
Nadelkissen n 276
Nagel m 80
Nagelfeile f 41
Nagelhaut f 15
Nagelknipser m 41
Nagelkopf m 81
Nagellack m 41
Nagellackentferner m 41
Nagelschere f 41
nahe 320
nähen 277
Näherin f 277
Nähkorb m 276
Nähmaschine f 276
Nahrungsmittel n 118, 130
Nahrungsmittel in Flaschen n 134
Naht f 34, 52
Namibia 317
Nascherei f 113
Nase f 14
Nasenbluten n 44
Nasenklemme f 238
Nasenloch n 14
Nasenriemen m 242
Nashorn m 291
nass 286, 321
Nation f 315
Nationalpark m 261
Naturfaser f 31
Naturheilkunde f 55
Naturreis m 130

deutsch

deutsch

deutsch

deutsch

Tandem n 206
Tangelo f 126
Tankstelle f 199
Tankstellenplatz m 199
Tansania 317
Tante f 22
Tanzakademie f 169
Tänzerin f 191
Tanzmusik f 259
Tapedeck n 268
Tapete f 82, 177
Tapetenkleister m 82
Tapezieren n 82
tapezieren 82
Tapezierer m 82
Tapeziermesser n 82
Tapezierschere f 82
Tapeziertisch f 82
Tapisserie f 277
Tarowurzel f 124
Tasche f 32
Taschen f 37
Taschenlampe f 267
Taschenrechner m 165
Taschentuch n 36
Tasmanien 319
Tastatur f 172, 176
Taste f 176
Tastenfeld n 97, 99
Tätigkeiten f 77, 183
Tätowierung f 41
Taube f 292
tauchen 238
Tauchen n 239
Taucheranzug m 239
Tauchermaske f 239
Taufe f 26
Tausendfüßler m 295
Taxifahrer m 190
Taxistand m 213
Team n 229
Techniken f 237
Teddy m 75
Tee m 144, 149, 184
Tee mit Milch m 149
Tee mit Zitrone m 149
Teebeutel m 144
Teeblätter n 144
Teekanne f 65
Teelöffel m 65
Teetasse f 65
Teich m 85
Teig m 138, 140
Teilchen n 140
Teiler m 173
teilnehmen 174
Telefon n 99, 172
Telefonzelle f 99
Telegramm n 98
Teleprompter m 179
Teleskop n 281
Teller m 65
Tempel m 300
Temperatur f 286
Temperaturanzeige f 201
Tennis n 230

Tennisball m 230
Tennisplatz m 230
Tennisschläger m 230
Tennisschuhe m 231
Tennisspieler m 231
Teppich m 63, 71
Tequila m 145
Termin m 45, 175
Terminal m 212
Terminkalender m 173, 175
Terminplaner m 175
Termite f 295
Terparybohnen f 131
Terpentin n 83
Terrassencafé n 148
Territorium n 315
Tesafilm m 173
Tesafilmhalter m 173
Text m 259
Thailand 318
Thanksgiving Day m 27
Theater n 254, 299
Theaterkostüm n 255
Theaterstück n 254
Theke f 142, 150
Therapeutin f 55
Thermometer m 45, 167
Thermosflasche f 267
Thermosphäre f 286
Thermostat m 61
Thermounterwäsche f 35
Thermowäsche f 267
Thriller m 255
Thymian m 133
Tiefe f 165
tiefe Ende n 239
tiefgefroren 121, 124
Tiegel m 166
Tierärztin f 189
Tiere n 292, 294
Tierfutter n 107
Tierhandlung f 115
Tiger m 291
Tintenfisch m 121, 295
Tisch m 64, 148, 167
Tischdecke f 64
Tischtennis n 231
Tischtennisschläger m 231
Titel m 168
Toast m 157
Toaster m 66
Tochter f 22
Toffee n 113
Togo 317
Toilette f 72
Toiletten f 104, 266
Toilettenartikel m 41, 107
Toilettenbürste f 72
Toilettensitz m 61, 72
Tomate f 125, 157
Tomatenketchup m 154
Tomatensaft m 144, 149
Ton m 275
Tonabnehmer m 258
Tonhöhe f 256
Tonicwater n 144

Tonleiter f 256
Tonmeister m 179
Tonne f 310
Tonspur f 255
Tonstudio n 179
Topas m 288
Töpfchen n 74
Töpferei f 275
Topfhandschuh m 69
Topfpflanze f 87, 110
Topinambur m 125
Tor n 85, 182, 221, 223, 224, 247
Torlinie f 220, 223, 224
Tornado m 287
Tornetz n 222
Torpfosten m 220, 222
Torraum m 221, 223
Törtchenform f 69
Torwächter m 225
Torwart m 222, 224
Touchdown m 220
Tourenfahrrad n 206
Tourer m 205
Tourist m 260
Touristenattraktion f 260
Touristenbus m 197
Touristeninformation f 261
Trab m 243
Trabrennen n 243
Tragbahre f 94
Tragebettchen n 75
Tragfläche f 210
Tragflügelboot n 215
trainieren 251
Trainingsanzug m 31, 32
Trainingshose f 33
Trainingsrad n 250
Trainingsschuhe m 251
Traktor m 182
Tranchiergabel f 68
Träne f 51
Transfer m 223
Transformator m 60
Transmission f 202
Trapez n 164
Traubenkernöl n 134
Traubensaft m 144
traurig 25
Trekking n 243
Treppe f 59
Treppenabsatz m 59
Treppengeländer n 59
Treppengitter n 75
treten 207
Trethebel m 61
Tretmaschine f 250
Triangel m 257
Trichter m 166
Triebwerk n 210
Trifle n 141
Trimester n 52
Trinidad und Tobago 314
Trittleiter f 82

Trizeps m 16
trocken 39, 41, 130, 145, 286, 321
Trockenblumen f 111
Trockendock n 217
trocknen 76
Trockner m 76
Trog m 183
Trommel f 258
Trompete f 257
Tropen f 283
Tropfen m 109
Tropfer m 109, 167
Tropfinfusion f 53
Troposphäre f 286
Trüffel m 113, 125
Truthahn m 185, 293
Tschad 317
Tschechische Republik 316
T-Shirt n 30, 33
Tuba f 257
Tube f 311
Tülle f 80
Tulpe f 111
Tunesien 317
Tunfisch m 120
Tür f 196, 209
Turbolader m 203
Türgriff m 200
Türkei f 316
Türkette f 59
Türkis m 289
Türklingel f 59
Türklopfer m 59
Türknauf m 59
Turm m 272, 300
Turmalin m 288
Turmspitze f 300
Turmsprung m 239
Turnen n 235
Turnerin f 235
Turnierplatz m 243
Türriegel m 59
Türverriegelung f 200
Tüte f 311
Typen m 205

## U

U-Bahn m 209
U-Bahnplan m 209
Übelkeit f 44
über 320
überbelichtet 271
Überdach n 266
Überführung f 194
Übergepäck n 212
überholen 195
Überholspur f 194
Überlauf m 61
übermorgen 307
Übernachtung mit Frühstück f 101
Überpar n 233
überrascht 25
Überschallflugzeug n 211

Überschwemmung f 287
Überweisung f 49
U-Boot n 215
Übungen f 251
Übungsschwung m 233
Ufer n 284
Uganda 317
Uhr f 36, 62
Ukraine f 316
Ulme f 296
Ultraleichtflugzeug n 211
Ultraschall m 52
Ultraschallaufnahme f 52
Ultraviolettstrahlen m 286
um 320
Umfang m 164
Umhängetasche f 37
Umlaufbahn f 280
Umleitung f 195
umpflanzen 91
Umschlag m 98
umsteigen 209
Umwelt f 280
Umzug m 27
Unentschieden n 223
Unfall m 46
Ungarn 316
ungesalzen 137
ungültige Schlag m 228
Uniform f 94, 189
Universität f 299
Universum n 280
Unkraut n 86
Unkrautvernichter m 91
unpasteurisiert 137
unscharf 271
unschuldig 181
unsichere Fangen des Balls n 220
unter 320
Unterarm m 12
unterbelichtet 271
unterbrochen 99
untere Kuchenteil m 141
Unterführung f 194
Untergrund m 91
Unterhemd m 33, 35
Unterpar n 233
Unterrock m 35
Unterschrift f 96, 98
Untersetzer m 150
Untersuchung f 45, 49
Unterwäsche f 32, 35
Unze f 310
Uranus m 280
Urlaub m 212
Urlaubsprospekt m 212
Urologie f 49
Urteil n 181
Uruguay 315
Usbekistan 318

## V

Vanille f 132
Vanillepudding m 140
Vanuatu 319
Vase f 63

# englisches Register • English index

english

english

english

english

english

english

english

english

english

english

english

english

english

# Dank • acknowledgments

DORLING KINDERSLEY would like to thank Tracey Miles and Christine Lacey for design assistance, Georgina Garner for editorial and administrative help, Sonia Gavira, Polly Boyd, and Cathy Meeus for editorial help, and Claire Bowers for compiling the DK picture credits.

The publisher would like to thank the following for their kind permission to reproduce their photographs:
Abbreviations key:
t = top, b = bottom, r = right, l = left, c = centre

**Abode:** 62; **Action Plus:** 224bc; **alamy.com:** 154t; A.T. Willett 287bcl; Michael Foyle 184bl; Stock Connection 287bcr; **Allsport/Getty Images:** 238cl; **Alvey and Towers:** 209 acr, 215bcl, 215bcr, 241cr; **Peter Anderson:** 188cbr, 271br. **Anthony Blake Photo Library:** Charlie Stebbings 114cl; John Sims 114tcl; **Andyalte:** 98tl; **apple mac computers:** 268tcr; **Arcaid:** John Edward Linden 301bl; Martine Hamilton Knight, Architects: Chapman Taylor Partners, 213cl; Richard Bryant 301br; **Argos:** 41tcl, 66cbl, 66cl, 66br, 66bcl, 69cl, 70bcl, 71t, 77tl, 269tc, 270tl; **Axiom:** Eitan Simanor 105bcr; Ian Cumming 104; Vicki Couchman 148cr; **Beken Of Cowes Ltd:** 215cbc; **Bosch:** 76tcr, 76tc, 76tcl; **Camera Press:** 27c, 38tr, 256t, 257cr; Barry J. Holmes 148tr; Jane Hanger 159cr; Mary Germanou 259bc; **Corbis:** 78b; Anna Clopet 247tr; Bettmann 181tl, 181tr; Bo Zauders 156t; Bob Rowan 152bl; Bob Winsett 247cbl; Brian Bailey 247br; Carl and Ann Purcell 162l; Chris Rainer 247ctl; ChromoSohm Inc. 179tr; Craig Aurness 215bl; David H.Wells 249cbr; Dennis Marsico 274bl; Dimitri Lundt 236bc; Duomo 211tl; Gail Mooney 277ctcr; George Lepp 248c; Gunter Marx 248cr; Jack Fields 210b; Jack Hollingsworth 231bl; Jacqui Hurst 277cbr; James L. Amos 247bl, 191ctr, 220bcr; Jan Butchofsky 277cbc; Johnathan Blair 243cr; Jon Feingersh 153tr; Jose F. Poblete 191br; Jose Luis Pelaez.Inc 153tc, 175tl; Karl Weatherly 220bl, 247tcr; Kelly Mooney Photography 259tl; Kevin Fleming 249bc; Kevin R. Morris 105tr, 243tl, 243tc; Kim Sayer 249tcr; Lynn Goldsmith 258t; Macduff Everton 231bcl; Mark Gibson 249bl; Mark L. Stephenson 249tcl; Michael Pole 115tr; Michael S. Yamashita 247ctcl; Mike King 247cbl; Neil Rabinowitz 214br; Owen Franken 112cl; Pablo Corral 115bc; Paul A. Sounders 169br, 249ctcl; Paul J. Sutton 224c, 224br; Peter Turnley 105tcr; Phil Schermeister 227b, 248tr; R. W Jones 309; R.W. Jones 175tr; Richard Hutchings 168b; Rick Doyle 241ctr; Robert Holmes 97br, 277ctc; Roger Ressmeyer 169tr; Russ Schleipman 229; Steve Raymer 168cr; The Purcell Team 211ctr; Tim Wright 178; Vince Streano 194t; Wally McNamee 220br, 220bcl, 224bl; Yann Arhus-Bertrand 249tl; **Demetrio Carrasco / Dorling Kindersley (c) Herge / Les Editions Casterman:** 112ccl; **Dixons:** 270cl, 270cr, 270bl, 270bcl, 270bcr, 270ccr; **Education Photos:** John Walmsley 26tl; **Empics Ltd:** Adam Day 236br; Andy Heading 243c; Steve White 249cbc; **Getty Images:** 48bcl, 100t, 114bcr, 154bl, 287tr; 94tr; **Dennis Gilbert:** 106tc; **Hulsta:** 70t; **Ideal Standard Ltd:** 72t; **The Image Bank/Getty Images:** 58; **Impact Photos:** Eliza Armstrong 115cr; John Arthur 190tl; Philip Achache 246t; **The Interior Archive:** Henry Wilson, Alfie's Market 114bl; Luke White, Architect: David Mikhail, 59tl; Simon Upton, Architect: Phillippe Starck, St Martins Lane Hotel 100bcr, 100br; **Jason Hawkes Aerial Photography:** 216t; **Dan Johnson:** 26bcl, 35r; **Kos Pictures Source:** 215cbl, 240tc, 240tr; David Williams 216b; **Lebrecht Collection:** Kate Mount 169bc; **MP Visual.com:** Mark Swallow 202t; **NASA:** 280cr, 280ccl, 281tl; **P&O Princess Cruises:** 214bl; **P A Photos:** 181br; **The Photographers' Library:** 186bl, 186bc, 186t; **Plain and Simple Kitchens:** 66t; **Powerstock Photolibrary:** 169tl, 256t, 287tc; **Rail Images:** 208c, 208 cbl, 209br; **Red Consultancy:** Odeon cinemas 257br; **Redferns:** 259br; Nigel Crane 259c; **Rex Features:** 106br, 259tc, 259tr, 259bl, 280b; Charles Ommaney 114tcr; J.F.F Whitehead 243cl; Patrick Barth 101tl; Patrick Frilet 189cbl; Scott Wiseman 287bl; **Royalty Free Images:** Getty Images/Eyewire 154bl; **Science & Society Picture Library:** Science Museum 202b; **Skyscan:** 168t, 182c, 298; Quick UK Ltd 212; **Sony:** 268bc; **Robert Streeter:** 154br; **Neil Sutherland:** 82tr, 83tl, 90t, 118, 188ctr, 196tl, 196tr, 299cl, 299bl; **The Travel Library:** Stuart Black 264t; **Travelex:** 97cl; **Vauxhall:** Technik 198t, 199tl, 199tr, 199cl, 199cr, 199ctcl, 199ctcr, 199tcl, 199tcr, 200; **View Pictures:** Dennis Gilbert, Architects: ACDP Consulting, 106t; Dennis Gilbert, Chris Wilkinson Architects, 209tr; Peter Cook, Architects: Nicholas Crimshaw and partners, 208t; **Betty Walton:** 185br; **Colin Walton:** 2, 4, 7, 9, 10, 28, 42, 56, 92, 95c, 99tl, 99tcl, 102, 116, 120t, 138t, 146, 150t, 160, 170, 191ctcl, 192, 218, 252, 260br, 260l, 261tr, 261c, 261cr, 271cbl, 271cbr, 271ctl, 278, 287br, 302, 401.

DK PICTURE LIBRARY:
Akhil Bahkshi; Patrick Baldwin; Geoff Brightling; British Museum; John Bulmer; Andrew Butler; Joe Cornish; Brian Cosgrove; Andy Crawford and Kit Hougton; Philip Dowell; Alistair Duncan; Gables; Bob Gathany; Norman Hollands; Kew Gardens; Peter James Kindersley; Vladimir Kozlik; Sam Lloyd; London Northern Bus Company Ltd; Tracy Morgan; David Murray and Jules Selmes; Musée Vivant du Cheval, France; Museum of Broadcast Communications; Museum of Natural History; NASA; National History Museum; Norfolk Rural Life Museum; Stephen Oliver; RNLI; Royal Ballet School; Guy Ryecart; Science Museum; Neil Setchfield; Ross Simms and the Winchcombe Folk Police Museum; Singapore Symphony Orchestra; Smart Museum of Art; Tony Souter; Erik Svensson and Jeppe Wikstrom; Sam Tree of Keygrove Marketing Ltd; Barrie Watts; Alan Williams; Jerry Young.

Additional Photography by Colin Walton.

Colin Walton would like to thank:
A&A News, Uckfield; Abbey Music, Tunbridge Wells; Arena Mens Clothing, Tunbridge Wells; Burrells of Tunbridge Wells; Gary at Di Marco's; Jeremy's Home Store, Tunbridge Wells; Noakes of Tunbridge Wells; Ottakar's, Tunbridge Wells; Selby's of Uckfield; Sevenoaks Sound and Vision; Westfield, Royal Victoria Place, Tunbridge Wells.

All other images are Dorling Kindersley copyright. For further information see www.dkimages.com